BERKELEY   MOYNIHAN
SURGEON

LORD MOYNIHAN
From a photograph taken in July, 1931

BERKELEY MOYNIHAN

SURGEON

BY

DONALD BATEMAN

WITH A PREFACE BY

LORD MOYNIHAN

LONDON

MACMILLAN & CO. LTD

1940

PRINTED IN GREAT BRITAIN
BY R. & R. CLARK, LIMITED, EDINBURGH

" I have gathered a posie of other men's flowers, and nothing but the thread that binds them is mine own."

(One of Berkeley Moynihan's favourite quotations)

PREFACE

THE normal relationship between a father and son must prevent the son from being a fair judge of his father's character ; the love and affection that he feels is too strong to allow of anything else, so it is my personal feeling that a son should not attempt a biography of his father, but should leave it to one who, outside the family circle, can give a fair and unbiased account of his life.

Because of my father's busy life I saw all too little of him in my early days ; he left in the morning before I was up, and came home long after I had been put to bed, yet he never failed to look into my room each day and see me awake or asleep.

At school, with one exception, it was always my mother who came to see me and who took me back each term ; the exception was my first visit to Winchester. On the way down I was trembling a little outwardly and a great deal inwardly. I was wondering whether I was going to be miserable, as I had been for four years at my preparatory school, or whether, as actually happened, I was going to be really happy ; yet all the time I felt how proud my father was, to be able to give me the finest education possible. He must have felt how different would his schooldays have been if he had had the same chances.

Apart from this, my chief memories of him were in Norway, swimming from his house-boat on the fjord among the hundreds of jellyfish, and of his perfect diving. It was always a great treat for me to swim with him and a great moment when I first was allowed to dive on his back ; and then the holidays at Leeds, driving down with him either to his nursing home where I sometimes waited hours for him, happily talking to his chauffeur Dowding, or to the Infirmary which I always thought really belonged to him and which was always known to my sisters and myself as " Daddy's Infirmary ". Here was my only contact with the Great War, talking and playing with the hundreds of wounded soldiers and carrying round cigarettes every Sunday morning.

It was not until my father's serious illness in 1928 that I really began to know him well. In that year and in the next, when we went to America together, I first understood him as a son should understand his father. When I married, my wife brought us still nearer together, and it was then that I began to realise that in becoming the great surgeon he was, he had had to sacrifice the home life and the love of his children that, till then, he had never had. He lived till his grandson was born, the crowning moment of his life, and he died happy in the knowledge that the name that he and his father had made would go on for at least two more generations.

His story is faithfully told in this book by Dr. Bateman, whom I now introduce to you. Decisions are often hard to make, and sometimes, unfortunately, the results are unhappy, but the moment Dr. Bateman accepted the task, I knew that the choice was right. I did not ask for a full-length biography — such a book would have been tedious to all but the specialist — nor simply a history of my father's surgical achievements — this would be too technical for the layman — but a book that anyone in whatever walk of life could read and enjoy as a story of a very human and great man.

To write this, the author must not only have known my father as a surgeon but also have visited him in his home and seen him with his family, and, most important of all, he must be a man who could be shown those intimate letters which all families treasure, and told those small details which unfold a man's character, when, otherwise, it would be misunderstood. All this, I felt, Dr. Bateman could do. As a great personal friend of mine from Oxford days, he had spent many a holiday at Carr Manor, and, as a young doctor, my father had become interested in him and in his contributions to the Medical Journals, and he had appreciated, more than anything, his capabilities as a writer of fine English, a quality which he considered was all too seldom found, but of which he himself was a great master.

I do not think that it is possible to get closer to my father's character than Dr. Bateman has done in this book. I shall always be grateful to him for giving the public a chance of reading, in so simple and straight-forward a way, the story of my father's life. In it, too, you will meet my grandfather, the last of eleven consecutive generations of our family to be in the Army as a profession, and you will see what accident prevented my father from following in his footsteps.

My father spent the greater part of his life in Leeds. This city is, and always has been, a loyal city, proud of its own great men, and when my father married the daughter of its most famous doctor, they turned out in their thousands to rejoice with Dr. Jessop on this happy day ; church and streets were packed, and by those who were there the cheering crowds will always be remembered.

On another occasion, the city turned out, this time not to rejoice, but to do honour in silent prayer to the memory of another great citizen ; at my father's funeral the streets were lined from Meanwood to Leeds, over four miles. At each house a little group of people stood bareheaded, watching the solemn procession, and at and near the church the crowds were unbelievable. Leeds honoured and deeply loved my father, and every particle of that love he returned. Even when President of the Royal College of Surgeons in London, which entailed much time being spent away, he would come back to Leeds on every possible occasion, happy to be in the city and among the people he adored. Leeds had given him his chance, and in return he would give them the service of an ever faithful citizen.

I hope that this book will be published simultaneously in England and America and I should like to write a few words to his friends over there. Ever since my visit to the United States in 1929 I have realised how very much those friendships meant to him during his life. The interest and encouragement of America's great doctors at a time when my father was just making his name were, perhaps, the biggest incentive he had to continue his fine work. Their love of him has bred in me a fondness which makes me consider their country as a second home. I do sincerely hope they enjoy this book as I have done.

*   *   *   *   *

A biography cannot be written without the help of many people, and it would be impossible to thank all those who, by giving us interviews or by lending us

Preface

material, have made this book possible. Among those we would specially mention are Sir George Newman, General Sir John Goodwin, Mrs. Eastwood, my father's secretary, Mr. Braithwaite, Dr. Oldfield, and all my father's colleagues in Leeds, and above all my sisters Dorothy and Shelagh.

MOYNIHAN

CONTENTS

LIST OF ILLUSTRATIONS

XV

PART I

HIS PARENTS AND HIS CHILDHOOD

His Parents and His Childhood

THE mists of obscurity quickly gather round the records of our forefathers. Where once was a forest of memories there now remain but a few tree-tops indistinctly outlined above the gathering mist. Gone are the shrubs and smaller trees that gave detail to the scene. As we gaze backwards, trying to create again the view, all too frequently we find that artifice is doing the work of memory. There remain gaps that we cannot fill. We are surprised that what was recently so real is now so vague. Hard authentic fact gives place to sentimental recollection ; which recollection in its turn is dispossessed by blank forgetfulness. Night falls. Behind us lies nothing but darkness.

Most families lack chroniclers. Aristocratic families there may be that, having for generations spent their lives in the public service, like aged ships collect upon their sides biographers numerous as barnacles. They are the exception. For most of us our ancestors live only in the family lore. They find expression in our day-to-day behaviour, in our sense of tradition, and in our exercise of those moral principles that, being bred in the fibre, we feel to be abiding. A man is not an isolated individual spirit. He is the historic focal point of those of his blood that have gone before him. In him is to be read the result of all their strivings, loves, and aspirations. He is the measure of the success with which they adapted themselves to the tangible and intangible needs of their day.

3

When, from the tumbling river of some unknown family, is flung out a man of greatness these things should be remembered. To the unthinking multitude such a man is a phenomenon. But to those of penetrating mind he rarely appears as a sporadic, inexplicable event. To them he is the owner of an unexpected talent, or even genius, that at the last owes its complete fulfilment to the family heritage underlying the man's whole character. The gift flowers beautifully only because the soil is rich.

Reaching into the past we seek the answer to the riddle of heredity. But all too often it eludes our grasp. Names on tombstones tell no story. Imagination may play round the writings in the parish register, investing the bones of history with a lively flesh. But let these ancestors of ours follow their known profession, be born, married, and die, as stated in the public annals — then we may dispose of them as we will. Snobbishness may surround them with the glow of social precedence ; sentiment may breathe romance and tender beauty into their marriages ; cynicism may derive a twisted smile upon encountering those broken branches that are found in every family tree. Fancy may so disport itself. Yet all this is speculation : a popular indulgence nowadays. It is the fashion to make biographical bricks with the minimum of historical straw. With such are built edifices that collapse before the lightest winds of accurate information.

*   *   *   *   *

The Moynihans had always cherished a great pride of family. More than the generality of people they seemed to exhibit in their lives a sense of the continued spiritual presence of their forebears. This was not vanity. It was as if, living beside these witnesses from the past, they felt impelled to impose upon themselves a standard of behaviour that had been bequeathed to them. This standard was to be as gratefully cared for as the material portion of their inheritance. But not that alone ; to them it was the greatest part. Others might find the essence of tradition in their estates, their works of art, their family documents. To the Moynihans this code, these ethics, were the prize. Indeed, at times it was their sole endowment. For generations the army had been their profession. Soldiers do not accumulate wealth. But down the years, in prosperity and in adversity, they conducted themselves in accordance with high principles and, in maintaining them, saw no occasion for self-congratulation.

Soldiers, infrequently as they grow rich, are even less often given to the pen. Of their intimate feelings they hand down nothing. At times, long separated from their homes, they put on paper something of their doings and of the events with which they have been in contact. That is all. They leave us nothing that gives insight into their intentions, failings, remote purposes, and the fundamentals of their faith. It is useless to repine. Had they left fuller matter from which later men might reconstruct their lives they would have been describing, not themselves, but men of different nature. Men having different wives and different children ; men, to the roots of them, different. No, incommunicative as they were, they were but living in conformity with their characters. This deficiency of theirs, though doubtless inconvenient to us, might not unreasonably appear of little gravity to them.

*   *   *   *   *

Berkeley Moynihan

On September 11th, 1709, was fought the battle of Malplaquet. Led by the Duke of Marlborough, the English forces there engaged in one of the famous encounters of their history. On that field there died on one day, within the space of a few hours, five Moynihan brothers. No details are known with which to ornament this isolated fact. One's fancy irresistibly plays around its circumstances. These brothers came from Tipperary. Imagination cannot turn away from that appeal ! There is a felicity about it that must provoke the feeblest romantic in us. They must have been a turbulent, tempestuous bunch. The English soldiers by their sides were probably as little to their taste as were the enemy. Their superior officers are likely to have dwelt as fervently upon the thought of Tipperary as we do now, but it can hardly have been with the same conclusions.

It would be foolish to assume that patriotic sentiment urged them to risk their lives for England. To say that they had stomach for the fight would be to use the phrase with more exactitude than allegory. Those were uncomfortable, hungry days in Ireland. An exiguous diet of potatoes and milk makes a man less sensitive to the niceties of patriotism. It is better, with a full belly, to serve in the ranks of the miserable English than, with an empty one, to pass the days at home in starved futility. One wonders, too, how the news of their death came home. In those days, when mails were carried on horseback and lesser news waited on word of mouth, it must not have been until many months after the event. Did some returning soldier, drifting home to Ireland when the wars were long over, bring the first sad intimation ? A little knot in the village street, a brief sharp flame of conversation, a rustle of horror — that

may have been all. The group breaks up, the scrunch
of feet on the highway grows faint and disappears, the
cottage lights go out. Already the brothers are lost in
the unreal past. The battle was remote, it happened in
unimaginable foreign lands : how can one long care
about such things ? To-morrow is urgent.

*   *   *   *   *

In family records, Malachi Moynihan described himself as " of the military profession ". He married Ann
Scott from Scotland. Their son Andrew, the father of
Lord Moynihan, was born in the Yorkshire town of
Wakefield on September 8th, 1831 ; he was the last of their
large family, and the only one to leave behind him issue
of his own. Malachi Moynihan died at the age of fifty-six
at his home in Sefton Park, Liverpool. His wife survived
him for another thirty-eight years. She was ninety-eight
when she died in 1875. She must have been a truly
remarkable old lady. Many years after her death, Lord
Moynihan made some enquiries about his ancestors at the
College of Arms in London. In November 1933 he received a letter from Mr. A. T. Butler, the Windsor Herald,
who wrote as follows :

" There is one point on which you may be able to
help, namely the identity of your father's mother, whom
we have hitherto supposed to be Ann, widow of Malachi
Moynihan ; the certificate of her death on April 6th,
1875, gives her age as ninety-eight which would make her
fifty-four years of age at the time your father was born in
1831. Is it possible that she was a second wife and that
your father was the issue of a previous marriage ? "

Lord Moynihan wrote back to say yes, there had been
a mistake, and a grave one ; his grandmother was indeed
the only wife of Malachi Moynihan, but she had been not

7

Berkeley Moynihan

fifty-four but fifty-five years old when Andrew Moynihan was born !

No letters written by these grandparents of Lord Moynihan now exist. No accounts of their doings, habits, or mode of life are to be found. It is not possible to build up a picture of their world. They seem to have spent the more settled periods of their life together in the southern parts of Lancashire and Yorkshire. Andrew Moynihan, though born in Wakefield, did not live there long. All references to his parents in later years imply that they had been living in Liverpool for some time past. Either Malachi Moynihan or his father must have been the first Moynihan to make his home in England. In all probability this immigrant, like many another Irishman before and since, arrived penurious in England and settled down at the port of his landing — Liverpool. The ancestral home of the Moynihans was Templemore, Tipperary, Ireland. But long before the first Moynihan came to England the family estates and fortune had dwindled. By the time Malachi arrived, there remained nothing but the memories of that life of dignity and affluence.

Andrew Moynihan's mother was, as we know, fifty-five when he was born. His father, who was then middle-aged, died when Andrew was six. The boy knew little of the pleasures of family life and little more of its comforts. The death of his father had left his mother in difficult circumstances. Those were the days when prosperity was coming to southern Lancashire. As the waves of the incoming tide lap higher and higher up the beach, so did class after class in Lancashire find itself becoming unexpectedly rich. It must have been hard for an elderly widow whose means were diminishing to maintain her

8

position in a society that was paying less respect to standards of birth as it paid more to those of wealth. Yet she seems to have supported adversity with dignity. With every temptation to modify the traditional family code of ethics into a form less exacting and more in keeping with that of those around her, she yet adhered to the principles and precepts of her forebears. She inculcated in Andrew a strenuous sense of duty and honour and one not easily to be reconciled with worldly ends. A high ethical code is an admirable thing. But few will deny that it is easier to follow when inherited with money than when it comes accompanied by the task of making one's own living. Yet Ann Moynihan was right ; she knew her son. She lived to see the whole life of that son, to see her teaching justified, her standards vindicated, and honour bestowed upon the family name.

Andrew Moynihan possessed most of the qualities of character that were later to make his son famous. He had a nature of singular sweetness. He was unfailingly gentle and considerate to all who came in contact with him. He was a living example of that romantic type, the chivalrous soldier. For long it was the accepted literary practice to attribute to the parents of great public figures most of the orthodox virtues. Even though the pendulum of biographical fashion has now swung far in the opposite direction, the memory of that insincere mode still lingers in the public mind. The reader of to-day is not inclined to believe that even the few among his ancestors adhered to the narrow and difficult way of life. But they did. To these few we owe much of what is fine and pleasant in our present world. Nor, indeed, were the virtues so few. Andrew Moynihan came to a maturity at a time when the conception of individual public duty was as high as it has ever been in our national life. The ideals of Victorian Englishmen may not have been of the pattern that we now admire. Nevertheless they were ideals for which the men of those times were willing to make sacrifices and pay service. The reward for a man's efforts along such paths was often suffering, hardship, and obscurity. This was the coin in which Andrew Moynihan was paid. He did not complain.

It is a temptation to think that we are different now. One does not easily resist it. When the talk in the market-place is of what England owes to each of us — then there is plenty of noise ; when it is of what we owe to England — then the silence is not comforting. True self-sacrifice does not envisage personal reward. There were, of course, great prizes in those days gone by ; but do not let us forget that they infrequently went to those who made them possible. Political acrimony, not spiritual satisfaction, often follows public service that does not receive material reward. Or so it seems. The appearance does, perhaps, deceive. The temptation disappears when one perceives that it has its roots in a fallacy. Persons of Andrew Moynihan's sort have always worked modestly in places withdrawn from the general gaze. The effect of their labours is not felt till after they are gone. During their lifetime, as now in ours, the stage was occupied by the discontented and self-seeking. Even to-day, in unlit places, one believes, a great tradition still has its followers.

No doubt Andrew Moynihan had his faults. But they must have been transcended by his virtues. Debits, as well as credits, find their place in family annals. There are always those who take pleasure in recording the shortcomings of those about them. In Andrew's case, however, they must have been hard put to it to find any mud to stir. His brief and arduous life was humbly lived and its burdens carried with fortitude. No mischievous stories surround his name. Later studies reveal nothing to occasion unpleasant astonishment. His stature is not diminished by the distinction of his son.

*   *   *   *   *

Immediately after leaving school Andrew followed the military tradition of the family by entering the army. The straitened circumstances in which he and his mother were then living did not permit him to seek a commission. He enlisted as a private in the 96th Regiment. In later times the 96th became the Manchester Regiment — which was destined to display in 1915 prodigious bravery in the early days of the Gallipoli campaign of the Great War. The young soldier rapidly advanced in his profession. At the time of his marriage in 1853, when he was twenty-two years old, he had attained the rank of sergeant. In those days his regiment was stationed in Lancashire, near Ashton-under-Lyne.

Ellen Anne Parkin was the daughter of Thomas Parkin, a cabinetmaker. By the skill of his hands he made a steady and sufficient living. The Parkins lived at Hurst, not far from Ashton. Andrew and Ellen had not known each other long before they were engaged. The marriage took place very soon afterwards in the parish church at Ashton-under-Lyne. The bride brought with her no dowry ; her husband had inherited no money. They were to have no permanent home and she was to suffer continuously the discomforts attendant upon moving about the world in the wake of an army. Yet these two were to know in the short thirteen and a half years of their married life together more happiness than many others, better placed but of less courage, enjoy in a lifetime.

Soon after their marriage they went with the regiment to Ireland. A few months later the futile and ill-judged Crimean War broke out. Palmerston, the English Prime Minister, and his associates, disturbed by the growth of Russian power and not disinclined towards a brief excursion into war, elected to engage the armies of the Czar on the shores of the Black Sea. It was a disastrous war : humiliating for England, tragic for the Englishmen that were to die in it. Trevelyan, the historian, writes :

" The course of the war exhibited the soundness of the British regimental drill and tradition, and the utter incompetence of the higher command, the lack of organisation and staff-work, the deficiency of the commissariat and medical provision. Half a dozen miles from our fleet in Balaclava Harbour, our soldiers starved and died because supplies were not brought up to them. . . . But the 25,000 lives that the country lost in the Crimea saved many more in the years to come. For the real hero of the war was Florence Nightingale, and its most indubitable outcome was modern nursing, both military and civil, and a new conception of the potentiality and place in society of the trained and educated woman. And this in turn led, in the 'sixties and 'seventies, to John Stuart Mill's movement for women's suffrage, which Miss Nightingale supported, and to the founding of women's colleges and the improvement of girls' schools, when at length some provision was made for the neglected higher education of one-half of the Queen's subjects. From the frozen and blood-stained trenches before Sebastopol, and from the horrors of the first Scutari hospitals, have sprung not only a juster national conception of the character and claims of the private soldier, but many things in our modern life that at first sight seem far removed from the scenes of war and the sufferings of our bearded heroes on the winter-bound plateau."

Away to this dreadful war went Andrew Moynihan. Married less than a year, unaware of the existence of Florence Nightingale but very much aware of the hardships of a winter campaign and the improbability of his safe return, he made his farewells and left for Russia. A notebook he then took with him is preserved to this day. It is a simple exercise-book such as is used by school children ; it has covers of stiff cardboard. Now over eighty years old it is yet in remarkably good condition. Though the leaves are yellowed and the threads that bind them breaking, it is hard to believe that the words on its pages were written by an English soldier, seated on Russian soil, in a bleak December so many years ago. In this notebook is to be seen the following letter : either the unsent original or a copy of one dispatched. Perhaps it is the former, for it finishes abrupt and incomplete. What stayed the hand that wrote — an affray in the night, or the light that died from the tiny fire ?

"HEIGHTS NEAR BALAKLAVA
5 December 1854

" MY DEAREST MOTHER,

" Here we are, thank God. I wrote you from Kingstown the day we sailed (Sunday, 19 November 1854) and we anchored in the harbour last night, and landed to-day. The passage was a most prosperous one as these dates prove and Captain Leech and his gallant crew were so considerate and kind to us that the Officers presented the kind, brave-hearted Skipper with a gold watch which was purchased at Malta. We took in coals at Malta where we stopped about 10 or 12 hours and about the same time at Constantinople for the same purpose. Poor Renell is blowing the embers of a wood fire into a

13

flame to enable me to write you this letter for it is now quite dark and damp and we have not a moment's spare time during the daylight. . . ."

*   *   *   *   *

The army settled down to endure the cruel winter that was to be more a battle with disease, frost, and rain than with the enemy. It is not easy to infuse significance into words from which the habit of constant usage has withdrawn the sting. Though one glibly writes of these afflictions one does not sense, without an effort, how horrible that winter must have been.

Hunger, that made the day drag by in weary misery ; cold, that made the tunnel of night seem endless ; the stink and pinch of slow disease that dallied with its victims ere destroying them : that was the soldier's lot. Add to this the bitter knowledge, which these men shared — that at home in England the war was little understood, and by many all but forgotten. Imagination may then bring one to the fringe of feeling what this army felt.

When the spring of 1855 had thawed out the opposing forces the campaign became more vigorous. The English and French troops advanced upon Sebastopol. Adjacent to this town the Russians had erected fortifications. A part of this structure was known as the Redan. It was built in the shape of a V, the apex of which faced the attacking English forces. Here the most vicious fighting took place. An attack was made upon the Redan on June 18th, 1855. It was unsuccessful. On September 8th of the same year, a determined assault was again made upon it. Andrew Moynihan was with the storming party. He was the first man to enter the fort. Almost at once the Englishmen were driven back ; they left behind them Lieutenant Swift, who lay wounded on the ground. Moynihan turned back to rescue the deserted officer. In the attempt he was twice bayoneted by the Russians and then taken prisoner. Within a few moments the English had again attacked ; this time successfully. Moynihan was freed. He and some others then held for some time a position inside the Redan ; a violent Russian onslaught eventually drove them back into their own trenches. In retiring, Moynihan was wounded several times. Once again, under terrific fire, he crossed the open ground to enter the Redan and rescue Ensign Maude, whom he brought safely back to the English lines. By the end of the day's fighting he had received twelve wounds.

For these heroic actions he was awarded the Victoria Cross, the highest distinction a British soldier can receive for bravery in the field. In addition, he was elevated from the ranks to become Ensign Moynihan. In the *Illustrated London News* of June 20th, 1857, is to be found a hand-coloured print ; the scene is Hyde Park, London ; there, in high summer, is taking place an historic event : Queen Victoria decorating heroes of the Crimean War with the Victoria Cross. The honour had only just been instituted ; never before had it been presented. There in that little group of men, the first ever to receive the Victoria Cross, stands Andrew Moynihan.

*   *   *   *   *

In the autumn of the same year of 1857, Andrew was promoted Lieutenant and with his regiment left England for India, there to take part in the quelling of the Indian Mutiny. The occasion was a mutiny of Sepoy troops in

British pay ; there was no rising of the civil population of India. Though the mutiny had been substantially overcome during the previous summer by faithful Indian troops and the British Army stationed in India, the fighting was to go on almost continuously for the next two years. In this fighting Andrew Moynihan took part.

His wife had accompanied him to India. She was expecting a child. In the previous year she and Andrew had suffered a sad experience when she had been delivered of male twins — both still-born. This time, to their great happiness, nothing untoward occurred. A girl was born to them on October 13th ; she was christened Ada Augusta. Mrs. Moynihan and the baby stayed on in India for the next two and a half years and sailed for home with Andrew in 1860.

The story of that voyage is told in the pages of Andrew's notebook. In neat laborious handwriting is set down a narrative bare but deep with implications. And what a tale it is ! As one reads it the picture of the ship and its company forms before one's eyes. One sees the smoky troopship wearily throbbing its way across the glistering seas. No luxurious amenities divert the officers and their wives ; no swimming-pool, gymnasium, or dinner-dance beguiles the torrid hours. Meals and the long dead vacuum that lies between them alone made up the days. With so much time for contemplation what apprehensive thoughts must have been engendered by the happenings that Andrew records ?

" Ship *Monica*

" Memoranda

" 5th April 1860. Thursday sailed from Calcutta about 12 o'clock noon. Anchored at 6 o'clock in the evening at a place called Aitchipure. Captain

16

came on board with the head stewart about 7½ o'clock P.M.

6th April Sailed from Aitchipure about 7 o'clock A.M. and anchored at Dimona harbour about 3 o'clock P.M. in the afternoon.

7th „ Sailed from Dimona harbour about 3 o'clock. The pilot refrained from wearing Topee on the plea that the wind was so strong and the Topee so large which combined together impeded the progress of the good ship *Monica*. Anchored at Vadgeree about 5 o'clock.

8th „ Mrs. Garrish died of cholera about 7 o'clock A.M. The funeral service was read and she was buried in the usual manner at sea — this took place near Lanyar Island. And a child of Corporal Lees No. 10 Company 2 years old. Which also took place opposite near Lanyar Lighthouse.

9th „ Clear of the Lands Head a boy by name George McEvoy of the 99th Regt. 11 months old died about 4½ o'clock and was buried at or about 7 o'clock the same night.

11th „ Sapper Alfred Griffith, Hospital Cook, died of cholera and was interred at 6½ o'clock the same morning. A woman Mary Overland died of cholera at 11 o'clock P.M. and was interred the morning of the 12th at 6 o'clock.

19th „ Found in Mrs. Overland's small box in the presence of Captain Meade, Assistant Surgeon Hatchett and myself £6 and 3 Rupees.

21st „ Died about 2 o'clock in the afternoon and was buried at 4½ o'clock P.M. same day Patrick Burke, son of Colour Sergeant M. Burke.

24th „ Died about 4 o'clock A.M. morning of the 24th child George Roberts aged 8 months.

27th „ Miss Dovedale 1/60 R. Rifles 9 A.M. 1 year and 7 months old. Daughter of Sergeant Dovedale.

30th „ George West 10 A.M. 1 year and 3 months of

age. Son of Lance Corporal West 1/8 Regiment."

And so, like this, the melancholy tale goes on. The rest is omitted. It continues until July 25th, when, presumably, the voyage ended. There are recorded the deaths of a further fifteen children under two years of age ; one of them being an infant twenty-one days old that had been born at sea. Five children under eight and two adults were also added to those named above. There is sad contrast between the minutely recorded details of the earlier deaths and burials and the stark recording of the deaths as horror mounted. The way in which blunt fact succeeds precise elaboration is movingly human. At the last all that is put down is the name of the child and the time of death. The parentage and time of burial are left out ; but never the regiment. The last entry, on July 25th, is this :

" Henry Joyce 1/60 Royal Rifles 5½ A.M."

Is that not touching ? For a moment a cold finger stops the heart. What must these days have been like for Ellen Moynihan ? Ada was only two years old. With so much cholera about one hardly dare hope the child would escape. And Andrew . . . he was always going down into the crowded quarters of the private soldiers and their families . . . no help for that . . . but even if he doesn't get it he'll give it to Ada . . . why can't he stay away from there ? why must it be always his job to go down there and comfort them ? . . . he loves his men, of course . . . but doesn't he love his own daughter ? can't he keep away for her sake ? . . . Then gentler feelings might prevail. One has a duty to perform . . .

their lot is even worse than ours . . . we have some comforts, they have none. . . . Andrew knows what they are going through, he has been through it himself . . . he must do his work the way he sees it, he wouldn't be happy any other way . . . they all love him so, he's the finest officer on the boat. — So must she have mused. Back and forth, the endless struggle between generosity and self-interest, the nights a torment of dread, the days a weary effort of fortitude. But happily the sword that hung over Ellen's head was not to fall. She and her loved ones arrived safely in England. Fate was to hold its hand for a few brief years.

In later days it was to be the desire of Ellen Moynihan's heart that her son should be a doctor. Many factors were to play a part in forming this desire. Some we shall never know ; some we shall later see revealed. But of those concerning which no written evidence, no word-of-mouth report, remains, this, surely, was one. Such horrors, matter-of-fact as they may have been in the lives of herself and her friends, cannot but have left a permanent and modifying impression on the minds of all those who endured them. To do something to terminate these tribulations, to spare others the agonies of fear through which she herself had gone — this must have been her spontaneous and natural desire. These events, coming on top of Andrew's tales of the squalor and misery of the Scutari hospital in the Crimea, would all but inevitably turn any woman's thoughts towards the practices of healing and mercy.

It is not easy for us now to realise what cholera was to ships' companies and to armies eighty years ago. Always likely to appear where men and women were crowded together, in hot climates its arrival was almost certain. On land in slums and hospitals its ravages were regular. It struck with a blow so vicious that those it assailed rarely recovered. Good health was no defence. It slew the vigorous as often as the sickly. To-day one was well, the day after to-morrow dead. No talk of going to the doctor the moment one felt ill ; too late, already one was too ill to move. Little better the doctor coming to you, too frequently were his struggles in vain. One was ambushed by an enemy intangible, ruthless, and everywhere present. And these are the days about which we sentimentalise, the days when life was quiet and gentle ! Ah, well, no doubt life then did hold graces and charms now lost to us. But what a price went with them ! Imagination, in fond reflection, reveals to us our great-grandparents enjoying their pleasure in the settings that now surround ourselves. It was not so. Diseases that you and I call rare, that people in the streets have never heard about, were then seen daily. So far have the researches of science advanced us down the paths of health that we now no longer even pause to count our blessings. We live longer than our forefathers and we live better.

*   *   *   *   *

The Indian Mutiny was the last fighting in which Andrew Moynihan took part. It had been varied and strenuous. He had been present at the defeat of the rebels in the ravines of the Chumbal ; he had assisted in the attack upon and capture of Bhugah and Sevrale. Serving in the Oude campaign of 1858, he took part in the vigorous fighting around the town of Sandee ; for this he was decorated. The rest of his life was to be spent in the peace-time occupation of armies. Soon after his return to England he was again transferred to Ireland. After this came a short spell in Gibraltar. The last few years of his life were spent in Malta.

*   *   *   *   *

Andrew and Ellen had two more children. Eva Ellen was born in Ireland when Ada was four. Being in Ireland gave the parents the opportunity of having the child baptized at Templemore, the earliest known home of the Moynihans. It was an occasion of joy for Andrew who was liberally endowed with the Irishman's nostalgia for the country of his ancestors. Three and a half years after Eva came a son. The delight of Andrew and Ellen was boundless. Berkeley George Andrew was born in Malta on October 2nd, 1865.

In the next year Andrew was promoted Captain. He was placed on the Staff and appointed Musketry Instructor for the Island of Malta. He and his family moved to a large and roomy house, the first they had ever had, and which — as Ada wrote long afterwards — " when arranged with my mother's exquisite taste, was a delight to the eye ". A year and a half of happiness followed. The children were full of fun. Ada and Eva were all over the place ; they were in great danger of being spoilt by the men, who all but worshipped their father. Andrew replied in kind. He adored his children and loved the regiment. He had four children, not three ; the regiment was his first child — without it life was unimaginable. Ellen was happier than ever before. Had she not everything she had longed for ? Andrew's success was established ; no one could tell how high he might not travel now. No war threw shadows of death across the nights ; she was the idol of her daughters ; Berkeley was beginning to toddle in the sunshine. What more could she want ? Here was everything she had waited for.

Suddenly the spell was broken. It had been too good to last. Andrew was taken ill with Malta fever. It was the custom to drink goat's milk on the island ; cow's milk was scarce. Through goat's milk, as we now know, the infection is carried. But in 1867 the disease was not properly understood. The importance of boiling milk was not then known. Andrew had been drinking fresh goat's milk. His illness rapidly became worse ; all efforts to assist him failed. On May 19th, 1867, at the age of thirty-seven, with the richest part of his life before him, he died.

*   *   *   *   *

Study of the lives of famous men inevitably awakens curiosity about their parents. It is not enough to know how a man became prominent ; one wants to know also from what fountain came his strength. It is natural to assume that distinguished men are but giving expression to their endowed qualities. The man's career and works are the flower of the implanted seed of heredity. It is no mere biographical convention that calls for description of his parents ; these people sowed that seed. We are inquisitive. What were they like ? Alas, how often are surprise and disappointment the reward of our enquiry ! It seems incomprehensible that such mediocrity fostered such rare ability. The riddle is insoluble. But stop — perhaps not entirely. Those observations are more true of esoteric genius than of that eminence that comes from fruitful efforts of a rich and varied nature. A single prodigious talent may bestow immortal fame upon a man ; his family before and after may be nothing.

But where many talents, deriving their force from inbred principles, make up a total not of genius but of greatness, then, perhaps, we may better expect to find some premonitions in the parents of the successes that await their child.

Here, at least, is this contention justified. Even those who expect to discover similarity between the generations must be surprised at the close resemblance time was to reveal between Andrew and his son Berkeley. Andrew displayed nearly all the qualities that were later to make Berkeley celebrated. Rather because of accident and opportunity than because of any difference in industry and energy did the son's fame outstrip his father's. And had the father's span of life been as long as his son's so might his fame have been as great.

Andrew must have been as much a dreamer as a soldier. One cannot imagine that he was contented. Happy in his love for his family and his regiment, yes — but not contented. His notebooks tell that tale. The totality of those odd jottings reveals a nature strangely compounded. There in those books is a queer mixture of recorded fancy and incident. In them, with meticulous accuracy, his accounts are transcribed. (One is provoked to a wry smile on reading such an entry as " Bridget Curran's employment with Mrs. Moynihan commenced on 17th January 1863. Was engaged at 7 P.M. o'clock on the 16th January 1863 at the rate of five pounds a year for the first three months and if she gives satisfaction for that period at the rate of six pounds." Think of it — five pounds a year !) In amongst these accounts, all over the place and in every empty corner, are written thoughts, quotations, and isolated words. This literary lumber-room contains the products of Andrew's intellectual life.

With these dusty relics as mental weapons he attacked the world.

Without the evidence these notebooks bear he would have come down the years in family talk as a soldier — brave, busy, and satisfied. But he was far from this. In those pages we find more of a poet than of a soldier. He had a love of words, sensuous and insatiable. Single sentences, in which one graceful word is underlined, are wedged in between the shillings and pence of domestic accounts. There, under the heading of September 1861, we read this curious entry :

> " 1st One bottle of brandy.
> 1st One bundle of cheroots.
> 3rd One bottle of Marsala.
> 5th One bottle of Gin.
> 10th One bottle of Marsala, 3 glasses of beer 1 of lemonade.
> 13th Gin.
> 15th Marsala. ¼ Cheroots 1/6."

And right across all this is written :

> " The noise or bluster."
> " One of the dingiest localities in the City."
> " With a ghastly jocosity that was far from agreeable."
> " And the Major followed it up with great pertinacity."
> " That dinner, which my young impatience thought interminable."
> " The talismanic words."
> " I read with an indescribable thrill the talismanic words."
> " Inexpressibly ludicrous."
> " The grave imperturbable demeanour of the . . ."

Now what does all this mean ? Can it mean anything but a delight in sonorous and felicitous phrases ? Groups of words that roll euphoniously off the tongue, sentences of concise description — they are here in hundreds. They make one long, as they must have done the writer, to stand up and speak them in public.

But not all the contents of the notebooks are as fragmentary as this. Some pages contain paragraphs of completed thought. Embodied in them are reflections on Andrew's day-to-day affairs. Sometimes these are in his own words ; sometimes they are conveyed through an apposite quotation from a favourite author. It is not possible to put them all down here. Together they build up a picture of the man. If not complete, that picture is at least suggestive.

Andrew Moynihan was reflective, even to the point of introspection. One imagines that he was a lonely man. Repeated separations from his family, frequent transfers from place to place, and his elevation from the ranks to association with new groups of men, conspired to cut him off from old friends and to make it difficult for him to acquire and retain new ones. Most men would feel this deprivation ; for Andrew it was especially painful. His emotional Irish nature made him long for the opportunities of self-expression that friendship gives. Frustrated in these desires, he made his notebook his confidant. In it he poured out his thoughts. Under the shadow of its covers he sloughed off the worries that enshrouded his mind. He never had the mastery of words that time was to give his son. Sentences of his own planning often gave him less relief than did quotations from the works of other men. He was impelled to transcribe phrases, quarried in casual reading, not for their beauty only but also for their sharp precipitation of his own experience.

He was a humble man. Nowhere in his writings are found expressions of arrogance, pride, or vanity. The ambition mirrored in these records is but that meed allowable to any man possessed of a strong sense of duty and a great love of family ; always is it tempered by his feeling for the rights of other men. Examples of this are many ; a single illustration speaks for all. He reads this verse about Napoleon and writes it down :

> His game was Empire, and his stakes
> Were Thrones.
> His table earth, his dice were
> Human bones.

This surely shows that he was not insensitive, not opportunist. It implies, too, that his conception of his task as soldier was founded on high principle.

He was a devout man ; much of his reading was in the Bible. But his religious views were simple — never forced on those about him. His faith was for his own consolation and comfort, not for the chastisement of others.

One cannot but marvel at the character of this gentle, brave, and modest man. Evidence of gross defect would enable one to paint his portrait in colours more naturalistic. It would show off his virtues to more brilliant advantage. But we must not invent shortcomings to tickle the reader's palate. Literary artifice might bestow on his character an aspect of greater reality. But that would not be fair. We must take him as we find him. We must permit rare virtue. No doubt he had his faults ; but we are not told of them. To invent them would be foolish. We must believe him to have been a fine man — with fewer failings than most of us.

In Andrew's day it was rare for a soldier in the British Army to rise from the rank of private to that of commissioned officer. Snobbery was rife ; it was allied to a sincere conviction in high places that a ranker was fundamentally incapable of displaying the qualities deemed needful in an officer. It was only a most exceptional man that could achieve this elevation. One may well suppose that a man, so promoted, would find his reception chilly ; that he would encounter constraint in the manner of those about him. Prejudice dies hard — and no more quickly in an officers' mess than anywhere else. Moreover the difficulties of a ranker officer would be increased rather than relieved by the concomitant addition to his pay. In the ranks he moved amongst men whose only money was the money that they earned. Now, himself without private means, he was to associate with men who regarded their salary as but a pleasant addition to their unearned substance. Whereas most of his fellow officers were men of moderate wealth, he had to support himself and his family out of his pay. It was impossible for him to entertain as he was entertained. To a man of his pride this would be distressing. He would be disinclined to accept a hospitality that he could not return in kind. Yet he would long to do so. Already tending to withdrawal into self, this economic separation would but accelerate that process. Inevitably a social sensitivity ensued. He was not alone in his position ; it was shared by others. Not all of them were inarticulate. Under the urgency of strong feelings, stimulated perhaps by recent slights, he must have copied out what follows. Here is his entry :

"MEMO FROM THE UNITED GAZETTE OF
10 JANUARY 1863

" The adjutants have another claim which applies to a very large proportion of their numbers. Many of them have been raised from the ranks, and if there is any case in which the authorities should be punctiliously conscientious in distributing the rewards of the Service it should be in that of men who have conquered all hindrances and by their talents and force of character have broken through the barriers of exclusiveness in the most rigidly aristocratic Army in the World."

Immediately after this comes a footnote — surely there must have been a slight ! — which goes like this :

" FROM MR. ODO RUSSELL TO EARL RUSSELL, 1862

" But that criticism was a matter of indifference to him so long as his own conscience and sense of duty were satisfied."

(Taken from *The Times*.)

Money, however, does not oil away all sources of social friction. An even greater distress can spring from the cruelties of snobbery than from the hardships of poverty. In all circles is encountered the vulgar mentality that estimates the gentility of those whose company it keeps according to their station rather than their natural qualities. To such it would be axiomatic that a ranker could not be a gentleman. Casual rudeness and petty insults follow invariably in the wake of this assumption. Mixing with men who had always belonged to the officer class, Andrew, new to their society, must have been continually exposed to this intolerant behaviour. It is not strange, then, that this passage from Whyte-Melville should have touched his fancy :

" A GENTLEMAN

" Our idea is, that neither birth, nor riches, nor education, nor manner suffice to constitute a gentleman, and that specimens are to be found at the Plough, the Loom, and the Forge, in the Ranks, before the mast, as well as in the Officers' mess-room, and learned professions, and the Upper House itself. To our fancy a gentleman is courteous, kindly, brave, and high-principled, considerate towards the weak, and self-possessed among the strong. High-minded and unselfish, he does to others as he would they should do unto him, and shrinks from the meanness of taking advantage of his neighbour, man or woman, friend or foe, as he would from the contamination of cowardice, duplicity, tyranny, or any other blackguardism."

One may imagine that there were occasions when the ill manners of his associates called upon his courage no less than did the dangers of the battle-field ; it is probable that his restraint was as great as had been his bravery. Let us hope that at least he found a few friends quick enough to realise his essential worth.

Andrew's mind was much occupied by thoughts about the nature of the hero. Descriptions of the heroic quality are a common feature in his notebooks. They vary in length from single sentences to long paragraphs. Here is one of them :

" Heroes who have been most distinguished for Fury in the fight, have been of tender heart as little children ; sharp their swords towards the foe, but gentle their hands towards the weak. It is the index of a noble nature that it can be majestic as a lion in the midst of the Fray and roar like a young lion on the scene of the conflict, and yet it has a dove's eye and a maiden's heart."

Truly a description in the grand manner ! It is difficult not to smile at the thought of an eminent soldier laboriously transcribing such sentiments. But the smile is misplaced. Though the style was high-flown the similes were sincere. Times, we must allow, have changed. Andrew was writing in the 1860's. The soldier's task was not then the destruction — from of course a safe altitude

29

— of defenceless women, children, and old people. He might indeed have claimed it was his purpose to protect such persons. He respected his enemy, and was capable of sparing his life once the immediate purposes of war had been fulfilled. This is not to deny that he may have been the instrument of unscrupulous individuals and governments ; but at least he was allowed to carry out his unpleasant task in an honourable manner. Perhaps it is all to the good that glory should cease to invest the soldier's task ; but if one has to be a soldier it must be comforting to wear a cloak of humanity, however threadbare.

To conclude that Andrew, because he wrote down accounts of heroes, was therefore intent upon being one is probably wrong. More likely is it that he was indulging a philosophic curiosity. In the history of all nations are to be found soldiers with a taste for abstract reasoning. We do well to admire them. They, no less than civilians, have made their contribution to the better welfare of the world. But, having neither the facility nor time for writing, they have often lacked the means and opportunity for giving permanence to their speculations. This was Andrew's situation ; and he knew it. Though the suggestion may seem perverse, one cannot yet resist the feeling that Andrew, fine and successful soldier though he was, would rather have followed a contemplative life. Point is given to this interpretation of his mind by one quotation in particular. It is found on a page that is headed " Self Assisted ". Here are copied passages that illustrate the difficulties a man has to contend with when, without the influential aid of friends or family, he is fighting his way upwards in the world. It runs like this :

" How can he find time to embody *his* own thought."

It is immediately followed by this :

" It was only when the sons saw themselves penniless and professionless, with the great battle of life all before them, and with no weapons wherewith to fight . . ."

Taken together, these two sentences seem to imply that Andrew was pondering over the frustration that necessity imposes on a man. But the easy explanation is not always the correct one. Perhaps no association between the phrases is intended. Perhaps it was not until his career was well advanced that the desire to embody his own thoughts arose.

Without the support of money or influence it is hard to make a mark in the world. It is much harder, given that starting-place, to achieve the same end with the preservation of honour. We are too ready to admire success without consideration of the means whereby it has been attained. We are quick to recognise the difficulties that have been overcome, but slow to appreciate the damage done to society on the way. The accolade should be for him who reaches the top by the narrow path. He has overcome the difficulties of the spirit as well as those of the world. Of this estimable little group Andrew Moynihan was one. With what thoughts he quit the trials that had been his mortal destiny we cannot tell. His had been an austere nature ; and one that had no doubt found comfort in the dignity of virtue.

He was not unalive to the limitations of his profession. Two more quotations out of his store doubtless found their way there because Andrew, like their original author, felt their full truth. The first of them is this :

"James described military glory in these terms, ' Honour, reputation, and fame acquired by military achievements ; that precarious splendour which plays round the brow of a Warrior, and has been collected by hard Service, extraordinary genius, and unblemished integrity ; but which may desert the greatest hero through one unfortunate failure occasioned by the fatality of human imperfection '."

And the second, which is headed " Death ", runs :

" We shall have a most disastrous war ere long, said he, and I may say in the words of Goldsmith, ' Go my boy, and if you fall, though distant, exposed and unwept for a time by those who love you, the most precious tears are those with which Heaven bedews the unburied head of the soldier '. Farewell, my friends, God bless you."

* * * * *

A private soldier in the modern army leads a very different life from that of his counterpart of eighty years ago. In those times no consideration was paid to his intellectual well-being or to what was to become of him when his period of service was over. At the beginning of the nineteenth century, Wellington had given it as his opinion that his private soldiers were the scum of the earth and that they had enlisted for drink. By the 'sixties things had improved a little, but even then the private soldier led a coarse life, and, when he left the army, did so scarred by the fires of indulgence and disease. By his illiteracy long cut off from life and friends at home, retirement, when it came, meant for him but penury and loneliness. The private soldier of the present day receives, in striking contrast, a general education that, for the purposes of his reabsorption into civil life, could not much be bettered.

When Andrew Moynihan went to Malta he took over the worst company in the regiment. They were known to the army in Malta as " the blackguards of Number 5 ". Not one of these men could read or write. The only one amongst them that was making any attempt at all to save money was the Sergeant. They were as slovenly in their habits as they were incompetent in their personal affairs. Andrew was dismayed ; but not cast down. With generosity and vigour he set to work to improve the men's condition and to restore their pride. He interviewed each man separately and asked him if he was receiving news from home about his family and friends : not one of them was. The reason was simple : not one of them could either read or write. Their relatives at home were probably in no different case. Andrew at once offered to start a weekly class in reading and writing ; he announced that he would write a letter to the home of every man that joined it, which letter would contain news about the soldier and would conclude with the information that in his own hand the man himself would be writing home before a year was out. Every man in the company entered the class. The Sergeant became infected with Andrew's enthusiasm ; he too took a part in conducting the lessons. The success these two met with must have surprised even themselves : not a man failed to be in a position to write home at the end of the year !

Nor was this all. The company's whole atmosphere changed, under Andrew ; the men enjoyed a self-respect that they had hitherto not known. Towards the end of his first year's command came the day of Andrew's greatest pride. It was the day of General's Inspection ; the company, in silent line, humbly awaited the great

D

man's coming. With Andrew by his side, the General entered the barrack-room of Number 5. By his bed, each man stood to attention ; each uniform immaculately brushed, each button polished like the sun. The General was impressed ; so most of all by the symmetrical neatness of the folded sheets and blankets on each bed ; such precision was remarkable — surely alone to be obtained by the previous stretching of the bedding on some flat surface. Turning to Andrew, the General said, " Did you yourself, Captain, provide the board on which they fold their sheets and blankets ? "

" No, sir, they use no board," came the reply. Andrew called the Sergeant ; the order was given for the bed-clothes to be undone and refolded. With the assistance of his neighbour, each man undid and remade his bedding ; the final order was as perfect as the first. The General turned back to Andrew.

" I congratulate you, Captain ; that is the way battles are won," he said.

But no more battles were to be won by Andrew. His death came soon. Too soon for him to make a greater mark upon the tablets of the army than that of the Victoria Cross, by which he has perpetual remembrance. When he died an account of his services was given in *Hart's Quarterly Army List*. It ends like this :

" This is a brief statement of the services performed in the field by this distinguished officer ; they are such as might be expected from a man who possessed in a very high degree all those physical and moral qualities which constitute the beau ideal of a model British soldier. He was powerfully built, capable both of undergoing prolonged fatigue and of making the most vigorous exertion. His intelligence was quick and penetrating. His character was decided and energetic and his habits exceedingly

simple and temperate. He possessed a minute knowledge of everything connected with the exercises and
management of infantry soldiers. To perfect the training and promote the welfare of the men under his
command was an object which absorbed every other
interest and to which he devoted all his time, all his
thoughts.

"There is, we venture to say, no Company in the
British Army more perfect in all its arrangements than
that which now records the loss of its distinguished
Captain — Andrew Moynihan. His body was interred
with military honours in the Ta Braxia Cemetery on
Monday the 20th instant and was followed to the grave
by all the officers of both Battalions of his Regiment and
by Major-General Atherby and the Staff of the Garrison
and by very many of the Officers of the Division and of
the Royal Navy."

* * * * *

When Andrew Moynihan died his family did not
immediately leave for England. Like him, his wife and
elder daughter were both ill with Malta fever. Eventually these two recovered and arrangements were made
for the whole family to return home. Their going broke
the last link that Number 5 Company had with the
Captain who had done so much for them, the Captain
for whom they had come to feel so much affection.
When the final preparations had been made, and the
day of sailing approached, the Sergeant of Number 5
Company called upon Mrs. Moynihan. He said that
the men of the Company had asked him to give them
an opportunity of saying good-bye to their Captain's
children. Mrs. Moynihan agreed to help him. The next
afternoon the three little Moynihans were taken by their
nurse to the parade-ground. Ada was then ten, and very
grown-up ; Eva was six ; little Berkeley one and a half.

35

They found the Company lined up, as if for inspection. The Sergeant was waiting to meet his guests. The two little girls walked down the lines and gravely shook hands with each man. When the nurse brought Berkeley up, the first soldier, stooping down, took the little boy in his arms and lifted him up ; dandling him for a moment he then turned, and passed the child to his neighbour. In this way Berkeley was passed right down the line of the Company from man to man. The occasion made a tremendous impression on Ada. For the rest of her life she remembered it and in old age often spoke of it. When she was nearly eighty, in giving an account of that long-gone afternoon, she wrote, " It all seemed so sad and solemn ! It was indeed very beautiful of them and quite unforgettable for my sister and me."

After a long sea journey the little party landed at Liverpool in the last month of 1867. They went to stay with Andrew's mother at Sefton Park, Liverpool. From there they went to Ellen's old home. The future had to be discussed and planned. Things were very difficult for the young widow. She had no money at all apart from the meagre pension, of one pound a week, that she received from the Patriotic Fund. This charitable organisation was her only official source of help ; there were, in those days, no pensions from the Government to the widows of army officers. With so little money she could not set up house on her own. Yet she was disinclined to reside indefinitely with her parents ; she feared to make herself and the children a burden to them. After the discussion of many possibilities a most happy solution was found. It was one that influenced the whole course of Berkeley's life.

Ellen had a sister a few years older than herself ;

36

these two girls, when children, had been deeply devoted to each other. This mutual affection had never lessened as the years went by, and had been maintained throughout the married lives of both of them. Mrs. Ball now lived in Leeds where her husband was a Police Inspector. To Leeds it was decided that Ellen and her young family should go. With the Balls, who had no children, they would take up residence ; of the expenses Ellen would pay an equitable share. In this way she would have the pleasure of companionship without the disadvantages of dependency. The house adjoining the police station in Millgarth Street was large enough to hold them all without discomfort. Here the children could kick their heels up and tease the policemen in the office at the bottom of the stairs. Here Ellen and her sister could solve the hundred and one tricky problems of domestic economy, chattering and laughing in the old happy way. Over them all, kindly and generous, Alfred Ball could preside. This good man assumed all the responsibilities of a father without either expecting or exacting the rewards of that position. It was his pocket that provided the money for the early education of the girls and it was he who helped Berkeley in his early student days.

*   *   *   *   *

In 1870 Leeds was riding to fortune on the woollen trade. Though hours of work were long and rates of pay were low, the working man was, by contrast with his harder past, a happy man. No doubt he occasionally drank too much, no doubt he spent Sunday morning up on the moors watching cock-fights instead of going to church, no doubt his children were poorly educated and did not enjoy the standards of living that we demand for them nowadays — no doubt all this : yet he was a member of a lusty, expanding industry and there was goodness about a world looking forward to a future full of hope.

His employer was in even happier circumstance. Possessing large factories and employing many men, he was his own master. The shadow of the industrial combine had not yet fallen across his mills. To the sweet music of high profits and negligible taxes he and his colleagues were making large fortunes. The environs of Leeds are still dotted with the tombstones of this accumulated wealth : those squat and solid mansions, sessile upon the landscape, standing for a way of life now gone. Here, with his family and many servants, the mill-master lived a life as rich and comfortable as his truculent Northern conscience would allow. The nonconformist spirit then flourished in Yorkshire. Sunday dinner might be a meal of gargantuan proportions, but it was proper to sit down to the enjoyment of it with the drawn, ascetic expression of one about to dine off a few husks. The joint of beef was vast ; its dispensation liberal. It was indeed a standard measure for both tastes and habits. Beauty took its cue from beef. Such art as found its way into these God-fearing houses called for a sturdy aesthetic digestion. Subtlety was regarded as effeminate ; such practice should be left to foreigners. For literature the Bible, for music *The Messiah,* for pictorial art a various and exhaustive study of the dying stag — these viands satisfied the artistic appetite.

But of this heavy-handed world the Moynihans saw little. Even had their inclinations been towards it they lacked the introductions to lead them there. They knew no one outside the family circle. They were a self-contained and intimately united family. The deep affection that bound them together may have sprung from innate characteristics or from lonely necessity ; whatever its origin, it was destined to continue with undiminished intensity throughout their long lives.

The two girls gave early evidence of being gifted with exceptional artistic ability. Ada had a quick masculine intelligence and a facile pen. She was a great reader and a rapid learner. Eva's talents were of a more egregious kind. She took delight in painting and had a genuine flair for it. In childhood she was a prolific poetess and continued so for the rest of her life. That her poetry did not appeal equally to all palates is perhaps understandable ; its uncompromisingly devotional quality cannot be congenial to all readers.

After the first few years in Millgarth Street the management of the household came more and more into the hands of Ada. Mrs. Moynihan's disposition was gentle and retiring. Ada's mind was able and dominating. She found the day long enough to perform the domestic chores with rare efficiency, to pursue her own studies and to give Berkeley his earliest schooling. The boy's debt to her, as being the initial formative influence in his life, was immense. To his mother he owed much ; but she gave him principles, not plans. Ada told him of undiscovered worlds and instilled him with the urge to conquer them. That Ada had vigorous personal ambitions of her own is unquestionable. But, considerable as were her scholastic attainments, she must have realised that her sex would always exclude her from most fields of intellectual achievement. She was born a quarter of a century too soon. Knowing this, she came to look upon Berkeley as an instrument for the vicarious satisfaction of her aspirations. While he was still a child she recognised his remarkable intelligence. To the fullest exploitation of that mind her life thenceforward became dedicated. It is possible that Berkeley's intellect was never quite as keen as his sister's. Those who knew them both will often take that view. They consider that the direction and encouragement Berkeley had from Ada throughout his childhood and schooldays was the most important factor in his life.

But the world in those days did not see what Ada saw. They merely perceived a jolly, mischievous, red-headed little boy who was doted upon by his three female relatives. A letter written by a friend in later years says that " Mrs. Moynihan was very proud of her children and used to dress Berkeley in a kilt complete with sporran and dirk, which with his thick red hair made him a striking little figure ". Pride was then a marked characteristic of the family. It had its roots in their poverty. They were conscious of their social and intellectual superiority to those about them whose circumstances were more comfortable than their own. They found the patronage of these people irksome. Inevitably they withdrew themselves behind the ramparts of the family circle. They were sufficient to each other. Few invitations were received and even fewer given. A visitor at that time came away from their home with two lasting impressions : the scrupulous order and cleanliness of the house and its many signs of unspoken privations.

*   *   *   *   *

When Berkeley was six he attended his first school. It was a small private school for boys and was housed in Brandon Villa at the top of Brandon Grove, New Leeds. Hydra-headed, it was presided over by the three Misses

40

Baxendale. They were its entire staff, full administrative board, and sole owners. Shortly after Berkeley's arrival there as a pupil, the youngest Miss Baxendale gave up her multifarious duties at the school for the no less strenuous task of being a vicar's wife. She married Mr. Fleming, the Vicar of St. Clement's. Persons of a romantic turn of mind have referred to Brandon Villa as a dame school. This appears to be unwise and incorrect. I did so myself to one who had part in those bygone days and was coldly informed that it was " not a dame school. It was a preparatory school for young gentlemen." With this distinction in mind it is yet possible to observe that the teaching there was mainly concerned with the three R's. No aggressive attempts were made to scale the higher educational peaks.

A fellow pupil in those days was J. B. Seaton. This boy was the son of a doctor in Leeds. He ultimately entered the Church, in which he reached high office. After some years in the Mission Field and as a vice-president of the Leeds Clergy School, he became Bishop of Wakefield, Yorkshire. In his later years he resumed his childhood friendship with Berkeley Moynihan. Of the days at Brandon Villa he used to say, " We were all terrified of old Miss Baxendale. Miss Emma used to teach the piano and Miss Jane did the cooking. We were always having rhubarb and tapioca. We hated it." No doubt they did ; as doubtless boys still do. Such was and is a staple of the English schoolboy's diet.

A time was to come when the Misses Baxendales' two old pupils, the bishop and the peer, were to sit beside each other at a public ceremony in Leeds. One was to turn to the other and say, " I wonder what Miss Baxendale would think of us now. Would you dare to stand up to her if she were here ? I don't think I should ! "

As the years went by, the awkward problem of further education for Berkeley became obtrusive. Mrs. Moynihan and Ada cherished ideas that were not in accord with the financial means at their disposal. Andrew Moynihan had left them no money for the fulfilment of these ambitious projects. Nevertheless it was through him that their desires were realised. The hard lot of the Moynihan family was brought to the notice of H.R.H. the Duke of Cambridge and the distinguished record of Andrew Moynihan recalled to his memory. The Duke was sympathetic. He secured for Berkeley a nomination to Christ's Hospital, the Bluecoat School. This school is one of the great institutions of England. It was founded in 1552 during the reign of Edward the Sixth. Its qualities are unique. All admissions to it are by nomination and election ; all its pupils are boys who would not otherwise have had the opportunity of enjoying an education of the same high standard. Its old scholars have occupied the highest places in the land. Christ's Hospital stands alongside the great public schools of the country. The traditional costume worn by its members is unusual and impressive. The belted monkish gown and its accompaniment of yellow stockings and buckle shoes are striking and unforgettable to all who have once seen them. They are the label of a remarkable foundation.

Berkeley entered Christ's Hospital in 1875. The qualities that were manifest in him in later life seemed well adapted to give him success in a big school for boys. But his record at school was not one of success. He did not stand out from the crowd ; none of his mentors saw the shadow of destiny fall before him as he paced the school yard. He was an ordinary boy amongst many

other ordinary boys. His career was utterly undis-
tinguished. He left no imprint upon the school in work
or play. His intellectual qualities appeared indifferent.
His athletic ability was not exceptional : he could neither
outrun nor outwit his fellows at games. Long memories
that reach back to those remote days report that the boy
was without distinction in any form. Five years after
his arrival at Christ's Hospital he left the school unsung,
unmissed, and fast forgotten.

We may explain this as we will. It is odd that it should
have been so. The boy was not shy ; he was always full
of quips and chatter ; he had all the exuberance that goes
with red hair. Perhaps his development was slow ; perhaps, lacking a particular ideal or focus for his ambitions,
his efforts were diffused and unobserved. One clue to this
pale beginning does exist. In it may lie the explanation
of these unmeaning years. Berkeley was not happy at
school. In his maturity it was a rare thing to hear him
refer to his schooldays. When he did so his words were
brief and apathetic. By some this was attributed to
snobbery ; they perceived in his manner a regret that
he had not been to one of those fashionable schools that
carry with their name the implication of social precedence. It may have been so ; the failing is a human one.
He may have been homesick ; but surely not sufficiently
so to take all colour out of his life for a period of years.
More comprehensible is it that his previous home life
had unfitted him for the ways of a big boys' school. He
had become accustomed to the assiduous attentions of
three women, all of whom adored him. It is easy to shine
in such company. It is almost inevitable that one should
become vain. Boys are merciless critics of their contemporaries. They will only tolerate vanity when there

is, in their eyes, justification for it. Berkeley must have
had some comfortable habits to break and some rough
lessons to learn in those early years. Yet though he was
left with no affection for Christ's Hospital that school
had provided a discipline that was urgently needed. It
strengthened his character and increased his adapta-
bility to the ways of others. If it did not alter his prefer-
ence for the company of women to that of men, for such
was his constitution to the end of his life, it did at least
teach him that there were discoverable delights in the
less gentle of these two worlds. He remained susceptible
to flattery but he developed a zest for the rigours of
intellectual interplay between men. Time quickly gave
him a chance to show that, while he brought nothing to
the school, he took away from it a useful armour in which
to face the world.

When he was fifteen, he was transferred to the Royal
Naval School at New Cross. A close association existed
between this school and Christ's Hospital. It was this
factor that made possible the boy's entrance into a new
school at an unusually late age. The change was justified
and was provoked by Berkeley's inability to settle down
happily at Christ's Hospital. The Royal Naval School no
longer exists in its old form or situation. In those days it
did not insist that its pupils should pass into the navy on
leaving school. There was never at any time the intention of entering Berkeley for the navy. New Cross was
then a green suburb of London. Now it has been
swallowed up by the industrial East End. The inquisitive
wanderer will find nothing to evoke memories of golden
schooldays. Over all hangs a drab pall of smoke, the
shroud that is the price of London's prosperity.

At the Naval School Berkeley settled down with a

contentment he had never known at Christ's Hospital. He did well at his studies and enjoyed athletics. In 1933, answering some questions about his activities in sport, he wrote :

" My athletic record is not worth discussing. At school the swimming prizes always came my way. I got the Humane Society Medal in 1882 for proficiency in swimming exercises with reference to saving life from drowning. I did the 100 yards in 1 minute 12⅖ seconds which equalled the amateur record. Which is now about 20 seconds faster with the crawl ! We did the old overhand and I was trained by Willie Beckwith who was the professional champion. I won the steeplechase, and the mile, too : but neither is worth mentioning. I captained the football and played casually at Blackheath, lured by Harry Vassal just down from Oxford where he had been Captain of Rugby."

This account does signify a rapid development in the but recently insignificant schoolboy. The swimming achievement is a notable one. To equal the amateur record at any sport is a considerable feat. It is one upon which men have rested their reputations for the remainder of their lives. Berkeley had reason to be proud of it. However transient the fame it brought him, the habit then created in him was a fruitful one. Of all outdoor sports swimming ever continued his favourite ; during the busiest years of his life it was the only one pursued with any regularity. He delighted in it.

* * * * *

When a boy reaches the age of fifteen his parents are looking for some plan as to his ultimate calling. By the time he is eighteen they are likely to be much agitated if a definite decision has not been reached. Berkeley

45

had never had in his own mind any doubt about his vocation. He had always been, was now and always would be, determined to be a soldier. It had been his intention since the day he emerged from childhood and the prospect of manhood found his mind unchanged. To his mother this had been the source of increasing distress. Of each day's burdens this knowledge was the greatest. She hated the idea. Her life had been spent hitched to the army wagon; because of it her most fruitful years had been rendered barren; and because of it, too, the high summer of her days had been chilled by loneliness. Now, when the sunlight was again breaking over the hills, she was again to be thrown back into the shadows. The great hopes she had for her boy were to go the way of all Moynihan hopes of old. Separations and fears were again to be her lot, and to these, as she herself had been brought, would her son's wife be brought. Bitter thoughts bowed her down. It seemed as if upon herself alone was imposed the price of a nation's security. Let others go out into the street and be thrilled by the sparkle of uniforms, by the undulant grace of banners in the wind, by the stirring, sad crescendo of the bands. All right for them. They returned to prosperous homes and large jolly families. All right for them to pat themselves on the back because they had done their share by paying a little extra on the income tax. She could think only of her two men, her husband and her son; the one gone, the other soon to go. But he must not go. She would not have it. She would resist it to the last.

She packed her bags and went to London. On her arrival there she went without delay to the Royal Naval School. She called upon the headmaster. He knew of Berkeley's fixed intention to enter the army. His own opinion was that the boy had exceptional ability in one subject only — Mathematics. This, thought the headmaster, equipped Berkeley to enter one of the Civil Services. He would particularly like to see the boy enter the Indian Civil Service ; the life was enjoyable, the chances of promotion good, and the lack of personal wealth no handicap.

This was a little better. Mrs. Moynihan would have preferred to hear the headmaster make a spontaneous suggestion in accordance with her personal wish for Berkeley ; but what he had proposed was the next best thing. What did she want Berkeley to be ? Ah — she had one passionate desire. Above all things she would like to see her son a doctor. This had, for many years, been the secret longing of her heart. Whether Berkeley was to become famous or remain obscure, whether he was to gain riches or continue in poverty — these would be matters of indifference to her so long as he was a doctor. The day on which he turned his steps to medicine would be a happy one for her.

In a little while Berkeley was called into the room. He knew of his mother's visit and easily guessed the occasion for it. He talked with his mother, with the headmaster, and with them both together. He remained obdurate. Nothing would make him change his mind. The Moynihans had always been soldiers. His father had been a soldier — a great one. He was going to be a soldier. The discussion rapidly came to an end. In the presence of such determination all arguments were useless. Mrs. Moynihan returned to Leeds, summoning up what resignation she could command to reconcile her to the future.

But coincidence was to prove a stronger weapon than

persuasion. In the spring holidays of 1883 a curious chance fell out. One afternoon Berkeley and a friend went swimming. Berkeley brought his friend home to tea with him. While Berkeley went to prepare himself for the meal his friend stayed in the sitting-room to talk to Mrs. Moynihan. As Berkeley returned to the room his steps were arrested at the door by a few words that reached his ear from the conversation going on within. Mrs. Moynihan was speaking of Berkeley's choice of an army career. In London her phrases embodied cold reason ; principles not personalities had been her theme. Now it was different. Now she spoke of all that this career would mean to her, of her ruined hopes, of the desolate prospect for her in the years ahead, of the endless poverty that was now apparently to be the lot of her daughters. It all came from her heart. Perhaps she was wrong ; but that is irrelevant. She was not discussing right or wrong ; she was allowing her tired mind to lay down its burdens.

The arrival with the tea of Berkeley's sisters, Ada and Eva, broke up the little moment. Before long the whole family were sitting round the table laughing and chattering. No one could share a meal with Berkeley without being drawn into the conversation by his rushing stream of jokes, disputations, and enthusiasms. Nothing delighted him more than to start a discussion of some abstract problem. He was like a puppy with a bone, a kitten with a ball of wool. As his sisters' inclination for this kind of diversion was no less than his own, the babble that arose from the table was terrific. Thrust, cut, parry — the conversation flashed back and forth across the whiteness of the cloth like sword-play. Voices were raised higher and higher. Sisters and brother bayed like hounds on the scent of the dialectic hare. Mrs. Moynihan lapsed into reverie ; she had followed this hunt, a hunt that never make a kill, too often not to be able now to foresee its every twist and turn — it held no surprises for her. She drifted away into the world of her own imaginings. With unexpected suddenness, breaking away from the general talk, Berkeley turned to her and said :

" Mother, something very important happened to me to-day ! "

" What was it, dear ? "

Dear Berkeley — something very important was always happening to him. Such was usually the preamble to a new sally. You asked what it was and at once he would pounce on you with his little joke.

" I decided to be the other thing."

" You decided to be the other thing . . . ? "

Ellen Moynihan's heart gave a flutter. Was he serious ? A bad subject for joking, this. No matter how hard she tried not to mind, it always gave that little stab of pain. In spite of strivings after philosophic composure, in spite of the ardent prayers of a devout mind, the defensive armour was never quite complete. But this time Berkeley's behaviour was somehow different. There was a sense of excited strain beneath the surface of boyish laughter. Was he, at the very last, to change his mind ?

The talk stopped. All perceived a change in the spirit that pervaded the room. Yet how like Berkeley ! How he loved the dramatic moment of poised tension — himself the centre of it ! All looked towards him.

" To be the other thing . . ." says Mrs. Moynihan. " What do you mean, dear ? "

" I mean I am going to save life, not take it. As we were coming back from swimming we passed the infirmary.

E

We stood and looked at it for a little while. It came on me all of a sudden that that was what I really wanted to do. The Moynihans have done enough killing. It's time they mended their ways ! And I'm going to be the first to do it. I'm going to be a doctor ! ''

There was no person in the room for whom those words did not have a peculiar significance. For ourselves, who were not there, they provide no surprise ; for us their freshness is spent. But for Mrs. Moynihan they were the startling consummation of all her hopes. In that moment, and for the rest of her life, she faithfully believed them to be the divine answer to all her prayers. Old disappointments and frustrations served only to enhance their sweetness now. Ada and Eva, too, found in them the answer to their own prayers. No less than their mother they rested their spirits in His providence. Before Ada's eyes was revealed in this instant a vista of the success that her brother was to command. Her teaching was not to be wasted. A rare intelligence was to win the admiration of the world. So Ada thought — and so have thought the sisters of a thousand brothers. And yet in Ada's thought was this distinction : there was in it that which forbids comparison with others. Her beliefs in Berkeley and in her projects for his future were wildly extravagant, fantastically ambitious. To her no ascent would be too difficult for him, no peak unscalable. From this viewpoint she never moved ; throughout her long life this attitude of mind was sustained. That a soldier's son, starting in hardship and obscurity, should rise to hold the highest surgeon's office in the land, that the King should grace him with nobility, that his fame should spread throughout the world — none of these things in their day surprised her. They were Berkeley's right, his minimum due. As each new honour befell her brother her only feeling was one of gratification at the world's good sense in recognising merit ; the only thing wrong in her eyes was that, perhaps, the honour was not quite as high as the merit deserved. For Berkeley the world held no accolade that could be commensurate with Ada's estimation of his worth.

Berkeley delighted in the sensation he had caused. He had assembled his characters, created a mood, and then, himself the central figure, had held the company in tense expectancy before divulging his secret. Perfect. Only one thing remained to round out the act ; an anticlimax like a cold douche of water. Nothing could delight him more. He plunged headlong back into the torrent of jests and nonsense. He would tolerate no serious discussion of his news ; all that could wait till the morrow. And so, while all wished to discuss the single subject of their thoughts, he, like a mischievous leprechaun, teased them until they could have fallen on him out of frustrated rage. That was a wonderful afternoon ! Here was a tale to last a lifetime ! He never wearied of its telling.

It should command our indulgence. The incident is felicitously apt. Here is displayed a little facet of the man ; but a little facet the sparkle of whose rays illuminate his whole character. That love of fun, that puckish mixing of the gay and serious, that thespian streak — how essentially Berkeley ! Time never robbed him of these qualities ; they were to be the delight and despair of all who loved him ; they were as engaging as they were irritating. By them he attracted friends and through them he provoked critics. They invested his nature with an elusiveness that was as charming to

some as it was annoying to others. It was the Irish in
him.

*　　*　　*　　*　　*

Our reaction to this sudden change of mind can hardly
be unanimous. Some will think it facile. In their eyes
Berkeley's fixed purpose was too easily undermined by
momentary emotion ; the new desire to please too easily
mastered previous judgement. Others again will not
escape a wave of disappointment. Is this how youthful
steps turn towards high calling ? Where is the dedication, the consciousness of singular vocation ? In the
general mind no pursuit is more hedged about with conventional illusions than that of medicine. We have
become accustomed to think of the great doctor as one
whose earliest childhood was invested with precocious
biologic curiosity. We like to read of how, at tender age,
he is discovered in the nursery not playing with toys but
engaged upon dissection of some modest mammal. But
a few years later on we find him gazing down the micro-
scope ; beneath its shining lenses he detects the vital
secrets of life's throb and flow. As youth expands to
manhood his scientific skill becomes entwined with
dedicated fervour ; he will release mankind ; shake
from its limbs the shackles of disease. Alas, — not so
are doctors made. In medicine, too, as in much else,
the novelist holds up the distorting glass to life.

Berkeley was no sad exception. Greater doctors than
he was have been first impelled by lesser inspiration. In
medicine the spirit grows by what it feeds upon. Increased awareness of the range and horror of disease
awakes the student's charity. Out of this springs true
devotion. Many a man, at his first entry to the wards
an uncouth fellow, has emerged from them a gentle

and compassionate healer. Few pass through that experience unmodified by sympathy and understanding. The journey through the wards is the journey through man's essential nature ; within their walls his spirit is nakedly revealed — comic, indomitable, pathetic, splendid. In the wards is first seen the mystic-silvery light that invests the grail towards which the great doctor ever after stumbling and groping strives.

*   *   *   *   *

Berkeley indeed had not undergone as remarkable a metamorphosis as the event implies. He had but removed by a few years his ultimate objective. He still intended to enter the army. But now it was to be as a doctor. For a few years longer, for just as long as it would take him to qualify in medicine, he would remain at home to comfort and delight his mother. These years were to be a filial offering, a token of affection, and a compromise between the conflicting wishes of himself and Mrs. Moynihan. To these ends he would make concession and for them face immediate difficulties.

Difficulties there were certainly to be. Even the most modest medical education demands prolonged expenditure of money. However small the total expense might be, it was an expense that the Moynihans could not then afford. Without outside help they could not manage it ; it would be impossible. But happily there were those who were willing to help Berkeley. Two people provided the money for his student days and the early years of his qualification : two uncles, both on his mother's side : Mr. Ball, the husband of his mother's sister ; and Mr. Parkin, his mother's brother. The disinterested generosity of these men first placed him on the threshold before

53

the door that was to open on success. That he opened it himself none can deny. But without them he might never have been in a position to turn the handle. To say that in spite of all obstacles Berkeley would have succeeded anyhow and anywhere is merest speculation. At one time or another this has been said of nearly all eminent men ; it is their present eminence as much as their inborn qualities that compels the observation. We must take the facts as they stand. It was not for Berkeley's benefactors to know over fifty years ago the rich dividend the world was later to reap from their investment. They, in their modest way, helped to make available some of the blessings that a great surgeon can confer upon the community. We may prize these blessings as we will ; not all will think alike. But let those whose gratitude to Berkeley now is high, those that in their own estimation owe to him their health and even lives, pause for a moment to remember gratefully the two men who rendered these things possible. Out of the fullness of their hearts those whom Berkeley sustained may well pay such a tribute.

PART II
THE STUDENT AND YOUNG DOCTOR

The Student and Young Doctor

In the autumn of 1883 Berkeley Moynihan entered medical school. He first passed through the doors of the Yorkshire College on his eighteenth birthday. He qualified as a doctor four years later. Those four years were spent in continuous hard work — remorseless, unrelieved ; during that time he lived in a little world bounded by the walls of his home, the Yorkshire College, and the Leeds General Infirmary ; in these places, working with beaver-like assiduity and unobtrusiveness, he laid the foundations of his great career. So soundly were they built that no strain imposed upon them by the later superstructure of his researches was able to reveal in them gaps or weakness.

* * * * *

The Yorkshire College was not a university ; it was not empowered to give degrees to its students. Founded over fifty years earlier, it was still only a collection of classes in various subjects ; its members could there take courses that entitled and fitted them to take the examinations and degrees of the University of London. Though the majority of its members were studying medicine its courses were not limited to that field. It was steadily growing ; the scope of its teaching was yearly being enlarged ; it ultimately blossomed into the University of Leeds, which is to-day one of the most vigorous of the

English universities. Now it has an ardent social and corporate life. In Berkeley's day the social life did not exist at all and the corporate life was but in embryo. There were no club-rooms, student associations, or organised athletics ; Berkeley and his fellow students met solely in the lecture-room and laboratories ; they took their meals at home ; there also they read and spent their leisure hours. Each student might acquire a little coterie of friends, but in no different way from any other walk of life ; not at all in the manifold and diverse manner that we now regard as one of the characteristic benefits of a university career.

That Berkeley made few friends during this period is not then surprising. Those that were intimate did not amount to more than three ; of these but one remained close in later years — the others were taken by circumstance beyond his frequent reach. W. H. Thompson — " Tommy " throughout the years — was the one fellow student with whom opportunity and inclination permitted Berkeley to transmute acquaintanceship into mature and enduring friendship. Dr. Thompson came to the Yorkshire College after Berkeley, but the two of them were not long in getting to know each other. Berkeley experienced a new happiness, for out of his childhood he had brought no treasured friends. Neither now nor in later life did he maintain correspondence or meetings with any of his school-mates. A striking feature of his life is the clean cut between all that came before his entry into medicine and all that came after. Of his early days he cherished but a single thing — his love for his mother and sisters, and the happy memory of times spent with them. His life began on that eighteenth birthday. Long before that for many of us the golden years have come —

and, alas, gone. Not so with Berkeley. For him it seems as though some shadow darkened infancy : it may have been his mother's lonely widowhood, his own lack of success at school, or the stringent grip of poverty upon a gentle home ; it may have been the fret of pride upon a mind jealous of social caste. But what it was he never said ; we cannot tell.

Whatever may have been that cloud, the arrival of Tommy pierced through it like a beam of the sun. It thawed out some of Berkeley's deep reticence. Here was a new adventure for an oddly compounded nature. Intensely gregarious, and always to be so, Berkeley was not often unreserved with men. The raw material of friendship is the interchange of inner thought ; the privacy that guards the mind must be relaxed. Berkeley was not forthcoming in this exercise. Perhaps he thought it weak ; perhaps he feared to give hostages to time. To natures such as Berkeley's true friendship is slow to come. Men do not reveal themselves to those who do not give in kind. Now, however, under this new influence, Berkeley advanced a step ; to the wonderful sparkle of his companionship he added warmth. Mutual affection came as the reward. To Tommy he took a portion of his troubles and with him shared the pleasures of success. And boundless was his delight in success ; no mock modesty dulled it. His love of it was childlike, never waning. Yet, even at its most exaggerated, criticism was disarmed by this very childishness. He had done it for you ; no less than his must be your pleasure. Tommy was always first recipient of special news. So he deserved to be. At each achievement of his friend his heart was full ; no tincture of jealousy entered in. For his simple devotion Berkeley loved him ; to him Berkeley gave as much of himself as it lay within his power to give to any man. As often happens, the solid basis of the friendship of these men was rooted in their differences. Berkeley was brilliant, filled with spontaneous enthusiasms, a great talker, passionately in need of friends ; Tommy was faithful, responsive to others, forgiving to vanity. To each other they were the support and complement.

It would have been sad if Berkeley's advance and the drift of the world should have come between him and Tommy to end their friendship. Happily no such thing occurred. When Tommy's training was completed he moved from Leeds to the neighbouring Yorkshire town of Bradford ; there he made for himself a wide reputation as a physician, and enjoyed a just respect. He remained at Berkeley's side until the end. The friendship of this abundant heart was one of the finest credentials of his worth that Berkeley carried with him out of this life.

* * * * *

The layman knows much about doctors ; but often less about the circumstances that attend their apprenticeship and qualification. About these he may be curious ; he may wonder how the wheels of medicine go round. Those, then, for whom these matters hold no mystery may here tolerate a brief digression for the sake of those who do not, yet would like to know, something about these things.

The medical curriculum has changed in details since 1883 but its fundamentals remain the same ; though the light of investigation has caused the introduction into it of some new subjects and has reduced the significance of some old ones, its pillars are still unchanged. What obtains to-day differs but little from what obtained in

Berkeley's day. In description of this kind the frills of difference can be left out.

The medical course is divided into three stages ; examinations punctuate the end of each. First come physics, chemistry, botany, and zoology ; second, the normal anatomy and physiology of the human organism ; third, the study of medicine, surgery, obstetrics, gynaecology, and pathology. The first two stages occupy a period of time approximately equal to the last. The passing of the examination that concludes the final stage is the mark of qualification. The first two stages may be taken at hospital or university ; the third stage can only be taken at one of the recognised teaching hospitals.

Various bodies conduct the examinations that mark each stage ; hence the various letters after a doctor's name that may signify his qualification. But, for any particular qualification, all the examinations must be taken with the same body. A student may elect to take the examinations of two bodies, and so obtain a double qualification ; this he does because, by so doing, he may hasten his qualification ; or, in the event of failure with one body, may proceed without delay to qualification with the other. In England there are three recognised routes by which a student may qualify. He may take the joint diplomas of the Royal College of Physicians and Surgeons — this entitles him to place after his name the letters L.R.C.P., M.R.C.S. ; he may obtain the licence of the Society of Apothecaries — he then becomes an L.S.A. ; lastly, and perhaps most commonly, he may take the degree of a university — this is the universally known M.B. The relative severity of the examinations is frequently argued. It is generally held that the university degrees are an unimpeachable label of proficiency.

Even between the different university degrees there are some niceties of comparative merit. But upon one point all are agreed : that there is no better degree than that of the University of London will not be contended by any. Its examinations are stiff but fair ; its graduates, as far as can be humanly controlled, sound and well-balanced. It was the M.B. of London that Berkeley set himself to take. The periodic visits to London that this entailed provided for him the only variant from his working life in Leeds.

These are the examinations that must be passed before, according to the laws of the land, registration as a doctor is permitted. But there are others too. They are the examinations that are associated with what are known in the medical world as "higher qualifications". These higher qualifications imply a standard of learning and experience of certain of the final subjects that far transcends that demanded for the qualifying examinations ; they are taken only by a small minority of the profession. For specialism they are the justification and recognition. There are so many of them that to give an account of them all here would be to weary and confuse the reader. Out of them I have selected for description the three best known, the three that are most frequently encountered. They are difficult to obtain and penetrating in their search of the candidate's knowledge.

The M.D. degrees of the universities may be taken in nominated subjects. The possessor of such a degree is one who has made a special study of one of the clinical subjects. An M.D. generally connotes a breadth of learning rather than a practised skill ; its bearer must first have been granted the M.B. degree of that same university. The Royal College of Surgeons and the Royal College of Physicians each bestow a higher qualification ; candidature for these is only accepted after the submission to the College of proof of specialised experience. The diploma of the College of Physicians is the M.R.C.P. — Member of the Royal College of Physicians. The test is one in medicine, exacting and prolonged ; out of the accepted candidates only a very small percentage pass each time. For appointment as physician to the staff of a hospital, where medicine is taught to students, this diploma is essential.

The diploma of the College of Surgeons is the F.R.C.S. — Fellow of the Royal College of Surgeons. The two examinations for it comprise one of the greatest intellectual tests in the world of learning. The first part is an examination in anatomy and physiology, the Primary Fellowship, commonly called the " Primary " ; more hearts have been broken over this, perhaps, than over any other English examination. Once over this hurdle the candidate, after surgical experience, is allowed to sit for the second part — a test in surgery. Here again, even though the sieve of the Primary has been passed, the failures are many. No person safely emerging from the twin fires of these examinations can be regarded as wholly unfitted for the practice of surgery ; to it the majority of the successful candidates are well suited. All surgeons on the staffs of teaching hospitals must now have the F.R.C.S.

Berkeley, having set himself to get the London M.B., was not long in fastening his eyes also upon the F.R.C.S. The Leeds of his day looked on this as high ambition.

*   *   *   *   *

Anyone with prolonged experience of a medical school must have noticed in particular one interesting phenomenon : the student who, coming from school or college totally without reputation for intellectual ability or effort, suddenly and surprisingly reveals unusual capacity. His work is respected and he passes his examinations with an ease that could not have been anticipated. So many separate and individual explanations for this have been offered that one inclines to the view that perhaps a single explanation covers every case. A simple and reasonable solution is available. Are not these happenings a manifestation of true vocation ? Is it not that these minds are now, as never before, working beneath the impetus of keen desire ? Is not this the secret of these new-found powers of achievement ? As a duck takes to water, so do many men take to medicine.

We cannot say that Berkeley, when he first sat in the lecture theatre of the Yorkshire College in that far-off autumn of 1883, was the subject of vocation. Indeed, we have evidence to the contrary. He had not relented at all from his purpose of entering the army ; he had but, for his mother's sake, postponed the realisation of those hopes. This, though, does not invalidate the thesis. In the mental composition of many men there exist, hitherto unknown, latent springs that are first released by the processes of a medical education. Berkeley found that the call of a whim discovered echoes deep in his fibre ; medicine evolved for him out of a means to an end into the completest satisfaction of his mind and spirit. Years were to elapse before this was self-admitted. But the instrumentality of this change was soon established.

From his initial opening of a medical book he knew no difficulty in comprehension or remembrance. He read quickly and with powerful concentration. While most of his fellows twice covered every page he need go over it but once ; but he neither presumed nor traded, as well he might have done, upon his memory ; he worked with tireless energy. He could have done better than his colleagues doing only half the work they did. Instead, he worked almost twice as hard as they. It was a claim of his that, as a student, he was rarely at his studies for less than fourteen hours a day ; before examination sixteen was his plan. The claim was not idle, it was many times confirmed. To those in competition with him this was heart-breaking. No day was long enough for them to get abreast of him ; even when they were able to maintain such working hours as he did, still, when the day was done, they could not show so great a profit. Endowed by nature with so many weapons, he could, however brave the hearts, out-distance all.

He had the classic gifts : those that are recognised as being a doctor's best : a retentive memory and all but limitless reserves of strength. His strength was not mere muscularity, it was that supple, integrative physique that knows no lassitude. He could do with little sleep and no more exercise than was encompassed by the day's activities. He took care of his body, but was not obsessed by it. He exacted from his mind tasks that would cripple most of us. Indeed, the word exacted may be wrong, for he performed the tasks with ease. He read and re-membered ; he saw and could for ever after visualise.

It would be unfair to hold him up to others as example. His virtues might be emulated, but not his fullest works. It would be impossible for one of common constitution, by sole propulsion of the spirit, to follow in his steps. He was richly blessed ; his credit is that not the smallest trickle of those blessings ran to waste. He played upon himself like a musician upon a subtle instrument.

His general aspect impressed itself upon all. He was about six feet tall, with the appearance as of greater height. His face had an opaque pallor ; no colour flushed his cheeks. His head was large and only just maintained the due proportions of his frame. It was surmounted by hair of a violent red. The contrast between this and the whiteness of his skin carved itself in the recollection of his friends. His step was light and his figure lissom. His gait was dignified, yet without heaviness. There was a delicate balance in his weight ; to this his breadth of shoulder and the smallness of his feet made contribution. He was good-looking ; but in no style of orthodoxy. His lithe mobility, the vivacity of his face and voice, the flame of his hair, were the compound of these looks. They were enlightened by the scintillation of his whole demeanour. He bubbled with good-humour ; a sense of fun infused his being. Little unmalicious jokes he loved ; he delighted in teasing, but never with un-kindliness. Provided that no bitterness of any sort crept in, controversy could never weary him ; the more abstruse the theme of talk the better pleased he was. Disputation of this kind is generally an academic pleasure, a cold gymnastic of the mind ; but Berkeley brought to it a humanising, warm invigoration, giving it fresh vitality.

Of extra-mural reading he did little ; he had no time for it. His love of literature developed later. Yet, though his taste was still unformed, its scaffoldings were visible. In Shakespeare's sonnets he unearthed a sympathetic mirror of his thoughts ; in them he found a satisfaction that communion with his friends did not promote. To

memorise them was easy ; to repeat them delicious. He
saw the spring in them, and not as yet the autumn they
concealed — that was for the future. They were the
solace of his youthful dreamings and, down the years, the
fountain of his apt quotation. They were the gate through
which he passed, as time went by, to the other glories of
the poet's flower-decked fields.

He had, even in those early days, an ardent love of
words. Dulcet phrases and mellifluous adjectives en-
tranced him. They matched the sweet depth of his voice.
No less for their music than their meaning did he cherish
them. Except within the confines of his home he had no
chance for recitation ; his family were the only audience
he could then command. But, from his first encounter
with the sonnets, his devotion was sealed ; he became
the acolyte before the shrine of words.

The only other seas of his literary voyaging were the
varied oceans of the Bible. Devoutly religious though his
mother was, he himself had no theistic bias. Not having
yet the need for spiritual comfort, nor having inherited
his mother's faith, religious exercises did not appeal to
him. It was the lovely English of the Bible that excited
him ; he did not then explore its philosophic content.
But those words, velvet and resonant — how he loved
them ! In them he had the artist's apprehension of
beauty — painful, intangible, ethereal.

For music, strangely, he had but little ear. Admittedly
he had no opportunity of hearing it. But even when his
better means brought it within his reach he took no
pleasure in it. Avid for cultivated joys he listened carefully, but answering emotion never came. Within the
narrow compass of the human voice he could appreciate
variants ; over the great scale he was insensible to tone.

Of this he made light ; nevertheless it irked him that, to him for whom so much was possible, this art should remain ever inaccessible. His only musical diversion was the singing of *The Messiah* at the breakfast-table. To this performance he brought great gusto and protean versatility, singing all the parts himself and being his own conductor ; in later years, when his own children surrounded the table, this matutinal display of virtuosity daily brought the house down.

In pictorial art he had no interest, nor such have medical students as a rule. In years to come when, during his travels, he visited most of the famous galleries of Europe he developed a facility for talk about pictures. Whether he ever really cared about them is doubtful — probably not. But he was grudging in any admission of incomplete appreciation of this, or any other, art. This for no reason of intellectual snobbery. It was a reaction analogous to that he had to music. Why should there be loveliness, and it beyond his grasp ?

When he could afford it, he went to the theatre. He sat up in the gallery with his mother or one of his sisters. When the lights went down he forgot the hard seat and the surrounding aroma of oranges ; the musky smell that blows across the footlights came to his nostrils carrying with it its own peculiar sense of imminent adventure, the world of fashion strutted before his eyes in charming mimicry — and into it, for just a little while, he stepped, out of his own grim world of examinations, empty pockets, and self-dependence. He was infinitely responsive to illusion ; his emotions had a truly Irish vibrance (and this though he was capable of a highly reasoned practicality at other times). Into the feelings of the represented characters he entered eagerly. As he grew older this capacity did not desert him and he never tired of going to the theatre. When prosperity moved him from the gallery to the stalls, he did not become the captious critic ; he was as excited as ever when the curtain rose, and he indulged in no foolish sentimentalities about the good old gallery days.

Of all the plays he saw his favourites were the operas of Gilbert and Sullivan. In his youth they were in their heyday ; their points were topical and their tunes fresh and unexpected. The simplicity of the melodies enabled him both to enjoy and remember them, partially tone-deaf though he was. He would go home and whistle them or, round a piano, sing them in chorus with his friends. Even though to hit the right note was with him a happy accident, he managed to make a great deal of noise, and had at least as much fun.

* * * * *

The mention of a particular calling arouses in the mind of the public an immediate reflex thought. A concept of its follower, derived from knowledge of his avocation, is at once to hand — ready-made, conventionalised ; the plumber is forgetful, the soldier arrogant, the lawyer sly ; for each pursuit there is an oft-used adjective. The medical student is well pigeon-holed. He is usually thought of as being rowdy and boisterous, callow and insensitive ; he and his fellows are notorious for their pranks and coarse-grained humour ; dividing their time between the tavern and the wards, they play out their parts in oafish comedy.

All this is nonsense. The rumbustiousness of Dickens is no more. Even if the Bob Sawyer type did still exist in Berkeley's day, Berkeley himself did not belong to it, for he was never cast in that conventional mould. His life was quiet, his days laborious. He had little time for anything but work. His indulgences were few ; he smoked little and drank hardly at all. He applied no special principles in these matters, and such little inclination as he had for minor luxuries was further tempered by the inadequacy of his means. In this he did not differ greatly from his contemporaries. Even then, for medical students, moderation was displacing old-time ribaldries. The evidence provided by his colleagues outlines a picture more of drabness than of gaiety. The need to replenish shallow purses caused all to think mainly of early and rapid qualification.

Some relief from the tedium of endless work was provided by the recurrent formal occasions of the student year. Of such was the Introductory Lecture that opened the Autumn Session of each year ; especially since it was usually given by some famous medical man. There was about the one of 1883, the one that opened Berkeley's very first term, a certain unconscious and prophetic prescience. The lecture in that year was given by Dr. Clifford Allbutt — later Sir Clifford Allbutt, and destined to be numbered among the great English physicians. Present on that occasion, as well as Berkeley, was the late Dr. Herbert John Roper of Leeds, also entering upon his first term ; the evolution of his friend Moynihan's life was to keep that lecture fresh in his mind. He tells us that Dr. Allbutt, a powerful orator, opened with these words :

" You students will be told to-day in a score of pulpits that you have cast in your lot with a noble profession. Do not suppose that the pulpiteers will hasten to add that you will make money by it — let him who hath notions

so sordid as that beware of our precincts. Look forward
to a noble but unappreciated existence. Your board
will be bare. You will not have the satisfaction of knowing that any medical man has been made a Peer, and
your food will be the bread of knowledge, and your
reward the consciousness of your lofty associates."

Well might Dr. Roper remember it! Berkeley's
board was to end by being far from bare, and his place
was to be in the House of Lords (where he was preceded
by Lister and Dawson).

There were other good things in that lecture too. The
passage that follows is one that is identical with Berkeley's
own later teaching. Perhaps this is when the seed was
first sown in his mind, for in the future he was to share
fully these sentiments of Dr. Allbutt's :

" As to your patient — put yourself in his place. He
may not know, as you do, either your skill or the vanity
of his fears. A cripple more or less — or a gravestone
more or less — is nothing to the solar system, but it is
all the world to him."

Dr. Roper was himself a man of considerable ability ;
he had a distinguished record in the medical school and
won many scholastic prizes ; indeed, he was Berkeley's
chief rival in that field. It is interesting therefore to hear
him speak of those times ; his memory of them was very
good.

" Years of Students, that is a batch of students appearing in one year, vary like vintage years. The year we joined
was a very good one. Moynihan at this time was a rather
tall, thin young man, with a pale serious face, and a shock
of red hair. He did not strike me in the first years of our
studentship as a man of outstanding brilliancy. There
were other men I thought much cleverer. He competed
for all the Medals and Prizes that were given at the end

of the Session, but, though he secured many, did by no means secure them all. He was a very hard worker. He could begin working for the next examination the day after he had passed one. Relentless ambition drove him on and gave him no rest. There was a Working Men's Club just below the old School of Medicine where students sometimes went to play billiards. Moynihan was never seen there. I remember one student from Sheffield was very good at the game — he achieved no success for himself in his profession, but became Mayor of his native town. (With what nice irony does Fate lead her rivers to the sea!) Moynihan was very regular and punctual in his attendance at lectures, and frequently stayed behind to ask the lecturer some question on his discussion. This delicate attention was much appreciated by the lecturer. He grumbled a great deal about having to attend lectures which he considered, and rightly, not to be of any use, but like all the rest of us he went just the same."

It is to be feared that the above " delicate attention " did not win for Berkeley an all-round favour ! But never mind — few of us have not paid service to the foible. Berkeley had humour ; so let us acquit him of Dr. Roper's veiled impeachment.

*   *   *   *   *

One of the most exciting moments in the medical student's career is that in which, with the examinations in anatomy and physiology just behind him, he first enters the wards of a hospital. Now, after two or three years of apparently getting nowhere, he feels that he has at last got his foot upon the good hard road of medicine. He sallies forth into the town and buys a stethoscope — delicious moment ! He hurries home and then, withdrawing to his room, tremulously applies the instrument to his chest. Cavernous, incomprehensible rumblings meet his ear. This — will one ever be able to make sense of this ? Is this poor thing the long-awaited voice of professional destiny ? The instant doubt is quick forgotten ; the next adventure hurries on ; in the morning, magnificently armed with the seal and emblem of his trade, he takes his place at the bedside — his first patient before him, his mentor gazing at him across the bed.

The months that follow are delightful. There is all the fun of medicine, and little or none of the responsibility. Halcyon state ! The next examination is remote ; too far away to confuse interest or trouble consciousness. New things are discovered every day. The wisdom of ages, slowly won and dearly bought, in a few vivid weeks unfolds itself before the student's eyes. The long, long drama of medicine is now replayed ; but all compressed, refined, the struggles of years yielded up in perfect epitome.

But, as the time goes by, the boundaries of medicine's cultivated lands force themselves upon the initiate's attention. Beyond them he sees the vast unbroken territories in which disease runs wild. Then only does he fully realise through what bitter efforts has the ground been won. Faintly he shares the tribulations and excitements of the pioneers ; their heartbreaks, frustrations, triumphs live in him again. He is inspired by their achievements and humbled by his own poor ignorance. Most of all does he feel these things when his work takes him to the very frontier, to the place where doctors are hacking ordered knowledge out of disease's twisted undergrowth.

In the 'eighties medicine was wielding a new tool. For long surgery had rusted upon its benches ; a crude implement, it had been used roughly and for gross purposes. By new hands it was now being polished and turned to an unexpected accuracy. It was being employed in a manner hitherto unknown. Its possibilities were immense and in the main untried. Many hands were at the work ; there was room and to spare for all. Barely had antisepsis staked its claim when the aseptic technique came pounding on its heels ; hardly had one operation justified itself before another, less risky and more subtle, rendered it obsolete. And yet each victory was but to climb a hill from which the view was greater, the vision of potentialities becoming even more immense.

It is just over half a century since, as a modest assistant, Berkeley first entered an operating theatre. In those few years surgery has been transmuted from a clumsy and dangerous craft into the deftest art ; in less than the span of a man's life it has transfigured the face of physical destiny. So little time ago enfeeblement, or even death, attended a thousand maladies ; yet now, by surgery, from out them all man is restored to health. No possible account can do full justice to the glorious wonder of it. It was Berkeley's privilege to watch this flood of healing pour over the parched fields of suffering.

That, with these things going forward, surgery should have from the first attracted Berkeley is not surprising. Here lay for imagination the greatest opportunity ; a world of enormous scope awaited it. Think but of surgery as practised in those student days. The operating theatre was merely a room set apart, differing hardly at all in structure or in fittings from other rooms about it, utterly unlike its modern counterpart ; standing in it Berkeley saw the surgeon enter in unchanged street attire, take off his coat and roll up his sleeves, then, having washed his hands, forthwith begin the operation. No cap or gown or mask was worn ; no snowy sterile sheets covered the patient ; precautions that we now regard as elementary were then not thought of. And yet, in spite of all these handicaps, the latent strength of surgery was being bared. Berkeley saw operations, newly conceived and newly dared, brought to a victorious conclusion. The words of his own recollection, spoken to an assembly at the end of his long surgical journey, tell of the impress made upon him in those days — the days of his studentship, house-surgeoncy, and early years of practice.

" When I entered medicine it was still with the idea of joining the Army Medical Service. But chance decided that I was to attract the attention of McGill, and to become his dresser. (The unqualified, student assistant of a surgeon.) A chance word of his, I remember vividly the circumstances in which it was uttered, turned my mind to surgery, created my ambitions, and controlled my actions. To this hour I can hardly mention the name of McGill without a throb. But in that I am not singular, for almost every student in my day was entirely and intensely devoted to him. He was in my judgement — and I may claim to be a travelled surgeon — the most brilliant of all intellectually, and with the limitations of his time, among the most deft and finished operators. His brain was so nimble that a needle of thought had no sooner entered it than it had penetrated, emerged threaded, and McGill had begun to sew. He gave me the first guinea I ever earned — and I can recall almost every incident of a most memorable day. In the impressionable years of early manhood the influence of McGill on my career was certainly the most penetrating. Certainly the most massive influence upon my character, the influence of largest scope, exerted for the longest period, was that of Mr. Jessop. Looking back upon the years in which I almost lived with him, I cannot but feel that he was the most considerable man whom it has been my privilege to meet. Absolute sanity and scrupulous rectitude seemed to me to be his characteristics. His views were wide, impartial and curiously modern, even to the end. His safe judgement was never swayed by prejudice nor swept by passion. The credit for any success I may have won belongs more to him than to any other.

I began my study of medicine under the auspices of Dr. Barrs, to whom I was out-patient clerk. It is true that I had previously encountered him when he failed to teach me physiology. From the time I first was influenced by his teaching I have never failed to be interested in the psychology of Dr. Barrs. The enthusiastic reply of a student to his question was often countered by a retort delivered with a curious flavour of caustic coldness. He endeavoured always to discover whether one's knowledge was one's own intellectual secretion, or the synthetic product derived from many text-books. He courted opposition in order to improve his marksmanship. A verbal contest with him was a sort of intellectual rifle practice. Of all adversaries I would prefer him first, for he offers the most obdurate and variegated opposition, and never fails in the long run to admit and to act upon the truth.

In my day Dr. Eddison was responsible for the lectures in medicine. I sat under — or as he would prefer to say, slept under — him for two years, and the coruscating brilliance of his discourses has never seemed to fade from my eyes. From him we learnt the many-sidedness of medicine."

*　　*　　*　　*　　*

It took Berkeley four years to qualify ; a feat that modern regulations render impossible. He went straight through his course without a failure, taking each examination at the earliest appointed time. He graduated M.B. of London University in 1887. On the way he had slipped the Primary Fellowship under his belt — thus preparing himself to step into the higher ranks of surgeons should his desires so continue to dictate.

The Primary was made memorable for him by a little incident after his own heart. It provided him with a story that gave him lasting satisfaction ; generations of students must have heard it from his lips. He was undergoing an oral examination in physiology ; his examiner was Michael Foster. Of the physiologists of the day none stood in more pronounced eminence than Michael Foster ; as teacher, writer, and thinker his position was outstanding ; his text-book on physiology was the standard work. To one of Foster's questions Berkeley gave an answer that Foster said was wrong. There was disagreement. The examiner was dissatisfied ; Berkeley maintained his facts to be correct. This dialogue ensued :

" What is the authority for your answer ? "

" Michael Foster's text-book."

" But I am Michael Foster ! "

" Then *you* are my authority. If, sir, you will have your text-book sent for, you will find my answer is the right one."

The text-book was duly brought, the relevant passage turned up, and Berkeley vindicated. And so through physiology he passed majestically. Later, when he related the happening to his fellows, his confident temerity was questioned — with so much at stake, how dared he run so arrogant a risk ? " Ah, but you see," his answer came, " I knew the whole book by heart ! " The little moral to this tale Berkeley quickly pressed : there is no excuse for failing any examination ; one should enter the examination invulnerably girded with the consciousness of complete command of the subject ; the ground

77

should have been so covered that not the smallest pebble had been left unturned. Inescapably, there was about these observations a certain cockiness — tolerantly acceptable from the old, but from the young provoking. It engenders in others a hope, expectant and malicious, that pride may take an early fall. Berkeley's fault was more of manner than of spirit ; his reply sprang from boyish exuberance. Nevertheless, when disappointment first assailed him, not in all quarters did he win sympathy.

In 1887 he stepped out into the world a doctor ; able, if not to earn a living, at least to keep himself. He was interested in surgery, but not absorbedly. He saw no reason to turn aside from the old path of his intention. To his friends and family he announced his purpose of applying for a surgeon's commission in the army ; by his forefathers he would take his place. But — once again — fate, chance, destiny, or what you will, stepped down from her throne to manipulate the players in her game. Berkeley had been too good a student to slip beneath the ropes so easily. Though, unlike all others whose achievements equalled his, he had turned his back on the hospital he was not to escape its grasp. Had he applied for one of the coveted house-surgeoncies at the Leeds General Infirmary he must, on the strength of his student record, without doubt have been appointed ; but he did not choose so to apply. But even more powerful than that was his record. Let him not seek the hospital, then would the hospital seek him.

Coming, a few days after graduation, down the steps of the Infirmary he encountered his beloved McGill. Together they walked a few paces, then, turning to Berkeley, McGill said, " We have just appointed you Mayo-Robson's house-surgeon." " But I didn't apply," said Berkeley. " I know," softly breathed McGill. Berkeley averted his head, biting his lip. It was on the tip of his tongue to say that had they appointed him to McGill — how different that would have been ! But he did not. Instead he allowed McGill's arguments to prevail and said he would accept the post. The die was cast. With a lingering glance over his shoulder, he abandoned the army. But when, in the spin of time's wheel, opportunity again caught up with the old desire he did not let it slip.

So, by these events, he returned to the hospital. The busy, satisfying life of a resident soon obliterated all regrets. Assisting at operations, taking notes, attending to emergencies — the days flew by, while interest took root and fructified. Now, without question, surgery held his heart. Eager, assiduous, he buttressed his student reputation. He confirmed the confidence that had selected him for rare attention. In those ensuing months he won the general favour.

His regret at not being with McGill was in great measure dissipated. Mayo-Robson won his respect. That surgeon was then making considerable contributions to his art ; he was doing much to adapt and modify the operations then available for the treatment of gallstones. When Mayo-Robson died in 1933 Berkeley said of him : " I came to him when he was in his formative stage, and the lessons he impressed upon a susceptible youth were quite unforgettable. Mayo-Robson must rank among the very greatest surgeons of all time. We who were his colleagues will for ever cherish the memory of a surgeon of the very highest rank, who was supreme in technical skill, adventurous in search of truth, restless in eager desire to seek better and still better methods of relieving the sufferings of mankind, of infinite resource, tender, compassionate, merciful."

In certain respects Berkeley's career was to follow closely that of Mayo-Robson. They both enjoyed, in Leeds, a great professional and financial success. In their maturity they were both urged to move to London. Some years before Berkeley was established Mayo-Robson had succumbed to this temptation, and in so doing met with many difficulties, some unforeseen and others unforeseeable ; he never entirely overcame them. It is probable that this, as well as loyalty to Leeds, influenced Berkeley in his decision when he himself was confronted with the choice between Leeds and London.

While he was with Mayo-Robson, Berkeley had the happiness of one more session with McGill. He was, in the absence of McGill's own house-surgeon, called upon to assist his hero. It was an historic occasion. For the first time, as they thought, in the story of surgery an attempt was to be made to perform an operation for prostatectomy. McGill had devised the ingenious and delicate procedure. All was successful. The result transcended their highest hopes. McGill's place in surgical annals was assured, more by this one operation than by anything else he did, great credit redounded to the hospital, and Berkeley subsequently maintained that of nothing was he more proud than of the privilege of having assisted at this operation.

As his learning was winnowed and tested by experience so did his love of surgery grow. Within himself he felt the stirring of individual capabilities. His habit of hero-worship did not detract from awareness of his own capacity ; it rather sustained it, for he discovered in himself a surgical facility that, but for the lack of training,

LEEDS GENERAL INFIRMARY

would have equalled that of those much older than himself. When in 1889 his appointment finished, he made the opportunity to go in search of new standards of comparison. With no immediate work to hand he left for a period of post-graduate surgical study in the clinics of Berlin ; for surgeons of the day Germany was then the accepted Mecca. Berkeley was duly impressed by what he saw. But he found his respect for Leeds enhanced ; in his opinion the surgeons at home could offer something no less good.

After some months abroad he returned to England in the early spring of 1890. There had fallen vacant at the Leeds Infirmary the post of R.S.O. — Resident Surgical Officer. On three special counts this post was a most important one in the eyes of those who aspired to it ; of those Leeds men that wished to follow surgery few failed to seek this office. It provided an opportunity for its holder to do much varied emergency surgery ; it gave him the chance to see the whole of the hospital's surgical staff at work, enabling him to compare their technique with their results ; it placed him, too, and most important this, in the direct line of succession for appointment to the permanent surgical staff of the hospital — when the time came to elect a surgeon the men who had been R.S.O. would always be considered first. Berkeley's candidature was successful. He took up his duties as R.S.O. in April 1890.

What were those duties ? They were administrative, supervisory, and surgical ; Berkeley had to control and regulate the admissions to the surgical beds of the hospital, he had to oversee the work of the house-surgeons, and he had to operate on all cases handed over to him by the honorary surgeons. Most of the surgical cases that came his way were those emergency ones of slight or moderate difficulty ; cases that, arriving in hospital at odd and inconvenient hours, called for immediate surgery, without, at the same time, presenting any great operative problems. Out of the handling of large numbers of cases such as these does a young surgeon build up a firm and reliable technique. When Berkeley entered upon his office he could hardly be called a surgeon at all ; when, three years later, he left, he was generally recognised as one of the most capable surgeons in Leeds.

As R.S.O. he was so busy that there was no time for him to do research work — even had he been so inclined. What he did was mainly to accumulate a large clinical experience in all branches of surgery ; his work was not restricted to any particular field. Nevertheless his interest came to be more and more concentrated upon the sphere of abdominal surgery. He seized every occasion that arose for performing, or assisting at, such operations. His skill became accepted. Operations of this nature were handed over to him in steadily increasing numbers. Though he was making no direct contribution to surgical knowledge he was rapidly making himself into an extremely competent surgeon ; and, on the way, relieving much suffering. The value to Berkeley of these three years could hardly be exaggerated. He lived right in the midst of his work — the only way to serve apprenticeship to medicine ; he saw the work of his masters and simultaneously brought himself to their notice ; he made friends of those in authority and won the admiration of students and nurses.

Of those students that passed before him one was to be a particular friend of later years. Carlton Oldfield was profoundly impressed by the gifts of hand and intellect of the young R.S.O. ; though inexperienced himself, he was convinced that here was an outstanding surgeon. He conceived an admiration and regard for Berkeley that ultimately drew them together. Berkeley, as his friendship with Oldfield grew, to these sentiments gave reciprocity. In the fullness of time Carlton Oldfield ascended to take his place beside Berkeley on the permanent surgical staff of the hospital ; there, in the department of obstetrics and gynaecology, he played a distinguished part in sustaining and adding to the new glory that Berkeley had brought to Leeds. The two men became close friends. When Carlton Oldfield's own son Michael was placed, many years later, upon the surgical staff, yet another link was forged in the chain of family tradition that has been one of the most pleasant features of the Leeds General Infirmary and Medical School ; it was to reawaken the fine surgical memories of the Heys and Teales, who, through father and sons, had carried the school to eminence : Carlton Oldfield's fount of recollections that has provided many of the details of this picture of Berkeley as R.S.O.

*   *   *   *   *

The years as R.S.O. saw Berkeley change from a youth into a man. Though never through all his life did he lose that perhaps the greatest of his charms, his fresh and sparkling youthfulness of spirit, yet those three years endowed him with an adult assurance and stability. Qualities so desirable in a surgeon, that after a lifetime's striving others never win, he showed with remarkable speed. Only a fear of the reader's intolerance causes one to hesitate before employing terms of eulogy. They are so widely endorsed, so fully deserved. It was truly said of Berkeley in those days that he " had everything ". To the skill of his own acquiring, nature had added bountifully so much that helps — so many attributes that lie beyond the power of cultivation. Good looks, fine voice, strength, and that infinitely potent indefinable — personality, all these were richly his. Combined with them, out of the well of education and heredity, was behaviour, moral and ethical, in the best vein of chivalry. And with all this was nothing facile, nothing shallow ; all was well-knit, solid, graciously dignified.

His body, previously somewhat thin, had now filled out. His manner had lost the lonely reserve that had been used to give it an aspect slightly forbidding ; instead it was suffused with a warm friendliness that yet did not overstep the bounds of privacy. Those in difficulties approached him with the assurance that a kind helpfulness would receive them ; he had a way of resolving their troubles and sending them away with renewed confidence in themselves. In hospitals the need for such support is frequent. Young men, suddenly burdened with the grave responsibilities inherent in their profession, find themselves faced with problems the gravity of which they cannot estimate. To their chiefs they do not like to go lest their fears should be shown to be but poorly founded, and themselves made to appear foolish ; yet, apprehensive of disaster, they badly need advice. To such Berkeley was always wise and courteous ; he redirected them, leaving their self-esteem intact. He was invariably cheerful and good-tempered. His equanimity was not ruffled by the ups and downs of moods. He was completely reliable and entirely competent. About a hospital there is something of the hot-house ; the heat of nervous strain and close proximity causes little jealousies and disaffections to flare into consuming flames. The presence of a comfortable nature, quiet and temperate, is then wonderfully soothing. That is what Berkeley was. He was master of every situation. In a room where stress and worry reigned, his arrival was a zephyr of relief — cooling, reassuring; the moment he came in all present felt that everything would be " all right ".

His own and others' burdens never weighed him down; they never took away the lightness of his touch. When work was done he could, in an instant, turn to play — and play as if he had not a care in the world. Each day, no matter how busy he was, there was always a few minutes for the children in the middle of it. Half an hour before lunch he would appear in the children's ward, there to laugh and romp for thirty uproarious minutes. Throughout his life he had a curious mastery of time. Never idle and never hurrying, his days flowed by with the smooth purpose of a broad deep stream. About him there was none of that scurry and flurry that, seeking to give impress of urgent affairs, some affect. He had time for everything. When, towards the end of life, the vast scope of his activities was marvelled at, he observed, " I have never been busy — merely occupied ".

Much was made possible by the clean precision of an orderly mind. Each activity was sequent and well-planned. He reflected in his person his mental tidiness. He was always neat, never ungroomed. At all times he had about him the fragrance of one fresh from the bath. He was meticulous in his physical care of himself. Washing, scrubbing, and brushing were with him frequent, pleasurable, essential; over his hands he took endless trouble. It was always after such tremendous ablutions that, glowing all over, he awaited his chiefs ; invariably dressed, as was the custom of the day, in morning coat, shining hard collar, and dark bow-tie. And later on, released from his duties, in sunny flannels and racket in hand, he would go swinging out of the hospital front door. His energy was prodigious. Indeed, it was highly needed. For his zest for life was prodigious too ; he threw himself heart and soul into everything, he was greedy for all untried experience. He was, none can deny it, a bit of a paragon — a very remarkable man.

The games of tennis were usually at the Jessops'. To their house Berkeley, when R.S.O., went with increasing frequency. They were a large gregarious family and he a lively and personable young man. He at once felt himself drawn to them — and they to him. Their cheerful disposition suited him admirably ; they brought him into contact with a type of family life he had hitherto not known. He was first introduced to them by the head of the family, and Berkeley's own chief, Dr. Jessop. Of Dr. Jessop it is impossible to write temperately. There was about him a deep and fruity richness that renders odious all critical analysis. Of the Leeds Infirmary staff, in Berkeley's younger days, he was head and shoulders the outstanding figure — massive and dominant. In the very life of Leeds itself he had come to be a towering monument. His name was synonymous with probity, industry, and generous dealing. And more than this, he was, as it were, a personification of the good warm heart of the North.

There is precise evidence that Jessops had lived in and about Leeds from the sixteenth century onwards ; there is ground for reasonable supposition that they were established in the district even earlier than that. They were always active in the social, industrial, and professional life of the neighbourhood. In the *History of Brighouse* — an environ of Leeds — there occurs the following passage :

" Richard Jessop of Low Mill, left impress on the trade and moral training of Brighouse from its juvenility. His son, of the same name, was a leading spirit in the local Sunday School Movement. Richard, the father, died in 1835, aged 78. Mr. Thomas Jessop, Registrar of Births, knew Brighouse from ' thread to needle ' and was connected with Messrs. Barber, Solicitors, and had much influence in legal matters. He died in 1879, aged 72. His son, Mr. Thomas Richard Jessop, F.R.C.S., whose name as a surgeon and Specialist is a household word within the wide radius of Leeds, we are proud to claim amongst our eminent natives."

Dr. Jessop was a figure so colourful that any attempt to imprint his picture upon the written page must inevitably result in but a poor, dull reproduction. He was of firm and stocky build and of a nature forceful, kindly, and energetic. He was all but universally loved for his professional integrity, infinite willingness, and broad humanity. That he should make a few enemies was unavoidable, since there were aspects of his character that were both positive and uncompromising. But he was a great battler and as often as not ended by routing his detractors. He was enormously successful in his profession, and that, as always happens, provoked antipathy amongst a minority of his less successful colleagues. His brain was clear, shrewd, practical, and penetrating. In surgical diagnosis and technique he displayed exactly the same qualities. He was of the type that wins the limitless admiration of its juniors. However much the words of Berkeley's maturity may have been spoken by lips that

87

had touched the Blarney Stone, there cannot be the very slightest doubt that anything and everything he said of Dr. Jessop came from the bottom of his heart — genuine, humble, and affectionate. It was patent that he was proud to do justice to one of the great men in his life.

Dr. Jessop was something more than a surgeon. He was the complete doctor. He was master of his calling and drained the glass of his powers to the very dregs. He worked mightily in the whole field of medicine. He was, as we have seen, a Specialist. He was something that has gone from the world we know. He could be consulted upon any subject within the whole gamut of medical knowledge. His advice was at all times sound and helpful, never merely eclectic or doctrinaire. He would give an opinion on a case of pneumonia as readily as on one of gallstones; he would treat a case of rheumatism as confidently as he would repair a broken leg. He was continuously sought after by the highest and the lowest in society. His word was oracular and his patients' faith in him utterly unstinted. Of his kind he was the last. The enlarging scope of medicine has made the feats that he performed, touching as they did the limits of individual capability, no longer possible. No more can one man pack into his single brain the vast known facts of medicine. But in his genre he was perfect — the epitome and epitaph — of the old-time Specialist.

He lived, as he worked, with unmeasured profusion. He made a great deal of money, spent it as quickly as it came, and, at the end, found himself left with little. His style of life was of that robust lavishness that only complete confidence in the future can command. He husbanded neither wealth, strength, nor spiritual vitality; of all he commanded he gave with both hands — giving munificently. He never took a holiday and rarely rested. He always thought the best of others and, to the limits of charity, condoned their mortal weaknesses. The proof of Berkeley's praise of him is that Berkeley, throughout his life, displayed the silver thread of practice that gave expression to the precepts of his young ideal.

The Jessop manner was in accordance with the man. Silk-hatted and with orchid in the lapel of his coat, each day he drove up to the hospital in a carriage drawn by a pair of bays. Alighting, he was met by his R.S.O. and students ; in royal progress the party marched through the corridors of the infirmary. Arrived at the theatre the great man stopped, and, drawing from his buttonhole the orchid, handed it to the theatre-sister. Then, after the usual preparations, on with the operation. With the steady speed of the inspired craftsman the work went forward, no bombast and no fireworks. So secure was his learning that he did not hesitate to ask, and where right utilise, the advice of his assistants. Like all the best of doctors he lacked that grudging intellectual pride that in its arrogance is but the mask of ignorance. Small wonder that, for those who knew him, even while Jessop was still alive, something of mythology invested the master's name.

He lived at Roundhay. His family, home and gardens were large and open-handed as himself. His house was the scene of many a party and jollification ; to the young doctors it was a second home. To none more so than Berkeley. There he became a visitor so constant that he passed out of friendship into family. The Jessops came to look upon him as another son, another brother. He suited them well, for, with his ardour, he was a man after Jessop's own heart. In him the old man saw a

continuation of his own spirit ; he saw one who, standing
on the threshold of medicine, came armed with those
same weapons, enthusiastic vigour and love of his fellow
men, that he himself had used to fight the world. He
took Berkeley under his wing and delighted in doing what
he could to further the young man's interests. He taught
and encouraged Berkeley, made opportunities to cultivate
his skill, brought him to the notice of those in authority
and those of potent influence, and opened for him the
doors into society. Jessop's efforts were misinterpreted
by some ; they accused him of not unselfish motives ;
they found in later happenings — happenings unforeseen by Jessop — a source from which to fortify their
accusations ; they said that by pushing Berkeley forward
Jessop was fostering his own affairs. But to Berkeley
Jessop's help was invaluable, although it did later on
bring to him setbacks that he might have otherwise
escaped.

*   *   *   *   *

From his first visit to the Jessop home Berkeley felt
himself drawn, in particular, to one member of the
family. Isabel — Isabella Wellesley Jessop — was then
in her middle teens. She was a lively child, vivacious,
jolly, and full of fun. Small and dainty, she had the charm
of a porcelain figure. She appealed to Berkeley both
through his love of children and of high spirits. But this
did not stand in the way of his treating her as an equal.
Though she was many years younger than himself it was
not long before he was telling her, as he had told no one
before, of his hopes, ambitions, aspirations. To speak
like this, to a woman outside his family circle, was for
Berkeley a new pleasure. He had always liked feminine
company, preferred it in fact to that of men, but, up till

now, had known few occasions to indulge his liking. Of his own class he had known few women, outside it none. Neither time, money, nor opportunity had allowed him to enjoy the society of ladies. But he "had a way with them". He had a remarkable, sympathetic understanding of their point of view ; and this they quickly discovered ; they could get round him, could soon win him over. His susceptibility to them put pitfalls in his way. He readily believed in them, and, when what they said ill-matched with later fact, was disconcerted. He was boyish, and his warm heart was at times too easily deceived.

But there was no deception about Isabel. Berkeley was, from the day they met, her hero. She had for him awed admiration. In her eyes everything he did was right. She was surprised, almost amazed, when she found that he returned her admiration. She was not an intellectual, could not follow the ranging of his learned, imaginative mind ; but she did understand him ; better perhaps than any woman he had known. She saw his weaknesses and the chinks in his armour. Young as she was, she knew in her heart that she possessed, as he might never do, a worldly knowledge that exceeded his. She saw how poor was his defence against sweet flattery and importunings. So, self-appointed, she became his ally and defender. When others criticised him she took his part ; she protected him against too much persuasion ; she warned him against his own inherent foibles.

The early days of their friendship passed light-heartedly, gradually maturing into intimacy. Together they played tennis, danced, and went to parties. Isabel was popular in young society, for she was a beautiful ballroom dancer and a tennis-player much above the average. The Jessops

lived a comfortable, carefree life. Seldom a week-end
went by without their house being full of young people.
Games, chatter, and laughter were the order of each day.
Every Friday evening Dr. Jessop took a box at the theatre
and there, surrounded by his gay and noisy family, sat in
patriarchal state. He always kept a seat for Berkeley;
and Berkeley, if his work at the hospital was finished in
time, did not fail to join them. In these years Berkeley
had everything he could desire : prospering work, friends
within the hospital and more without, all the entertain-
ments that he loved his but for the asking, and, giving
all most piquant flavour, a heart falling in love.

For falling in love he was. Isabel soon became something more than just the jolly, ever-teasing friend. She
was " Tiny ", the darling and constant undercurrent of
Berkeley's thoughts ; Tiny, upon whom he focused every
hope that lay outside his work. The whole tremendous
force of his nature became engrossed in her. She gave
him a support unlike any he had known before ; as time
went by he felt it irreplaceable. In her small person
was contained all that he looked for from a wife. Young
as she was, fears filled him lest another should, before
he spoke, steal her away from him. Yet to propose he
hesitated. He could offer her nothing but his record and
its pointers to the future. In the latter he had bounding
faith — but would others have the same ? Would they
regard it as sufficient dowry ? For his age he had done
brilliantly, the medical school could show no one like
him ; on all sides he received professional encouragement. In 1890, by passing the Final Fellowship and so
becoming F.R.C.S., he had equipped himself to apply
for the next surgical vacancy on the hospital staff — he
would probably get it. He did not doubt for a moment

that his success as a consultant was assured. It was not long to wait — surely he might speak now ? But, Berkeley being Berkeley, such reasoning was unnecessary. Here was something that he wanted, and wanted badly, he *must* have it — in the end he would make everything all right ! So he proposed to Isabel.

Or rather, he did not propose to her — at least, not yet. Beside the path to Isabel stood the figure of Mr. Jessop — though loved, still haloed by the fearsomeness of student days. To ignore it on his way to Isabel, unthinkable, impossible. First, then, he must speak to Mr. Jessop. To all, Jessop was simply and invariably known and spoken of as " Mr." ; the word of " Mr." was the law. Berkeley's close contact with the Jessop family must have led him to expect a cordial reception. Even though " Mr." should turn him down, he would, one was sure, do it kindly. Nevertheless the coming interview was frightening. One does not just stroll up to one's chief and, without a qualm, ask for his daughter's hand in marriage. And when one's chief is " Mr.", the giant of one's world, how much more frightening !

But perhaps Berkeley was not going to give " Mr." as much of a shock as he thought. In large families little goes unobserved ; young men do not there pay court without, as they descend the front-door steps, mothers and sisters whispering in the sitting-room. Rumours about Berkeley's intention quickly travelled far, and before long to others his mind was known. On March 14th, 1892, Berkeley received a letter from his brother-in-law, the Reverend A. N. Claye, his sister Ada's husband, which, after some general matter, concluded with these words :

" . . . I don't know what deity you surgical and

medical officers worship, but it seems to me to be one
who demands from his devotees human sacrifices from
time to time. I believe you are a bit of a fanatic, but
don't let these hundred more beds persuade you to cast
yourself under the wheels of his chariot. But I'm glad
to know there is someone you care to *live* for.

" Yours sincerely,
" ARTHUR N. CLAYE."

So, a few months later, he took the plunge. He went
up to Roundhay Mount and bearded the lion in his den.
Of that day he wrote to Ada in these words :

" THE GENERAL INFIRMARY
AT LEEDS
June 6, 1892

" DOVEY,
"The interview with Mr. Jessop is a thing of the past.
The interesting event came off yesterday afternoon at
about 3.20 P.M. All of them were in the garden, so I
told Isabel I wanted to speak to Mr. Jessop for a moment
and told her to wait outside. I popped into the dining-
room to Mrs. Jessop, told her I was going in to Mister.
She seemed took all aback and quite nervous like. I
felt that the cucumber was a detail of coolness to myself.
I felt as I often feel, that I will *make* things go as I want
them. I asked ' Mr.' if he could spare a few moments
as I wanted to speak to him about Isabel. He drew up
a chair for me and we began. He said she was very
young, 'quite a child in fact', and so much *younger* than
May (thank God for that, says I to myself) and he had
thought of sending her away for a year. I smiled at
that and thought ' no you don't '. He said that she
would make a good and loving wife and he thought we
should be very happy. Asked me if I'd thought it well
over. Did I intend starting in Leeds? I said yes and
told him I hadn't a farthing of my own. He said he
preferred it. A man who had his way to make was much
better than one who had something to be going on with.
Then came the sounds of Praise. He would rather have

94

me for one of his daughters than anyone. He had had every confidence in me and my honour. That he knew I had every quality destined to make a successful man and to have a happy home. That he would do his utmost to help me whatever our relations were. He then said that he would not stand in my way if I wished to speak to her. I said (knowing I'd got what I wanted) that I didn't wish in any way to go contrary to his will. He shook hands, said 'you have my very best wishes' and went. Told Mrs. Jessop, she went in to 'Mr.' and he said more nice things while I walked unconcernedly and tried to look as if nothing had happened. I am off to London on Friday for the ring, back on Saturday to take the plunge and am going to stop at Roundhay till the 17th over Isabel's birthday. I don't know what to give her for her birthday, shall look out the 'Venice' when I'm there. — I wish Mamma had known her. I'm sure they're alike in many things.

> " Love to you darling,
>> " B."

With this hurdle behind him Berkeley hurried forward. The world was at his feet. What " Mr." had said to him topped even the best he had expected. To be spoken to like that by " Mr." — well !

On the morning June 13th, 1892, in his twenty-seventh year, he wrote from the Jessops' home at Roundhay Mount to his sister Ada, this letter :

" DOVEY,

" I sent you a p.c. on Saturday afternoon containing the good news — hope you got it all right.

" When I came here on Saturday I found them all in the schoolroom and Mrs. Jessop in bed with a bad throat. The music room was in a state of upset owing to cleaning but was rapidly getting ship-shape. I washed, shaved and otherwise beautified my person and went and chatted with Mrs. J. in the boudoir, till the music room was ready.

Then I called Isabel and took her in and we sat on the couch. I put my arm round her and told her something, she went as pale as a sheet, so I kissed her and went on till she nodded her head and gave me a big hug. Then she was very quiet for a moment, and suddenly took her arms away and turned her face away and said, 'No, I'm not good enough' and began to cry. I soon turned the tears into smiles. Then I put the ring on. *Such* a beauty—the most beautiful I ever saw except H's which cost £70. Then we went to see *Mother*. Ise threw her arms round her and said, 'Oh, mother, I'm the happiest girl in all the world'. Then on to see Ethel, Connie and Maud kissing them all on both cheeks. They were all so pleased and are smiling all over still, especially Ethel. She is the only one who takes kindly to calling me Berkeley and she does it as though she were used to it. The others haven't managed it yet. Ise still says 'Mr. Moynihan' so I reprove her by saying 'Miss Jessop'. Gladys said she couldn't believe it and two or three times in the evening Ise kept saying 'I'm like Gla— I can't believe it'. She cried poor little mite when she got to bed, but she looked so happy and 'restful'. I read your letter to her. I have bought her a lovely pearl shamrock ring for her birthday like this [then follows a drawing] with one small diamond in the middle of each shamrock and I'm going to give her the Christening Cross. — We went to church yesterday morning.

"So happy. Goodbye lovey
"Thine,

"B.

"Mr. Jessop says '*He seems quite used to it*'."

* * * * *

And there it was : a great decision made, undertaken, and pursued to consummation. He was engaged to a young woman, the better part of ten years his junior, not now and never destined for a culture or cultivation like his own, and a person who had never known difficulties to compare with his. Yet he was right. Right because his essential values were well found. In his wife he sought the companionship and comfort that, in spite of his outward self-assurance, he badly needed. His intellectual life was self-contained : for it he needed no domestic sustenance ; troubles, too, he could manage : he had learnt how to deal with them. But someone believing in him to the last, someone to soothe the turbulences of a nature Irish, and of flaming hair — that one he sought, and, at the issue, chose well. Vicissitudes that came to Berkeley and Isabel, together or between, never destroyed, or by a fraction minimised, his first devotion. To some, in later life, their union was hard to understand, for they seemed so different. Here is its explanation : Isabel gave to Berkeley a faithful, loving loyalty, and, what he lacked himself, a resilience of spirit that lifted him over the rough and broken ground of all his early years in practice, and, in more distant years, steadied a mind oft tending to o'ertop itself. All this, in the wisdom that underlay his outward exuberance, Berkeley realised, remembered, and to the end was grateful for. The surface of life showed how much Berkeley gave to Isabel — wealth, titles, and success. But let no one suppose the bargain was one-sided. With these gifts came for her burdens, not to be seen by all. And, in the depths, the seeing eye may find revealed those things she gave to him : things not to be held and measured, but which made it possible for Berkeley to obtain much that otherwise might have lain beyond his grasp. She gave him happiness.

When a young doctor, whose intention it is to make a name for himself as a specialist, marries his chief's

H

daughter — and when that chief is the most influential
member of the hospital staff — then the young man
exposes himself to criticism. Berkeley was no exception
to this rule. Hard things were said about him ; he was
accused of opportunism ; it was said that he had tried,
by unfair means, to seek advancement. And these remarks were not without sound precedent : behaviour
such as Berkeley's had been known before. But, suggestive
as was the superficial evidence, it dwindles on closer
study. Berkeley's habit was always one of self-reliance.
Deep in his heart he knew his success was certain ; it
required assistance from no adventitious aids. Jessop,
indeed, might help him to the staff, but, to do justice to
" Mr.", he would do that anyway ; for that one did not
need to be his son-in-law. He might introduce Berkeley
to a larger practice than early comes the way of most
young men ; but that would be merely to hasten a
process that must, in due course, eventuate. In more
substantial ways he could not help ; this Berkeley knew.
Berkeley knew, too, that to be " Mr.'s " son-in-law was
of itself to render hostages to the near future ; in obstruct-
ing Berkeley, the enemies of " Mr." would find vicarious
satisfaction. Berkeley stood well with all ; by this
alliance to one camp he lost rather than gained. Taking
it all in all, this closer bond with " Mr." must help
more than it hindered — but not much ; its value could
be easily exaggerated.

And then these letters — they are the touchstone.
What Berkeley wrote to Ada, had it been known to all,
must have destroyed criticism. His words are genuine ;
in them remote consideration has no part. There lies the
proof that Berkeley was urged by no ulterior motive.
The reader's time is almost wasted by these unravellings

of thought : the impregnable needs not this little labour of defence.

* * * * *

In 1893, after three years as R.S.O., Berkeley set forth to make his way in private practice. Those three years had been intensely busy, full of interest, and more free of care than any he was now to know for long. Living in the hospital he had borne no household burdens, the fret of domestic economy passed him by ; his salary was all his own, for expenses he had none. In hospital he did not have to seek his work, it came to him ; he did not have to consider the patient's means, he had only to get on with the job. Now he had to enter that which in every medical school is called " the cold, hard world " ; he had to pit his skill against that of others, to test himself in open competition. In hospital praise may come from every side, breeding a sleek self-satisfaction ; but once get outside, where the patient pays in kind as well as praise, then no overcoat, in those first draughts of isolation, is more than thick enough. And yet even to practice there is a brighter side ; there is no thrill more pleasant than that which comes to the young consultant called to his first private patient ; it is a compound of new experiences : of new, complete authority, of sole responsibility, of apprehensive tremors. Pleasant, perhaps, is not the very adjective ; although there is no better. The occasion is unique, and so should be the word for it. And when the case is all tucked up, disease controlled and pain alleviated, how deliciously light are the feet of the doctor as he turns his steps towards home ! Yes, there are compensations.

Berkeley engaged consulting-rooms at 33 Park Square, Leeds ; practising from the same house as " Mr." . . .

There he awaited his patients — awaited the crumbs that fell from the master's table. He filled in his time by setting the keystone to his scholastic achievement, as during this lean period he read for, and passed, the examination for M.S. — Master of Surgery — of the University of London ; this test is comparable, though academically more stringent, to the examination of the F.R.C.S., and the distinction it confers is of like greatness. With this final degree added to his others Berkeley applied, when the vacancy occurred, for the post of Assistant Surgeon at the Leeds Infirmary.

To many readers the ways of consulting practice may be obscure ; they may not know how a consultant's life is ordered. So for the sake of such people a brief, explanatory digression may be here interpolated, for without full comprehension of a consultant's life Berkeley's career cannot be understood.

After prolonged and varied training within his specialty the would-be consultant seeks permanent appointment upon the staff of some hospital. He seeks for an appointment that will allow him to work within the field of his own past study. The most coveted appointments are those upon the staffs of teaching hospitals, for there the consultant enjoys the stimulus of teaching and, by making himself known to the doctors of the future, spreads abroad his reputation, which is his source of practice ; his ability becomes known and spoken of, doctors recommend him to their patients, patients to their friends, his advice and help are sought. Without such an appointment his task is very hard ; he has difficulty in making himself known, he lacks the circumstance for the continuous practice of his art, and his contacts with the eager minds of medicine are reduced.

But it is not easy to find appointment on the staff : its numbers are strictly limited. Vacancies thereon are few, coming only upon the deaths or retirement of its present members ; the candidates are many and the competition of great intensity. When a vacancy does arise, the aspirant for election has a busy time. He has printed for distribution amongst the governing board and medical staff of the hospital a series of testimonials and a form of application ; he then calls upon every member of the staff, separately and individually, and before them submits to question and discussion ; finally, at the fixed day, the medical staff meet and from their conclave send forward to the governing board the recommended name or names, and then the board, after more discussion, make an election and a candidate is appointed to the staff. Once on the staff definite duties, consisting of regular attendance at the hospital on certain parts of certain days, are assumed by the new consultant. This work is unpaid ; the consultant makes his living in his free time, out of his private practice or paid appointments.

Berkeley applied for a surgical post in 1894. He had reasonable and justified hope of election. That is to put it low : in the eyes of others there was every expectation that he would, in fact, be elected. His scholastic record was brilliant ; his ability, in the light of his age, tremendous ; he was known to many as a gifted teacher ; the credentials of his faithful service to the hospital were irreproachable. But man is man, fallible, swayed by the winds of jealous passion, perceiving justice through the lens of his own distorting eye. Berkeley was not elected ; another was appointed. His successful rival was a man of honest capability, deserving of fortune and true to his office. Berkeley's disappointment was not due to his

own deficiencies and it was a bitter pill, a cruel, unexpected blow for him ; in his professional life it was his
first great setback. He took it very hard. Worse than
the injury to his hopes was the damage to his pride. He
did not easily get over it.

His failure sprang, but in small part, from his own
shortcomings. It arose from the internecine warfare of
the staff. That body was split into two factions : Jessop
commanded one, his enemies the other. The latter group,
by downing Berkeley, sought to humiliate the former.
Berkeley's new relationship to " Mr." served but to
enhance their delight in the discomfiture of " Mr." Just
so are keen young hearts disposed of ; through tangled
barbs like these must science and humanity press on
their cause. It was said that Berkeley was over-young,
his turn would come ; that he tended to arrogance and
that chastening would be beneficial ; that — but reasons
innumerable could be adduced, all of them facile, all
cloaks for the hidden sword.

There was specious force behind all these objections.
Berkeley was indeed young, though his career displayed
the irrelevance of counted years. He was, too, filled
with some self-importance ; he knew himself to be remarkable, and in fancy grew irresistible. He did, both
he and others since have said, think a bit too much of
himself. But, even so, the punishment outran the crime.
Its harmfulness none then could estimate. That Berkeley
rose above it is to his credit, not to theirs ; had he not
risen, then the narrow motives that put him down must
have done irreparable harm. So be it — the past has
gone, the old scar heals. Out of frustration Berkeley
welded strength. He never in opinion confirmed the
justice of his fate, but he came to say that the experience

was salutary, that it taught him a lesson that he was glad to have learned then rather than later, and that favours in this most imperfect world are not, and never will be, scattered according to the letter of the book. After the first shocked moment, he took it well : most of us would be satisfied, finding ourselves in like position, to make so brave acquittal.

During his first two years in practice he made his living in various ways. It is probable that he was self-supporting, though members of his family may still have been helping him. From his private practice he was making a little money ; but the main part of his income came from other sources. Chief of these was his assistant-ship to Mr. Jessop. He assisted " Mr." at all the latter's private operations, prepared his instruments for him, and undertook the private work that, coming " Mr.'s " way, " Mr." would not or could not do ; for this Berkeley received a small, but steady, yearly salary — an invaluable aid to a young consultant. He also drew a modest salary for his duties as Prison Surgeon for the Leeds area ; this entailed attendance on the prison sick. It also entailed another duty, to Berkeley so distasteful that, as soon as his means permitted it, he resigned from his post — it demanded his presence at every execution performed in the Leeds gaol. Lastly, he was paid for the work he did as one of the official teachers of anatomy in the Yorkshire College, to which position he was raised in 1894. That work gave him great pleasure ; he had always had a natural flair and fondness for anatomy, and early recognised the supreme importance of its detailed knowledge to the surgeon.

By these hand-holds on the face of medicine he managed to get along. He was saving for his marriage and await-

ing, not without anxiety, the next vacancy upon the
staff — due in about two years. His case-book tells the
story of the progress of his practice ; it makes interesting
and revelatory reading. His first case came his way
exactly one week after he opened his rooms ; he could
hardly have expected better. He was called to see a
schoolboy, who, by hitting himself with a cricket-stump,
had inflicted on himself a cut of one inch long beneath
his eye. Berkeley dressed it ; the patient subsequently
twice visited him at his rooms. For the entire conduct
of the case Berkeley charged one guinea. His second
casé was one, handed on from " Mr.", of suspected
spinal tuberculosis. There are extensive notes about it,
written in Berkeley's neat and graceful hand ; there were
ten visits, after which the patient was sent to convalesce
at Blackpool — five guineas was the fee for all. His third
case was one of gout, his fourth of deafness. After two
more minor cases comes one of lung tuberculosis, a strictly
medical condition — so do young surgeons live ! Five
months after opening practice came his first private operation, for drainage of a suppurating gland of the groin ;
the operation, eleven visits and many careful dressings
of the wound by the young specialist, cost the patient
thirty-five pounds and fourteen shillings. In less than a
month came another operation, for removal of a little
boy's adenoids ; the fee — ten guineas. The practice
grew — slowly, but with steady increment. In the month
that opened his second year of practice he saw four
patients ; that year saw a rapid improvement. The
extensive, redundant, sometimes verbose case - notes
gradually declined ; there were no longer so many hours
of waiting to fill in ; their place was taken by brief,
concise account of facts. The notes he made in later

years were sparse, at least when judged by some of the standards of to-day ; but they were sufficient, and he had a wonderful memory. He could remember, as if perpetually, the history and exact details of each case. In the January that came in his third year he entered on a year that was to bring him, in so far as we can judge by his books, a hundred and twenty patients ; upon a great many of these he operated.

That he had an early struggle is accepted : the story of his school and student days shows this ; his need, as a young surgeon, to visit cases of phthisis and pneumonia proves it. But, in trying to make his greatness glow, we must not exaggerate those difficulties ; others have known much worse. He started in practice with the good-will and admiration of the majority of those associated with the largest hospital in a large town, he was popular in society, and he was assistant to the most successful surgeon in the place. He did very well the thing he had to do. We can admire his greatness to the full without inventing for him hardships that never came his way.

* * * * *

His marriage took place in 1895. The Jessops had a great many friends ; the affair was a considerable one. The account that follows is taken from a Leeds newspaper of the day :

" MARRIAGE OF MR. G. A. MOYNIHAN
AND MISS ISABEL JESSOP

" The marriage of Miss Isabel Wellesley Jessop, the second and eldest unmarried daughter of Mr. T. R. Jessop, F.R.C.S., of Roundhay Mount and 32 Park Square, Leeds, with Mr. Berkeley G. A. Moynihan, surgeon, of 5 Woodhouse Square and 33 Park Square, son of the late Captain Moynihan, V.C., 8th (King's) Regiment, took place yesterday afternoon at Leeds Parish Church. Very rarely has such a pretty wedding been witnessed in the city. Great interest was taken in the occasion, and for a couple of hours the vicinity of the church was the scene of great animation. The marriage ceremony commenced at two o'clock, but long before that time every portion of the church set apart for the general public was thronged. Many hundreds, who came later, expecting to find accommodation, were doomed to disappointment, and had to console themselves with glimpses of the wedding party as they arrived and left. The interior of the church, beautiful in its ordinary aspect, had a most charming appearance. Magnificent plants, palms, and exotics had been unsparingly employed in decorating it, while the bright, kaleidoscopic hues of the ladies' dresses completed the picture. As the bridal party entered, the organist, Mr. Alfred Benton, played the prelude and March from *Lohengrin*. The bride, who was escorted by her father, wore a handsome dress of white satin with Court train, trimmed with pearl passementerie, and a veil of embroidered tulle with sprays of orange blossom. Her bouquet was composed of white roses, lilies, orchids, shamrock, and edelweiss. Miss Jessop was attended by Miss Winifred Brown and Miss Gwynette Cliff as train-bearers, their frocks being of white satin with cream lace, while their large white hats were trimmed with bows of white and pale-green ribbon, and ornamented with gold and pearl pins, the gift of the bridegroom. Master Neville Wilson, attired in a Claud Duval coat and three-cornered hat, acted as page. The bridesmaids were Misses Maud, Constance, and Gladys Jessop, sisters of the bride ; Miss Moynihan and Miss Frances Parkin, sister and cousin of the bridegroom."

After the wedding Berkeley and Isabel went to stay in Madeira ; the sunshine and the perfect bathing delighted Berkeley ; he fell in love with the place. In his later years he frequently revisited it, finding delight again in its charms and the sentimental recollection it impelled. On returning to England, Berkeley and his wife took up residence in a small house in Leeds — Number 5 Woodhouse Square. Much as he had loved the sunshine of Madeira, Berkeley was ready to come home. It was characteristic of him all his life that, after the first short respite of vacation, he longed to be back at work : he might pretend regret, but, as he re-entered consulting-room and hospital, his step was light, his spirits high. He always claimed he was at heart an idle fellow, that to fritter away the days in games, chatter, and reading was all he wanted, that to work he had to make some self-controlling effort. In the face of his tremendous industry many will doubt this. But he was probably speaking the truth. His whole attitude to life was one of search for mastery — over himself, his work, and his surroundings. Ambition overcame his idleness.

In 1896 there came again a surgical vacancy upon the staff of the Leeds General Infirmary. Once more Berkeley applied. He sent out a letter of application and many testimonials. Not often can Leeds have seen such testimonials. Out of them all I select the following, which paint a picture, even allowing for flowing brushwork, of a considerable young man :

" 33 PARK SQUARE
LEEDS

" GENTLEMEN,

" I beg to offer myself as a candidate for the post of Assistant Surgeon to the Infirmary. I am 30 years of age, and was educated at the Leeds School of Medicine, where I obtained prizes and certificates in the following subjects : Anatomy (Junior and Senior), Physiology, Materia Medica, Midwifery, Gynaecology, Medicine, Forensic Medicine, and Clinical Medicine.

" I am a Fellow of the Royal College of Surgeons of England, and a Licentiate of the Royal College of Physicians of London. At the London University I have taken the degrees of Bachelor of Medicine, being placed eighth on the honours list ; of Bachelor of Surgery, being placed fourth on the honours list ; and of Master of Surgery, the highest Surgical degree. In this latter examination I was fortunate enough to obtain the Gold Medal, a distinction gained only seven times by London men, and never before by a provincial student.

" After qualifying I was appointed House Surgeon to the Infirmary for twelve months ; afterwards I held the appointment of Resident Medical Officer at the Ida Hospital, and from April, 1890, to April, 1893, I held the post of Resident Surgical Officer to the Infirmary.

" In addition to the time passed at the Leeds School of Medicine, I worked for six months in London, and for some months in Berlin under Professors Von Bergmann and Von Bardeleben.

" From April, 1893, I have been in practice in Park Square as a Surgeon, and since December, 1894, I have held the post of Surgeon to Her Majesty's Prison, Leeds. In August, 1894, I was appointed Demonstrator of Anatomy in the Yorkshire College.

" I beg to submit for your consideration Testimonials from the members of the Honorary Staff of the Infirmary.

" Should you decide to confer upon me the post of Assistant Surgeon, it shall ever be my first care to devote to the services of the Infirmary the best energies at my disposal.

" I have the honour to be, Gentlemen,
" Your faithful servant,
" B. G. A. MOYNIHAN "

" From J. E. EDDISON, Esq., M.D., Consulting Physician to the Leeds General Infirmary, Professor of Medicine in the Victoria University

" Mr. Moynihan has asked me to express my opinion as to his fitness for the post of Assistant Surgeon to the Leeds Infirmary, and I readily comply with his request. In my opinion he possesses every qualification for such a post, and throughout his student career as well as since he passed his examinations he has displayed unusual ability and energy. It is no exaggeration to say that he has shown himself to be one of the most brilliant men that the Leeds School of Medicine has produced.

" JOHN EDWIN EDDISON "

" From EDWARD WARD, Esq., M.A., M.B., B.C. (Cantab.), Surgeon to the Leeds General Infirmary ; Lecturer on Practical Surgery in the Yorkshire College and Victoria University

" 22 PARK PLACE
LEEDS, July 7th, 1896

" The bare record of Mr. Moynihan's brilliant career would of itself be ample demonstration of his entire fitness to assume any professional distinction or responsibility which he may hereafter seek.

" But it would be quite inadequate to convey any proper impression of the character and the qualities by which his successes have been achieved.

" He is a man altogether beyond the standards by which professional attainments and success are ordinarily measured.

" His academic honours, superlative though they are, have come to him without effort, and indeed, were mere incidents in his swift acquisition of the wide information and the varied experience by which he has early developed into a surgeon of high scientific culture and knowledge, and of unusual technical skill.

" He has consistently justified, and more than justified, the high expectations which he aroused at the very commencement of his professional education.

" Indeed it may now be confidently said that the addition of Mr. Moynihan's name would strengthen and distinguish the staff of any hospital, and for obvious and special reasons his appointment as Assistant Surgeon to the Leeds General Infirmary would be a peculiarly fitting and fortunate event which would be received with wide-spread satisfaction.

" EDWARD WARD "

" From T. R. JESSOP, Esq., F.R.C.S., Consulting Surgeon, Leeds General Infirmary ; Member of Council, Royal College of Surgeons

" 33 PARK SQUARE, LEEDS

" *To the Election Committee of the Leeds General Infirmary*
" GENTLEMEN,

" In recommending Mr. B. G. A. Moynihan for the appointment of Assistant Surgeon to the Infirmary, I may lay claim to the possession of exceptional knowledge and experience of his general qualifications, of his special fitness for the office he seeks to obtain.

" Shortly after he entered upon his studies at Leeds, he was pointed out to me by my late friend, Mr. McGill, who was a close observer, and a daily companion, of the students, as one who could not fail to distinguish himself, being, to use Mr. McGill's own words, head and shoulders above the men of his year. Success after success achieved at the Yorkshire College, as well as the oft-expressed views of my colleagues, reminded me again and again of Mr. McGill's opinion and prophecy, until in 1887 Mr. Moynihan obtained his first resident appointment at the Infirmary, and then came directly under my own observation.

" His work at the Infirmary, when House Surgeon, and during his three years' tenure of the post of Resident Surgical Officer, more than confirmed the good opinion I had heard expressed.

" Mr. Robson, whose House Surgeon he was, will testify to the character of his earlier work ; of my own

110

knowledge I am able to say that a more efficient Resident Surgical Officer the Infirmary has never possessed.

" Since he commenced practice in Leeds I have been in close constant association with him, he has done much of my work, including important operations ; and now I can depute to him professional work of any kind with a feeling of the most perfect reliance.

" Mr. Moynihan's latest achievement in winning the London University Gold Medal in Surgery stamps him at once as the most brilliant student the Leeds School of Medicine has yet produced. I am not committing a breach of confidence when I state that one of his examiners told me he had never read papers which evidenced at once so complete a grasp of the subject discussed, and the possession of knowledge so wide, general, and comprehensive.

" Men of Mr. Moynihan's stamp are very exceptional. The Infirmary staff would be enriched by his addition to it.   " I am, very faithfully yours,

" T. R. JESSOP "

The election meeting came. Berkeley was appointed. He took his place upon the surgical staff of the Leeds General Infirmary. To that institution, through all his active life, he dedicated his whole attention ; there he made all his observations ; there tried out all his new ideas. Upon his private practice and the Infirmary he lavished all his industry. He was proud of the Infirmary, proud too of what he did for it, jealous of its reputation, and — above all — had for it a deep affection. When he came to leave it, having climbed to take his place by " Mr." in its annals, he left it, despite all outward vanity, with a humble and sorrowful heart. It had seen and had the best of him : there, if anywhere, reposed his memory ; there, should there be one, stood his memorial.

PART III

ON THE ROAD TO SUCCESS

On the Road to Success

THE years 1896 to 1914 were the period of Berkeley's scientific efflorescence. In 1914 the outbreak of the Great War interrupted the smooth and steady flow of his labours ; when, at its close, he came to take up the threads again, his fame was so great that the world pressed too heavily on him to permit him to continue in the old way ; more and more of his time had to be given to public activities and less and less to quiet thought and pursued investigation. Even his great energy could no longer find time for everything. In choosing, from then onwards, to dedicate himself, when the calls of private practice had been fulfilled, to the care of surgery in its domestic, social, and political aspects he chose wisely. However fertile and ingenious the mind, there comes, inevitably, a time when the spring of originality ceases to bubble with its pristine force ; it is then foolish to waste the years in kneeling, cup in hand, before its ever-dwindling stream ; the wise man knows when to start watering his ability from the spring of another's genius, and, by so doing, prolong its vigorous life.

So it was that between the ages of thirty-one and forty-eight Berkeley made his original contributions to surgery. In those years he made himself world-famous. His fame rested not solely, or even primarily, upon his surgical discoveries ; it was due to his transcendent many-sidedness. There was no department of his work in which his capabilities were not outstanding ; in more than one of them he was, by universal consent, the best. To talk about " the best surgeon in the world " is to drive discussion into the bogs of dialectic ; there it sticks and no good ever comes of it. There is no best surgeon in the world because, of course, there can never be agreement upon how to distribute credit amongst the qualities. But, since Berkeley had in some meed every quality, he as nearly approached being the complete, the perfect, surgeon as many of us will ever see. If he had genius, it was the genius of versatility. That genius may take this form is a thesis that cannot be acceptable to all. But, if ever that thesis can be sustained, it can find no greater justification than in Berkeley Moynihan. Wherever Berkeley's critic takes his stand the essentials of his view remain the same ; he sees, from every place, a big mind. Above the hazy indefinables of low-lying detail it rises clear-cut as a snowy peak. About the approaches to the mountain one may argue, but about the summit — never. It is there to be seen by all.

That Berkeley's fame should have about it something nebulous — for such indeed it had — was perhaps because its essence was this versatility. His fame was vast — but vague ; comprehensive — but intangible. He was as widely known as any doctor of his day, yet with less manifest cause for this repute than was apparent in any of the others. In their case eminence could be pinned down to some new operation, a crucial discovery, or a practice amongst illustrious names. But with Berkeley it was different ; no diagnostic tag was pinned to him. When his name came up in conversation someone would say, " Moynihan — ah, yes, the famous surgeon, everyone knows him " ; but when that someone was pressed to explain why Berkeley was known to all he would fumble and flounder only to conclude, "Well, I mean, he's a famous surgeon, everyone knows him". And everyone did know him, but so many people for so different reasons. To one he would be known for his masterly execution of an operation upon a friend or relative, to another as an inspiring teacher, to another as a writer of a text-book of clarity and stimulation, and yet to others as brilliant orator, dynamic organiser, or merely commander of high fees. It is to his credit, and to the public's too, that no narrow label was in fact attached to him, for, had it so been, a disproportionate estimate of him must have then emerged. He was a tremendous all-rounder ; he took surgery in his supple hands and lifted it bodily, leaving it firmly established at a new high level.

What did he really do ? What fundamentally can we associate with him ? He did these things : he turned the surgical operation from a thing jerky, and of rough parts, into a smooth, harmonious unity ; he taught doctors how to diagnose and treat a ubiquitously common ailment, hitherto unrecognised ; he simplified, and clearly wrote about, the whole of abdominal surgery, thus bringing it within the grasp of a thousand surgeons to whom, before his day, its theory had been obscure and its practice impossible ; he made the layman conscious of surgery's power to heal, so bringing him to surgery while life could yet be saved ; he brought together, in new societies, surgeons from every part of the land that they might, by discussion and dissemination of ideas, come to a fuller understanding of their work. Nor was this all ; along with these large wheels did many lesser wheels revolve, innumerable minor endeavours that assisted the

major works. He travelled frequently abroad, always
returning with something new to plant in the garden of
English surgery ; he supported, by tongue or pen, every
endeavour that sought the physical betterment of his
fellow countrymen ; he poured the rich fuel of his
enthusiasm upon uncountable struggling little fires of
surgical aspiration, causing them to blaze up and give
revitalising warmth to poor, sick men.

It is not my purpose to describe surgical researches in
the phraseology of ward and lecture-room ; those who
want the clinical minutiae of Berkeley's studies will know
better than to look for them in a book intended for the
general shelf ; those who wish for operations performed
beneath a lurid, novelistic light must seek elsewhere, I
shall not cater for them. This is but a slender account
of Berkeley the man, it is neither a surgical primer nor
a titillating account of operations performed upon the
fashionable. As far as surgery goes I shall but tell, quite
simply, of how Berkeley dealt with the problems that
confronted him.

*   *   *   *   *

In 1896 Berkeley had a good practice. For a surgeon
who had only just been appointed to the staff of a hospital
it was a large one ; comment was made in Leeds, at that
time, on Berkeley's astonishingly rapid advance ; no one
could remember an instance of a young man in Leeds
being so well-placed so early in his career. He was seeing
more private cases than many of his seniors and his
opinion was increasingly valued and requested by doctors
of all ages. He was earning a steady income and, while
he and his wife did not enjoy many luxuries, there was
no reason to suppose that these too, in fast-increasing

5, WOODHOUSE SQUARE, LEEDS
Lord Moynihan's home from the time of his marriage till 1904

numbers, would not soon be theirs. Berkeley was a handsome and clever young surgeon ; he had a wife who could bring him into contact with the well-to-do, and a father-in-law who had both the power and inclination to spread his name within the profession that, to his profit, would invoke his aid : the ball was at his feet. To understand this is important. Against this background Berkeley had, for the first time in his life, to make a choice between two courses without the whole weight of financial necessity being placed entirely within one scale. Placed as he was he could, by directing his full attention exclusively to his private work, make of his career, as it rolled down the glittering fields of easy, fashionable practice, a fast-growing snowball of wealth. (That he did ultimately make a lot of money is true ; but, as this early state of his reveals, he had the opportunity of doing that and that alone.) On the other hand he could, while giving reasonable and economic consideration to his practice, yet by an effort set aside a portion of each day for the pursuit of surgery as an art and science, and not as trade alone. That he did adopt this latter course is to his credit ; it commands our respect. What the ultimate fruits of this immediate sacrifice of time were to be Berkeley could only guess ; his choice, in its setting, was disinterested.

Research does not necessitate monastic withdrawal into the laboratory. It is in medicine rather an attitude of mind than a circumscribed employment. Nor does it require genius ; intelligence and application will suffice. Genius usually, though not always, leads the great advances, but the researches of intelligence provide the humble, though essential, communications without which the attack could not be made. The scientific discoveries of genius are alone made possible by the accumulated researches of lesser men ; from this material the genius draws the matter for his interpretation. The more we know the less clear becomes the line that separates the discoveries of genius from those of other men. Pasteur was without doubt a genius, Lister may not have been ; yet, for the health of man, their efforts were equally beneficent, their researches equally justified. So, when Berkeley allocated to research a little of his day, he did not go in search of the dramatic ; rather, like some laborious gardener turning and weeding the soil, he sought to keep the grounds of surgery fertile, to prepare them for the sowings of fruitful thought.

This research attitude of mind, what is it ? It is a disinclination to believe that the signs, symptoms, and pathology of disease are cut and dried, that all is well classified and docketed. Each day the doctor sees something that does not fit, something a little odd ; not once but several times a day the thing unusual, by the textbook standard, comes his way. All these he may dismiss ; they are like rough pebbles in his path making the way slow and difficult, but not wholly arresting progress. But, should he care to, he may record, collect, and classify these observations. Then, when he has sufficient evidence before him, he may upon analysis find that these oddities have running through them some common factor, large or small, and from it he draws a simple, logical conclusion. His cases, analysis and conclusion, he publishes in one of the medical journals, and there all doctors read them. He has removed one small stone from the path of medicine ; he has, by the taking of a few special pains over his daily work, made the way a little easier for those that come after him.

Researches of this kind, from his first day in practice, Berkeley set himself to do. He did not postulate some particular explanation of a tremendous surgical problem and then spend many years in trying to prove it — a policy that would have coincided well with the popular estimate of research. Rather did he conduct a ceaseless, guerilla-like research along the whole front of surgery, making repeated little advances all along the line ; so that, at the end, he had, by his endeavour, advanced the entire frontier of surgery. He was his own general, leading his own mass attack.

A picture of the variety and rapid accumulation of Berkeley's researches is given by the recorded dates and titles of his early works. I do not refer to books, only to papers published in the different medical journals. Between 1896 and 1900, during his first four years on the staff of the Infirmary, he published papers on the following subjects : appendicitis, tuberculous skin disease, mesenteric cysts, strangulated hernia in infancy, ruptured kidney, dermoid cyst, excision of scapula for sarcoma, subclavian aneurism, the operation of gastrorrhaphy, the anatomy and pathology of the rarer forms of hernia, the prevention or anticipation of shock in surgical operations, the surgery of chronic ulcer of the stomach. Many of these titles will be meaningless to the lay reader, but he may take my assurance that they endorse wide interest, wide learning, and continuous hard work. Right up until 1914 an increasing stream of publications of this nature came from Berkeley's pen. If any difference in the years existed it is perhaps this, that the titles show a progressive focus of interest upon affections of the gall-bladder, stomach, and duodenum.

It has been said of Berkeley that he had not the true

research mind. To attach a definite and specific meaning to that vague phrase is difficult, but there is one of somewhat general acceptance : it is often taken to imply a capacity to form original concepts as to the nature of disease and, by experiment and investigation, prove the concepts correct. If we accept this meaning, then the observation about Berkeley many would hold to be correct. Observation is, too, the proper word — not criticism ; the possession of a research mind in that mould is an endowed quality, not a thing to be acquired by industry. Into the nature of disease Berkeley did not make the flashing penetrations of a truly intuitive mind. He did in fact do little more than the capacities of any of us, given similar circumstances, would have enabled us to do. Bluntly, he had not the genius of originality. But he did achieve a very great deal more than most of us, standing in his shoes, would have achieved. And this he did because he had upon his side the henchmen of genius — scrupulous attention to detail, unflagging interest, and a mind of perfect tidiness. He did, as we have seen before, by a complete control of self fully exploit each tiny spark of genius that he had. His sensitive imagination was alive to research's authentic thrill and potency ; to the extreme of his abilities he followed its star. When we review his work it is fair to remember that, in the original field, he did everything that lay within his power to do.

While all the foregoing papers were being prepared and published, other work, of even greater weight, was taking shape upon Berkeley's desk. With his old chief Mayo-Robson he undertook the writing of two books ; these were published in 1901 and 1902. The first was on *Diseases of the Pancreas and their Surgical Treatment* and the second on *Diseases of the Stomach and their Surgical Treatment*. These two books reviewed the existing knowledge of their subjects, incorporated the original thought of their two authors, and presented their themes with force and clarity. They became accepted as standard works, enduring so for a decade. The book on the pancreas, indeed, was so excellent in form, substance, and style that it has permanent value as a model of medical book production ; in its modest way it is a " classic ".

These two books served also another purpose. To them more than to any other of his written works belongs the credit for initiating Berkeley's American fame. His work on retroperitoneal hernia had brought his name before a few American surgeons, but these books brought him a far wider public, they carried his name into all the great surgical clinics of America. Dr. William B. Coley of New York, himself an American surgeon of great fame and distinction, having read the book on the stomach, wrote to Berkeley, " It is the most valuable work on the subject, and I have learned much from it ". This was high approval for a young surgeon not yet forty. It was not an isolated event, several other letters from America and England expressed the same feelings.

In 1904 Berkeley published a book on *Gall-Stones and their Surgical Treatment*, this time entirely from his own pen. It received immediate approval in the surgical world and established securely Berkeley's place amongst the notable English surgeons of the day. Its publication was opportune. Coming soon after Berkeley's first visit to America, it confirmed in American eyes the considerable impression he had made while over there. His visit to America came about in an interesting manner ; it was the result of his courteous reception of an American visitor to England, and of the great impression he had made upon that man.

In the summer of 1902 Berkeley had welcomed several American doctors to Leeds. They had been drawn there by the learned authority of his papers and of the two books of which he was joint writer. Berkeley found their company stimulating and congenial ; he found in their attitude to surgery a close resemblance, indeed almost an exact identification, with his own. They were inquisitive and progressive, yet of a young enthusiasm and warm humanity : a compound of qualities exactly like that which coloured Berkeley's own being. In their company he was even more at home than with his fellow English surgeons ; their outspoken keenness, affection, and admiration were in tune with his own nature and manner. These men, with their ardent interest in surgery, set less store by professional precedence than by ability ; they respected the traditions of English medicine but were not impressed by the superior air of patronage with which London surgeons were in the habit of speaking of the work of their provincial colleagues. Berkeley was encouraged by their quick approval. In their presence, whether speaking, demonstrating, or operating, whether entertaining or taking part in simple acts of friendliness, he was always at his best. He was uplifted by the consciousness that they, with him, were fellow travellers in the great adventure of surgery.

With these visitors there came, in July of 1902, Dr. Andrew Stewart Lobingier, a surgeon of Los Angeles. He had been travelling round Europe, watching surgery in various clinics, and was now rounding out his trip with a visit to the surgical centres of Great Britain. He went to Leeds and felt himself at once drawn to Berkeley ;

he respected the man and admired his work. Before returning to America he wrote to one of the American medical journals that, on the Continent and in Britain, three young surgeons had impressed him most : Petersen, working with Czerny in Heidelberg ; Paul Lecene, with Hartmann, in Paris ; and, in England, Berkeley Moynihan. This report, and others substantially the same, caused the American Surgical Association to send Berkeley an invitation to read a paper at their meeting in Philadelphia in May 1903 ; Berkeley accepted. He appreciated the honour they had extended to a man not yet thirty-eight years old.

The trip was a great success. Berkeley made friends everywhere. His beautiful diction, friendly charm, and exuberant vitality impressed all those at every gathering to which he was invited. The main event of his visit took place on the evening of May 11th, 1903 ; it was a meeting in the hall of the College of Physicians of Philadelphia. The minute paper must have, for Berkeley's American friends, a certain historic interest. It reads as follows :

Dr. W. J. Mayo, of Rochester, Minnesota, will read a paper entitled " A Review of 303 Operations upon the Stomach and First Part of the Duodenum ".

The paper will be discussed by Dr. Albert Vander Veer, Mr. B. G. A. Moynihan, Dr. John B. Murphy, Dr. J. M. T. Finney, and Dr. J. Chalmers DaCosta.

A most awe-inspiring collection of famous names, a company in which Berkeley would be tested against the best. But — such was his perfect self-confidence — his composure was not disturbed and he spoke with graceful force and logicality. His words met with general approval. They introduced him to friendships with Dr. Mayo and Dr. Murphy that were to give him happiness for many years to come.

He came home to England again delighted with the success he had enjoyed and with many new ideas upon which to work. In matters of surgical technique especially he had seen much that made him change his views. Before Berkeley came on the staff at the Leeds Infirmary it had been the practice of the surgeons there to operate in their ordinary clothes, covered merely by an apron, and without gloves on their hands. Before going to America Berkeley had introduced the practice of wearing a white coat in which to operate. The habit had brought him much ridicule, but he bore it with the quiet patience of conscious rectitude ; he knew that soon the other surgeons would follow suit. On his return from America he brought back with him several pairs of rubber operating gloves that had been presented to him by a surgeon over there. These he produced in Leeds where they caused even more fun to be poked at him than had his white coat. This verse taken from a song in the Leeds student festivities at Christmas, 1903, shows what the hospital was thinking about Berkeley :

We see the surgeons turn aside, to test the latest germicide,
  To stop the wily microbe's least infection ;
They've sterile clothes from top to toe — moustaches now
    have had to go,
  And even just to speak will bring correction !
But not content their hair to hide, when on the nurses fair
    they've spied,
  They'll order caps too hideous to mention !
Lest when they're on a mighty list, *their* doings may be slightly
    missed,
  And *you* should claim the gallery's attention.

On the Road to Success

There's no doubt it must impress
To thus cover up each tress,
But I think it's cutting things a bit too fine . . . ah !
For quite soon they'll want to veil
Every face from gaze of male,
  You'd be better far in convents out in China.

The author of this ditty was himself unconsciously a
prophet, for the faces of nurses were to be veiled during
operations at no distant date. And white coats and
rubber gloves could ride the waves of satirical laughter.
The difficulty with the gloves was getting them on and
keeping them in condition ! Rubber gloves, even when
helpful advice is at hand, are difficult to put on at first.
They are easy to tear and have a disconcerting way of
slipping through one's fingers and landing on the floor —
after which there is an embarrassing wait while they are
re-sterilised ! Berkeley had great difficulty in getting
them on, his task not being made easier by the sniggerings
of his critics behind his back as he struggled with the
slippery things. When he had got them on they made
his work, by reducing the sensitivity of the feeling in his
finger-tips, for the time being more laborious and slower
— another source of criticism. Then, being unused to
them, he would frequently prick or cut them with his
instruments and, as a rubber glove is without virtue
unless entirely free from holes, frequent repairs were
necessary. Rubber gloves being then unobtainable in
this country, Berkeley had to make his own last as long
as possible. At the end of the year they were so patched
and mended that the original gloves were hardly dis-
cernible ! He deserves much credit for the way in which
he persisted in these reforms ; he never could bear being
laughed at, and yet, in spite of knowing that his own

actions would provoke such behaviour, he continued in his adopted course.

*   *   *   *   *

Back in Leeds from America, Berkeley undertook more work than ever. His practice was beginning to extend beyond the confines of Leeds ; patients from all over the North of England came to consult him. His appointment-book was full, and the rest of his day occupied by his duties at the hospital and nursing home. But still he found time to address medical societies and to write papers and books. The latter work was done nearly all in the early morning. He would rise at six and write for two hours before breakfasting at eight. During 1903, 1904, and 1905 these early hours of his day were given over to the preparation and writing of his largest book, in the opinion of many his greatest book — his *Abdominal Operations*. This book was a masterly survey of the diagnosis and treatment of all surgical conditions of the abdomen. It excluded only obstetric, gynaecological, and genito-urinary problems. It was a revelation of new surgical command over a hitherto dangerous field. Only just over ten years ago, when Berkeley was R.S.O., half the patients that had been submitted to surgical opening of the abdomen had succumbed to the operation. Here in this book, so soon afterwards, he demonstrated how more accurate diagnosis, more careful preparation of the patient before the operation, and a more skilled, more gentle, operative technique could, between them, so reduce the operative mortality as to change the face of abdominal surgery. He showed with what safety certain operations could be embarked upon, how the dangers of others could be enormously reduced, and how the

surgeon of confident capability, unrestrained by the fears
of ignorance, could save innumerable lives by having the
courage to operate before the patient was so far gone as
to have lost all recuperative power. Before the publication of *Abdominal Operations* patients had died because the
surgeon, knowing how dangerous was the operation, had
feared to open the abdomen until the patient was *in
extremis*, thereby multiplying the strain the operation
threw upon the patient. He had not dared to operate
earlier in case, the patient appearing to his friends but
moderately ill, a fatal issue should ensue, and for it
the surgeon be blamed. If, however, he waited until
the patient was manifestly in grave straits, then, though
the operation might be of no avail, none would blame
the surgeon for the patient's end. He might, with the
poet, say :

> . . . Diseases, desperate grown,
> By desperate appliance are removed,
> Or not at all.

But this, though a good alibi, was hardly productive
surgery. Berkeley in this book, published in his fortieth
year, showed that the earlier operation, in the hands of
a technical master, was easier and of almost infinitely
less risk ; early and well-judged operation might save
the lives of uncountable patients. It was the purpose of
the book to demonstrate to surgeons why, when, and how
to operate upon the abdomen. The style of the book was
immaculate, its language simple, lucid, with a serene
impetus, and its form of publication a model of text-
book production.

The effect of the book upon the surgery of its day
cannot be finally assessed. The good it did, in the
relief of suffering and the saving of human life, can be

estimated only by a guess. A saying of Berkeley's own
invention, one of his favourites, concerning the pioneer
of aseptic surgery, ran : " Lister has saved more lives
than have been lost in all the wars of all the ages ". That
anyone should say the same of Berkeley would, perhaps,
transport his spirit for ever into delight ; with an ideal
like that before him he laboured all his life. *Abdominal
Operations*, though it provoked no revolutionary change
like Lister's, did permanently alter the surgeon's attitude
to abdominal complaints ; with the fear of fumbling
interference lifted from his mind, and a new awareness
of his own potential competence, he approached these
maladies in the conviction that he could cure them.
Berkeley " threw open the abdomen to all surgeons " ; he
taught them how to operate upon it with certitude and
safety. All those sufferers that by operation have been
saved from acute abdominal disease, owe to Berkeley in
part their lives ; he blazed the trail along which all
abdominal surgeons now march. In surgery, though
Berkeley stands lower than Lister, the great man's hand
yet rests upon his shoulder.

Soon after the publication of *Abdominal Operations*
letters of congratulation, from all over the world, began
to reach Berkeley. They are too long, and too much alike,
to bear repetition here ; they are all full of praise. From
Europe two letters especially pleased Berkeley, coming as
they did from two of the surgical masters — Garre of
Breslau and von Eiselberg of Vienna. Both of these men
told of their keen approval of the work. But it was from
America that most of the plaudits came. Berkeley's
friends and admirers there received the book with open
arms, introducing it at once to the widest surgical public.
With affectionate courtesy, that so characteristic feature

of the best in American medicine, they wrote to tell him of the pleasure that his book had given them, in letters full of gratitude. I resist the temptation to reprint many of them ; but excerpts from three, they being so representative of all the rest, I must put in. They came from different sections of vast America, from surgical centres separated by hundreds of miles.

The first of these letters came from Dr. J. B. Murphy. At the beginning of the century this Chicago surgeon was one of the outstanding figures in American medicine ; he was an ingenious thinker and a brilliant operator. This is his letter :

" My dear Mr. Moynihan,

" Some time ago I received from W. B. Saunders & Co. a complimentary copy of your work on surgery. I had already purchased a volume. To-day I received the further information from Saunders & Co. that the volume was sent to me with the compliments of the author.

" I assure you I greatly appreciate the courtesy and prize the volume additionally on account of the personal remembrance, but nothing could make me value it more highly as an exposé of abdominal surgery than I do. The medical profession is greatly indebted to you for placing in its hands such a practical working guide to abdominal surgery. Then, too, it has so much of your personality and your work, that one feels he is observing you in your clinical arena in Leeds.

" I have just returned from the Mayos, Rochester, Minn., where we had the meeting of the American Society of Clinical Surgery, and they gave us a grand display of surgical work. Your book was one of the interesting topics of conversation at that meeting, for you have many admirers in that Society, and justly so, for you have been the pioneer of so many important changes.

" Trusting I may have the pleasure of seeing you the

coming summer, and with compliments to Mrs. Moynihan, in which Mrs. Murphy joins, I am,

" Very sincerely yours,
" J. B. MURPHY "

Berkeley was delighted with this letter. It substantiated an earlier remark of Murphy's, made some time back when Murphy had been watching Berkeley operate in Leeds. The American had then turned to another onlooker, a friend of Berkeley's, and had whispered to him that it would have been worth while coming from America to England if the sole purpose of the journey had been to see Moynihan at work — never had he seen such skill. Berkeley was glad to think that the impression then made on Murphy had endured.

The next letter is one from Dr. Robert Le Conte of Philadelphia, Secretary of the American Surgical Association. The main portion of it is set down here :

" MY DEAR MR. MOYNIHAN,

" You continue to shower upon me gifts of inestimable value, and I hardly know how to thank you (so I shan't try) for the Report on Surgical Treatment of Non-Malignant Diseases of the Stomach, and best of all that splendid book on *Abdominal Operations* which reached me this morning. The excellence of the paper, printing, illustrations, etc., is a worthy garment for the knowledge it contains. For the past two hours I have been reading its pages, lost in an intellectual treat. What a pleasure it must be to have produced so excellent a work. . . . ' The Book ' for the present will rest on my desk until I have read every word of it. Thanking you for your kind thought of me,

" I am very sincerely yours,
" ROBERT G. LE CONTE "

From the Dean of the Kentucky School of Medicine

132

came the third letter. Apart from the omission of a middle
portion that dealt with some niceties of operative detail,
I reproduce it here in its entirety.

" MY DEAR DOCTOR MOYNIHAN,
    " I have made a very careful study of your work
on Abdominal Surgery, and I write to congratulate you
upon the production of the best work of this kind that
has been published in the English language. Other
works have embraced more subjects, including pelvic
diseases, but I am so familiar with all questions relating
to Gynaecology that I much prefer a book with the
omission of these subjects.
    " I am specially interested in surgery of the upper
abdominal cavity, which you have reduced to such great
simplicity, giving your own views with originality, but
quoting from the best writers upon the subject. . . .
    " While many men have done good work in Gastro-
enterostomy, you have done the best, and you are the
pioneer in improvising the correct method in making
the attachment, anatomically, physiologically and me-
chanically.
    " With the hope that we may see you in this country
in the near future, I am,
                        " Faithfully yours,
                            " W. H. WATHEN "

Gastroenterostomy is an operation whereby the
stomach is joined to a lower part of the intestine, thus
rendering it unnecessary for food to pass through the
duodenum, which lies between the two. It is for this
reason that the procedure is often called a " short-circuit "
operation. It has various uses ; the one in which
Berkeley most employed it was in the treatment of
duodenal ulcer.
    If Berkeley's name is to be associated, particularly or

exclusively, with any one disease, then pre-eminently it should be connected with his work upon duodenal ulcer. Although this complaint was known to exist before Berkeley came along, its diagnosis was hesitant, inaccurate, and infrequent, the treatment of it was clumsy and uncertain, and the ultimate outlook for the sufferer from it one of chronic ill-health and shortened life. What Berkeley did was to place the diagnosis upon a simple and formal basis, to standardise treatment, and to offer to sufferers from duodenal ulcer the prospect of a long life, free from pain. At the last, in the eyes of many, his views on all matters relevant to the disease erred towards bigotry. But this I take to be of small significance ; his work was by then done, it had passed into the hands of the profession, for them to adjust and refine ; in his terminal opinions we must permit the acknowledged master a little licence if he wishes to gild his gingerbread.

Gastric ulcer, isolated ulceration of the stomach wall, had been the subject of much study in Berkeley's student days ; a good deal was known about its nature, its symptoms and their treatment. About duodenal ulcer much less was known ; relatively much less thought and attention had been paid to that condition. Some doctors contended that the only certain diagnosis of duodenal ulcer was with the eyes, that in fact it could only be diagnosed at operation or at necropsy ; they argued that it was impossible to separate its symptoms out from the complaining rigmarole of the dyspeptic patient. Other doctors, and many of them, regarded the condition as but unimportant, a mere appendage of gastric ulcer and undeserving of special attributes ; a trivial incident in the welter of chronic indigestion.

In 1903 Berkeley published a book on *The Surgical*

Treatment of Gastric and Duodenal Ulcers. In the years
that followed he endeavoured, by correlating what he
saw in the duodenum at operation with the patient's
original complaint, to find a regular, consistent chain of
symptoms leading up to a regular pathological change ;
he would then be able to say that one special group of
symptoms, out of all those associated with indigestion,
must inevitably and invariably imply the existence of a
duodenal ulcer. He came to lay enormous importance
upon the appearance of the living tissues he saw at operation. The abnormalities seen then, he said, were what
gave rise to the patient's pain. Post-mortem examination was well enough but it told only of the last results
of illness ; it did not reveal what was wrong at the time
of onset of ill-health, at the time when a cure was most
desirable and at the only time when a true repair was
possible. In pursuit of this study of the ravages of disease
upon living tissues Berkeley became greatly engrossed.
At the end of each operation he would draw with coloured
crayons, upon a thin white sheet of cardboard, an exact
picture of the abnormalities he had seen while operating ;
this he would accompany with illustrations and descrip-
tive matter explaining the curative methods he had
adopted. He had a swift, light touch that made his drawings very clear ; in an incisive way they told more than
copious written notes could do. These little sketches
were bound in the volumes of his case records. There,
with the notes of the patient's progress after operation,
they provided his analytical material. In them was the
essence of every case : the first complaint, the pictured
disease, the method of handling, and the degree to which
health and strength were in the end re-won. It was not
long before Berkeley had collected a large number of these

cases in his records. At the end of the century's first decade he was able to survey a larger number of upper abdominal operation cases than had ever before been performed by one man. In them was contained evidence that substantially proved all the theories he had held about duodenal ulcer.

He gathered together, out of his records, a group of cases in which the characteristic feature was severe abdominal pain after food. This pain did not come on until over an hour after the meal had been taken ; the sufferers from it discovered, of their own accord, that they could rid themselves of the pain by taking more food, by drinking a glass of milk, or by taking a dose of alkaline salts in water. Berkeley selected these cases because the history of their symptoms differed so much from the classical complaints in gastric ulcer cases, in which the pain after food is rapid in onset and not easy to relieve. Then, with his cases chosen, he referred to his drawings, seeking to establish a common causative factor in operative findings. This he successfully did ; in them all he found pictures of duodenal ulcers seen at operation. Then he applied the reverse investigation to another group of cases ; a group in which his drawings of them all showed duodenal ulcer disclosed at operation. What symptoms did these cases have ? If they had pain, relievable by food — the so-called " hunger pain " — coming on some time after food, then he could claim that his own theory, that duodenal ulcer symptoms differed radically from those of gastric ulcer, was fairly proved. His enquiry bore him out ; the cases did have pain, it was delayed, it was relieved by food.

Satisfied with his work, he published, in 1910, a book entitled *Duodenal Ulcer* in which he expounded his views, his cases, and his proofs. It was his most important piece of original study, his greatest claim to prime discovery. The existence of duodenal ulcer was already known, the set of symptoms had been previously recognised, but the integration of the two into a single picture of early identifiable disease was new. For that reason is Berkeley's name permanently linked with duodenal ulcer. His book was well received and brought in its train much admiration. But, at the same time, it started much controversy. All paid Berkeley tribute for his contribution to knowledge in making the diagnosis clear ; but not all agreed with him on what he considered the ideal mode of treatment once the diagnosis had been secured. Berkeley advocated operation. The physicians contended that the cases could be cured without resort to such drastic measures. The battle of conflicting treatments raged for long, still in fact rages, and even now still drags in Berkeley's name. And that is the point : his productive investigation is obscured by his controversial advocacy. Whether Berkeley was right or wrong about treatment is, to some extent, irrelevant ; what is important, and what he deserves great credit for, is that he did show how to diagnose duodenal ulcer with exactitude. Others may evolve the proper treatment in due time. But, and this is a wise old piece of medical lore, there can be no treatment without diagnosis. He who identifies disease is no less our benefactor than he who shows how to treat it ; the one cannot exist without the other. Every person that is successfully treated for duodenal ulcer, by whatever means, is, it may not be unjustly claimed, in Berkeley's debt.

*　　*　　*　　*　　*

It is a striking feature of research, and one with which all workers are acquainted, that investigation of a single issue reveals, at the same time, many others which, though hitherto in existence unsuspected, have all exciting possibilities. So Berkeley found during his study of duodenal ulcer. He quickly came to realise that not alone in that condition was visual examination of living disease important. Surely, he thought, less attention should be paid to the morbid pathology of the post-mortem room and more to its vital counterpart seen in the operating theatre. It was his view that the surgeon's time was at least as well employed in trying to discover the earliest changes caused by disease as in noting its end-results. There were things to be seen upon the operating-table that could never be seen elsewhere ; either recovery took place, or else the condition changed out of all recognition before post-mortem examination took place. The more Berkeley's mind played round this subject the more significant it seemed. He became convinced that what he had done in the elucidation of duodenal ulcer was but a fraction of what could be done in the realm of abdominal surgery by employing the same technique. Note the symptoms, look at the lesion, apply the treat-ment, watch the patient : that was the programme. It could be applied with almost endless variations to an almost endless series of conditions. Inestimable were the potential uses for it. To this new approach to the old problems he gave the name " pathology of the living ". He preached this method with all the force of his enthusiasm.

This is how he pleaded for it in his own words ; the passage is taken from the end of a closely reasoned medical address that, because of its difficult scientific terms, is not

BERKELEY MOYNIHAN
January, 1911

suitable for reproduction in its entirety in this setting. He said :

"In this very imperfect recital of a few of the results which have come from the work of the surgeon I hope I have said something to convince you that the study of morbid conditions within the abdomen during the progress of an operation has materially increased our capacity to make a more certain and an earlier diagnosis, and has accordingly equipped us with a more efficient therapeutic power. It is, I submit, by a close study of the anamnesis followed by a careful investigation of the parts implicated in the disease, *during the life of the patient*, that the surest foundation for accurate diagnostic power can be built. The surgeon, after hearing the detailed story of an illness, has not to wait until death comes to the patient before he can lay bare those pathological processes which have given rise to all the symptoms. He can see and handle the organ or organs affected at the time they are exciting the sufferings of the patient ; not at the time, months or years later, when all bounds have been overstepped by the unchecked extension of the disease, in parts laid waste by a late infection. At the time when symptoms are being caused, the pathological changes are open to examination ; *that* is the advantage which comes from a study of the pathology of the living. So far as abdominal diseases are concerned, he is the best diagnostician who spends much of his time in the operation theatre. The lessons there to be learnt are far greater in number and far outweigh in value those that can be learnt in the *post-mortem* room, in so far as they bear any reference to the treatment of the living. . . . I would, therefore, urge upon all those engaged in practice the desirability of following their patients to the operation table whenever the opportunity occurs. The lessons there to be learnt will in practice be of a value beyond all reckoning, and interest in the daily work will be thereby quickened to an unaccustomed degree."

His emphasis upon the pathology of the living and his contribution to medical knowledge of duodenal ulcer he regarded as his most important scientific works. But though he was proud of them he could speak of them in modest terms. In a speech he made in 1917 he said of those who worked upon the problem of duodenal ulcer :

" The earliest records of duodenal ulcer are found in connection with stray cases, or in those where perforation or haemorrhage had occurred and caused death. The earliest mention was by Travers in 1817. Abercrombie in 1870 gave the first connected account of the disease, and recorded a few cases. In 1894 the first successful case of operation for a perforated ulcer was recorded by H. P. Dean of London. In 1900 Weir of New York gave an excellent summary of all the cases of perforation then on record. But of duodenal ulcer as a cause of continued or recurrent dyspepsia, or as a pathological lesion to which were attached a series of symptoms capable of recognition during life, there is nothing. The first ascription of a group of symptoms to the definite structural lesion in the duodenum is to be placed to the exclusive credit of English medicine."

Though in his private life Berkeley was human enough to speak freely of his own original studies he was, in public, as these words show, capable of a more dispassionate view.

* * * * *

It is difficult to convey to those who have never seen an operation a proper idea of the impression a surgeon makes upon the onlookers. When the latter are critical they will remember the surgeon's false moves long after they have forgotten the better part of his technique ; they are quick to perceive any attempt to achieve the brilliant when that endeavour is not in accord with the patient's interests. But before untrained eyes the surgeon may win applause for many a spectacular move that would have been better left untried. That is why, for those with special knowledge, an operating theatre is, indeed, a great place in which to test character. There the surgeon has it all his own way ; he is in complete authority and, in a dramatic setting, may give free play to his flamboyant instincts ; do what he will, no one may criticise him at the time.

During this period of Berkeley's life much cheap admiration was being won by surgeons. Acting on the assumption that the shorter time the operation took the better was the patient's chance of recovery, they tried to do each case in as short a time as possible ; with one eye on the clock and the other on the wound, they ruthlessly cut their way to a swift conclusion. To do an operation in a few minutes less than one's colleagues took to do it was to score off them ; by so much one thought oneself the better surgeon. The majority were of the opinion that the rough handling of the patient's tissues, an unavoidable concomitant of this search for speed, was a price worth paying since brevity of operation was all-important. But a small group of surgeons never accepted this doctrine. They could not convince themselves that a few minutes saved were a fair recompense for so much violent usage of the injured part. They came to believe that greater gentleness, while doing less harm, would promote a quicker healing ; that a slightly longer operation would be followed by a shorter convalescence. Of this group Berkeley became the leader. He became the great protagonist of " gentle surgery ". He believed in the elimination of all harshness from surgical procedure. He advocated only such speed of operation as was com-

patible with the exclusion of all strain. To summarise
his faith he used the word " caress ". At operation every
touching of the tissues should be a " caress " ; there
should be no dragging or pulling of the parts exposed,
only " caressing ". It was his opinion that an operation
should be as fast but no faster than this measure would
allow.

Berkeley trained his hands to a remarkable degree of
subtle accuracy. In the days of his early surgery it was
his habit to go about at all times with a short piece of thin
string in his pocket ; this, in idle moments, he would
take out and, never looking at it, endlessly tie and untie
it as he talked ; looping it round the arm of a chair he
would, with the fingers of one hand only, knot it and then
undo the knot. He practised until there was nothing to
choose between the skill of his two hands ; he was as
clever with the one as with the other. With his usual
fondness for alliteration, he would speak of the " digital
dexterity " needful in an able surgeon. Himself he had
it to a phenomenal extent.

His hands were rather broad and rather short. They
were not fat, nor were they thin and angular ; they had
the appearance of firm muscularity. The fingers were
wide, not tapering, and slightly incurved towards the
central line of the hand. The nails were squarish, suffused
with fresh vitality. They reminded one of the hands of
a great pianist ; not the long, thin, " artistic " hand of
ignorant convention, but the short, solid, knuckled hand
that so often goes with manual genius. Berkeley took a
religious care of them. Each week they were manicured.
Never would he use them for rough purposes about the
house or garden. It was his pleasing habit to go about
his daily business with them always clothed in new-

washed gloves of pale material. His hands were his livelihood and his joy ; he was not ashamed to guard and cherish them. He was pleased when others spoke of them. He was elated when, on being presented to King George V, his sovereign said, " I am proud to shake the most skilful hand in all the world ". Here, indeed, was justification for all his solicitude.

When he operated the movements of his hands were flowing, continuous, unhesitant. He did nothing suddenly and was unshaken when the unforeseen arose. He was a quiet operator, setting great store by the maintenance of a concentrated hush in his theatre. If he sought drama — and his instinct was dramatic — he found it in the sacramental devotion with which he surrounded his every operation. He would allow no unnecessary talking while he worked. When he spoke himself it was quietly and without sharpness. If he had to correct or reprove one of his assistants, he did so, if possible, in private ; if to do it in public was essential he would usually content himself with some mild phrase like " We don't do things that way here, do we, So-and-so ? " The words were not severe, but the implied rebuke that underlay their soft restraint was detectable by all. The offence was not committed twice.

While the certainty of Berkeley's movements took away from all his operations the appearance of haste, his work was never slowly done. The onlooker was surprised that what had seemed so leisurely was, by the clock, so quickly finished. There was about his technical manœuvres a marvellous assurance, a sense of utter mastery that inspired in all present a restful confidence. Never in doubt himself, he relieved all others of their doubts. His complete knowledge of anatomy, his careful application of physiological principles, his unequalled

" digital dexterity ", and his profound self-confidence, made him a truly great operator. When his friends claim that there had never been before so great an operator, their contention is hard to refute. Certainly there had never been a greater one.

The reactions of those who watched him operate are the source of many a story. Around the names of all surgeons of repute anecdotes collect with the tenacious frequency of limpets upon the rocks. These tales have, as often as not, very little basis in actual fact ; the same story is told of many surgeons. Of those about Berkeley no doubt the usual number are apocryphal, adapted though they may be to his needs. But two, told of a Frenchman present in Berkeley's theatre, have a charming comicality that makes one hope they are true. This visitor saw Berkeley arrive and prepare himself for work ; he saw the washing and the scrubbing, the changing of out-door clothes for white operating ones ; he was, before this unusual spectacle of those days, deeply impressed. But when, the final touch, Berkeley discarded his leather shoes for white rubber ones, the Frenchman began to smile. Turning to his neighbour he remarked in an undertone, " Does he then stand in the abdomen while he works ? " Later, when the party had moved into the theatre and the operation was in progress, Berkeley repeatedly spoke of the care he was taking to reduce the incidental haemorrhage to a minimum. He did in fact, the Frenchman thought, a little labour the point. When next it was made the visitor observed to Berkeley, " Is your English blood, then, so precious ? "

But more satisfying are the sincere expressions of admiration that came from other masters of his craft who saw Berkeley operate. We know what Murphy thought, what he said when standing in Berkeley's theatre. Writing in a letter at a later date he also said, " I am looking forward to our visit to England to receive an additional injection of enthusiasm by witnessing your work in your operating arena. How you are able to accomplish so much, having only the same number of days as the rest of us, is scarcely comprehensible." Not only J. B. Murphy wondered how Berkeley fitted in so many things into a twenty-four-hour day ; it was, all Berkeley's life, a source of speculation to all who knew him. He did it by never idling, dallying, or frittering away the minutes here and there. Every nook and cranny of his day was carefully filled ; no minutes wasted anywhere.

But, returning to his craftsmanship, here is another letter — written to Berkeley in May of 1913 by Dr. W. J. Mayo. In surgery the name of Mayo is synonymous with supreme authority the world over. Nowhere has American surgery flowered more finely than in the clinic that bears the Mayo name. After spending some days in Leeds, Mayo wrote to Berkeley :

" MY DEAR MOYNIHAN,
        " I had a very fine time in Leeds as I always do — the character of your work is of the type I try to do myself but not so well do I succeed — painstaking care and conservation of all the patient's forces have taken the place of speed and show of the old order of things and the results are definitely better and more satisfactory in every way.
        " I fully appreciate as never before your aims and ambition. To leave as a heritage to Leeds a school of surgery based on physiological chemistry and on physiology as well as pathology and technique is a great purpose. . . .
                " I am sincerely yours,
                        " W. J. MAYO "

Another writer to Berkeley was H. W. Keen of Philadelphia, who himself had played a distinguished part in the literature of surgery. He did, as many of his letters show, conceive a great admiration for Berkeley. Berkeley held him in affection and esteem. This following letter has a double significance ; not only does it reveal Keen's respect for Berkeley's surgery but it also tells of the variety of interests the two men shared. Berkeley had an ebullient interest in almost every one of man's activities ; books, sports, history, architecture, it did not matter what the subject was, about them all he was inquisitive, and of them all spoke with the sparkling ardour of enthusiasm ; he was never so happy as when in the company of another whose interests were as diverse and as vigorous as his own. For this reason the hours he spent with Keen were always happy ones.

" R.M.S. *Calypso*
August 1905
" MY DEAR MR. MOYNIHAN,
" We enjoyed so much our visit to Leeds that we should be very thoughtless did we not express to you and Mrs. Moynihan our sense of your delightful friendly attentions. Rarely indeed have we passed two more delightful days. Moreover I want to express to you my appreciation of your masterly surgery. I felt it a great privilege to witness your operations and to add to my surgical knowledge.
" To-day I have read two copies of the *Outlook* which when my daughters have finished I shall send you. You remember our talk over the work of the Department of Agriculture which is now one of the most important and useful departments of the Government and of which the head is a member of the Cabinet. In one of the numbers you will find a most interesting statement of its work far more in detail and far more complete than I could give you. In the other you will find a most interesting and

illuminating account of the Destruction of the Russian fleet by George Vernon (?) which throws much light on that wonderful achievement. Some of the other articles may also interest you if you have time to read them.

"We are looking forward with great pleasure to seeing you and Mrs. Moynihan in our home in Philadelphia.

"With kindest regards I am,

"Yours sincerely,

"H. W. Keen

"*P.S.*—We have had a delightfully *smooth* passage.

"*P.S.*—You will be interested also in the article on education in the Philippines. We are doing a splendid work for civilization there following your example in India.

"Many thanks for the Report on Non-Malignant Disease of the Stomach. I have read it with much profit."

In 1912 Berkeley was to have his portrait painted by von Herkomer. The artist, to get a better impression of his subject, was invited to see Berkeley operate. What he had to say about the occasion is interesting in that it shows a layman's reaction to the sight of Berkeley at work. He wrote :

"My dear Moynihan,

"I never adequately thanked you for the extraordinary sight I was privileged to witness.

"Your running commentary was so valuable — and don't *you* talk about anyone else being a better lecturer — it was just a perfect demonstration lecture, and it *did* seem so easy ! My right-hand neighbour said one must see someone else do the same operation to appreciate your master hand.

"One thing struck me forcibly, how the whole personality of the patient was obliterated ; it was simply a living organism upon which you worked locally. Many

other little observations I made, of which I will tell you
when we meet. . . . I send you the two volumes of *The
Herkomers*. You may have some moments when you
could read the history of the man you love and saved.
"Ever yours,
"Hubert von Herkomer"

It is useless to draw out description in an endeavour
to place the reader in what Murphy called Berkeley's
" arena ". Mayo's letter really tells it all. Berkeley
himself summarised his surgical faith in an address which
he gave in 1920 ; he entitled it " The Ritual of a Surgical
Operation ". It was a very celebrated talk ; one that
was both repeated and reprinted. It dealt with the
bacteriological aspects of an operation, with the surgeon's
costume, with asepsis and antisepsis, and with the
technical conduct of the case ; it discusses the relative
merits of different sorts of disinfecting solutions and goes
at length into the value of the use of rubber gloves.
These are matters of narrow interest. But it also speaks
of the surgeon's attitude of mind, of the considerations
that he should most carefully maintain :

" The ritual of an operation commences before, sometimes long before, the incision is made, and may continue
for a long period after the wound is healed. In the
transition of a patient from ill health to sound health the
operation itself is only one — though it may be the most
important — of all the factors concerned in this fortunate
event.
" In this discussion we are not asked to deal with two
essential preliminary propositions, the necessity for the
most careful clinical enquiry into all aspects of the
patient's history and condition, so that accuracy of
diagnosis may be achieved before operation ; and the
exact relevance of the proposed operation in the par-

ticular conditions recognised by this enquiry, or discovered during the course of the operation itself. A great many mistakes are still made in both these matters. It is useless, to say the least, to perform the most perfect technical operation in conditions which do not call for it ; and the test of a successful operation is not restricted to the healing of the wound, but to the ultimate effect of the procedure upon the disorder of the patient. . . .

" Surgery should be a merciful art. The cleaner and gentler the act of operation, the less the patient suffers, the smoother and quicker his convalescence, the more exquisite his healed wound, and the happier his memory of the whole incident, to him probably one of the most important in his whole life. The results of the ritual are therefore expressed not only in the mortality — where the difference may be slight — but also in the quality of the healing of the wound, and in the quality of the recovery from the operation, in respect of security, rapidity, smoothness, completeness and finality. . . .

" The most important person present at an operation is the patient. This is a truth not everywhere and always remembered. It is our duty to make the operation as little disagreeable as possible for him. To many patients it is a dreaded ordeal. Our patients to-day are terrified by the tradition that clings to the word ' operation ', a tradition started in the days when it must indeed have been a terrible procedure, without anaesthetics other than those stupefying drugs, alcohol, and tobacco, with patients strapped down or held by assistants, and all the other horrible accessories. To-day an operation can, and should, be made a very simple matter, devoid of entirely anything repellent or disheartening. . . .

" Every detail in every operation is of importance, and should be conceived, practised, and tested with unwearying patience by the operator himself, and by him in conjunction with all his assistants. Was it not Michael Angelo who first said that success depends upon details, but success is no detail ? In surgery, at least, success may well depend upon the scrupulous, exacting, and unceasing supervision and close scrutiny of every smallest detail of procedure. In respect of surgical work there may be some truth in Blake's assertion that all excellence is in minute particulars. Surgery is nowadays no longer the work of an individual, but of a ' team ' in which every member plays his exact part, in which all contribute to success, and in which each may bring about disaster. The well-trained team should display that mastery which is implied by ease in smooth and efficient action. In every phase of its work there should be, not merely the casual observance of a ritual the meaning of which is lost and the deeds of which are only a faded counterfeit, but acts of full devotion to principles which have been tried and proved, acts which are the witnesses to a living and perfect faith.

" It is of course a platitude to say that a good surgeon is not merely one who operates well. The qualities required to make our ideal surgeon are many : gifts of character, leadership, wisdom — even worldly wisdom — compassion, and the finest technical skill. In respect of the latter we remember that surgery is not only a science but an art, work demanding the highest craftsmanship, and a knowledge of all the ' tricks of the tools' true play'. In all the movements of the surgeon there should be neither haste nor waste. It matters less how quickly an operation is done than how accurately it is done. Speed should result from the method and the practised facility of the operator, and should not be his first and formal intention. It should be an accomplishment, not an aim. And every movement should tell, every action should achieve something. A manipulation, if it requires to be carried out, should not be half done and hesitatingly done. It should be deliberate, firm, intentional, and final. Infinite gentleness, scrupulous care, light handling, and purposeful, effective quiet movements, which are no more than a caress, are all necessary if an operation is to be the work of an artist, and not merely of a hewer of flesh. For every operation, even those procedures which are now quite commonplace, should be executed not in the spirit of an artisan who has a job to get through, but in the spirit of an artist who has something to interpret or create. An operation should not only bring relief or health to the patient, but should give a glow of keen delight to the artist himself, a thrill of joy and a sense of complete satisfaction to a critical spectator.

" Ours has been a necessary profession ever since man's body was subject to enmity and casualty. All who practise it will need the gifts of which Thomas Fuller spoke — ' an eagle's eye, a lady's hand, and a lion's heart '. Of all of us who labour honestly may it at last truthfully be said, as it was said of James the Fourth of Scotland, ' Quod vulnera scientissime tractaret ' — ' He was most skilful at the handling of wounds '. "

*   *   *   *   *

When Berkeley was appointed to the staff of the Infirmary he gave up smoking entirely. It had been his habit to smoke cigars occasionally, but now, contending that it impaired the acuity of his senses, he gave it up. For the rest of his life he never smoked at all. Half in jest and half in earnest he used to say to those of his surgical friends that smoked, " I never knew a really good surgeon who smoked ". It is probable that in his younger days he never much enjoyed the indulgence ; to give it up was no real hardship. But deep in his heart he really did believe that, for a surgeon, tobacco was a deleterious drug, and, therefore, one to be avoided.

He was not a teetotaller. But he was very abstemious in his ways. He liked light wines and especially enjoyed good port. He would never drink more than a small glassful of wine, and if taking port was usually content with a bare half glass. Though not a collector of wines he did, over the years, lay down a fair amount of port. He was, for all that there was sentimental in his nature, a shrewd man. He derived a pleasant satisfaction from the realisation that his port was growing in value as it matured in flavour. His palate was keen and he took a boyish delight, as indeed he took in nearly everything he did, in discussing vinous subtleties. He loved others to enjoy the wines his table provided ; and, though taking so little himself, he was yet not unwilling that others should drink more freely than he did. But he had a poor opinion of those that, by however small a margin, over-stepped the bounds of moderation. His enormous pride and satisfaction in the alert perfection of his own senses and physique forbade his doing anything to injure or dull them ; it seemed to him incomprehensible, and a little contemptible, that others could find pleasure in anything that entailed loss of supreme self-control.

He did in fact, despite his kindly generosity of heart and mind, not wholly understand his fellow men. He could interpret the behaviour of women with far greater exactitude than he could that of men. Unavoidably conscious as he was of his superiority in intellect and capability to other men, he could not share their feelings. This sometimes troubled him. He felt himself unwanted in the gregarious convivialities of his friends. His acquaintances were, in truth, never completely at ease with him. They, knowing themselves frail, sometimes tired and often worried, found comfortable refreshment in the congenial atmosphere of smokes, drinks, and humorous chatter ; but, when he was there, they were never entirely sure that in the hidden places of his mind Berkeley did not look down on them, thinking a little less of them. He who was so utterly sure of himself — needing no support and relying on no other — was like the ghost of a moral reproach at the feast. He did not obtrude his rectitude, but his companions were aware of it ; it was an irksome reminder of the call of their own better selves. Berkeley, feeling no need of reassurance, could not relax with them into those intimately exchanged confidences that are the bastions of friendship. Self-revelation is the hostage that we offer up to fortune as the price of true friendship ; it is not a commodity that can be bought without equal sacrifice from either side. Berkeley was about fundamentals reticent, perhaps so by nature rather than by set intention, but the quality proved an obstruction in the path of friendship. As has been said of him by another writer, " Moynihan was a man with many friends but he made few friendships. He rarely talked of his difficulties to others. In the words of Carlyle, ' He consumed his own smoke '."

He certainly had many friends if viewed in the light of those sentences. Nor did he neglect the bonds that bound them to him. He had a wonderful memory for anniversaries and special occasions of all kinds ; and though many of these events had no personal importance to him, he would remember them because of their significance to his friends. He would cable affectionate birthday greetings to surgical friends in all parts of the world, surprising them by his yearly remembrance of their day. On the anniversary of their operation he would write, to those patients of whom he was specially fond, letters of friendly reassurance and encouragement. This practice was one that was susceptible of misinterpretation ; but, to anyone who knew him well, it was clear that in this instance he had no thought of self-advertisement ; it was alone spontaneous cordiality. He was a great writer of little notes of all sorts. He would use the time when journeying in car or train to dash off a few brief notes to those who, at the moment, were foremost in his thoughts. It was an endearing habit. That one so busy should do what other friends did not, was naturally impressive. It caused him to be held with special affection in many a heart.

* * * * *

How he found time to write any letters at all during the busy, creative years of 1896 to 1914 is surprising. His appearance of having "time for everything" was illusory. There were a great many things that he was far too busy to do. Apart from a little tennis and some swimming, he took no time away from work. When, after having passed the age of forty, he took up golf and played with regularity one afternoon each week-end, he observed to one of his friends that never before had he with any frequency not worked on both Saturdays and Sundays. He had not had time to play. He was not, he said, financially out of the wood until his fortieth birthday had gone by.

When he was first married he and Isabel had been able to afford nothing better than their small house in Woodhouse Square. They lived in the modest style their means compelled. At the turn of the century, a few years later, their finances had improved and they moved into a house of medium size not far from the nursing home to which Berkeley sent his private patients. They needed a larger home. Berkeley, like his father before him, had two daughters and then a son. Dorothy, Shelagh, and Patrick were born within ten years of his marriage. Though he had little time to spend at home, he was, as often as he could be, with his children. As in the old

154

days in hospital he was never happier than when he had a child upon his knee. He was tremendously proud of his children and anxious, perhaps unreasonably so, that they should make a mark upon the world no less than he himself had done. When his son was born he wrote to his beloved sister, Ada :

" My DARLING ADA,
    " The baby boy arrived this afternoon at 3.45. Patrick he is to be, of course. . . .
    " The boy is a picture, rotund and perfect. Judging by his voice he must, I think, be an Irishman. Let us hope he may be as good a man as either of his grandfathers.
                            " With all my love,
                                    " thine,
                                            " B."

Another letter a week later was much concerned with the boy's name. Berkeley, proud of family and full of sentiment, wanted to please himself and everybody else.

" My DARLING ADA,
    " The boy has done splendidly during the last week. He has eaten well : gained weight, slept peacefully and behaved himself, in all respects most perfectly.
    " My feeling with regard to names is in favour of ' Patrick Berkeley ' only. I don't know where Andrew would fit in : and I have no *special* affection for the name. Moreover we have already an ' Andrew Moynihan ' in the family ! and I have not the smallest doubt that he will worthily uphold the name. We haven't yet settled names, godfathers, or date of christening. Isabel is, and has been all the week, very well indeed.
                    " My bestest love,
                            " thine
                                    " B."

The Andrew Moynihan he refers to is Ada's own son — A. M. Claye. He was quite right in his prognostications. The boy, in later life coming to Leeds as a medical student, did very well ; he rose, through no abuse of avuncular influence, to become a member of the staff of the Leeds Infirmary.

In years to come the career of Patrick Berkeley, too, was to exercise Berkeley's mind. He was aware of the difficulties that pursue all sons who try to follow in the steps of famous fathers ; only a sense of avocation in the son no whit less strong than had been the father's can render the journey safe. If in his father's profession the son succeeds, then the critics say that he owes all to paternalism ; if he makes no great mark, then, in contrast with his father's fame, he is dubbed a failure. In the days ahead, when for surgery Patrick showed no inclination, it was not without relief that Berkeley perceived the situation.

But all that was still a long way off in the early nineteenhundreds. The sunlit romping of Berkeley's children was unshadowed by adolescent problems. On holidays in England or abroad, often with Tommy and his wife, sometimes with other friends, Berkeley's untroubled gay vivacity was tireless. He was, on those occasions, a perfect companion. Swimming, walking, playing tennis, he hustled and hounded his friends along. Then, when the evening came, his effervescent talk was always entrancing ; his old delight in argument was undiminished ; he loved an intellectual set-to. About everything he did there was pulsating zest, an insatiable avidity for life. Once, when walking along the cliffs of North Wales with Tommy, he flung himself down upon the grass and lying in the sunlight said, " Ah, Tommy, why do we waste our time in work ? We should spend our days sitting in the sun, talking and enjoying the beauty of the world."

To judge of the happiest period in another man's life is rash ; there is too much we do not know. But there is compelling urgency about the thought that here, for Berkeley, lay the best. The happy family, the fruitful work, the admiration of great surgeons, and prosperity's fast-incoming tide — all these were his. By the world he was as yet but little touched. The flattery of foolish voices — a siren-call often too much for him ; the blandishments of fashion — not easily resisted when youth had been so hard : these he was yet to know. The accumulated tasks, work and duties of later years, were to leave him with but little time to spend before his hearth ; he loved his children dearly but, as they grew up, was inevitably less with them ; the calls of his practice and public life left him too little time. Isabel and the children, in sufferance of long hours of loneliness with him away at work, had, too, in later years to make their patient contribution on the altar of Berkeley's fame. Isabel, who relied on her husband so much in every way, never became quite reconciled to the busy occupation of his days ; for some things she thought Berkeley could pay too great a price, and fame was one of them.

But in these early days he had adequate leisure at home. He and Isabel went about with their friends. They were both fond of tennis and played together frequently. To the whole family the jolliest part of each year was the summer holiday. For the ten years that preceded the war Berkeley owned a house in Norway ; his sister Eva looked after it, and to it the whole family repaired for a month each summer. It was, most appropriately, called

Holiday House. Wonderful family times were had there. Berkeley could swim to his heart's content, and in games with his children, away from all care, he could refresh himself.

In May of 1914 his friend W. J. Mayo, while travelling, went to visit Eva Moynihan. He wrote to Berkeley :

" DEAR MOYNIHAN,

"We are just leaving Christiania after a most delightful afternoon with your sister where we have been greatly entertained in walking about your garden looking at the fjord and imagining the fine time you have here during your summer holidays—Holiday House so correctly named. Miss Moynihan resembles you in many ways ; artistic to her finger-tips, one sees everywhere about the place evidences of her personality.

"We have had an intensely interesting trip. Moscow and St. Petersburg were well worth the visit. Professor Ott and his clinic were the chief surgical attractions. Professors Federoff and Ziedler were also interesting. In Helsingfors Krogriss had some of the divine spark of surgical genius. In Stockholm Professor Berg and his associates are doing advanced work.

"Christiania you know so well and so much better than I that comment would be superfluous. I am greatly grieved that you are not to visit America the coming September. We have much to show you, not so much surgically perhaps but a gradual betterment of the clinic, a crystallization of dreams and the growth of an ideal. We hope we have found means of perpetuating it. I should have been glad of your advice. Perhaps later you will find yourself able to come. . . .

" Faithfully yours,

" W. J. MAYO "

Eva Moynihan was a magnificent housekeeper — almost too good. She was so tidy and so particular that the children, and even Berkeley himself, hardly dared

to enter any room for fear of being reproached for dis-
arranging the furniture. It was all very neat, and
correspondingly uncomfortable. But as long as the sun
shone, which it usually did, this mattered little as all the
daylight hours were spent down on the houseboat on the
fjord. Eva, too, had the most rudimentary money sense.
Berkeley had taken Holiday House because he thought
it would be a pleasant and economical solution of the
holiday problem ; but he found that while it was the
former it certainly was not the latter. The drain on his
pocket was continuous. Nevertheless with things going
so well in England he put up with it until the war broke
out. Eva was a poetess, with several published works
to her name, so perhaps she had more important things
than domestic accounts to think about. Which, for
Berkeley, was rather a pity.

*   *   *   *   *

When he was forty Berkeley found himself, not without
pleasure, being occasionally invited to speak in public.
As soon as his gift for witty and felicitous oratory became
known, the invitations arrived with increasing frequency.
Berkeley was unaffectedly delighted. He took endless
trouble in the preparation of his speeches, writing them in
his consulting-rooms when the day's work was done, and
whenever possible committed them to memory before
delivering them. He was always nervous before he got
up to speak, but, once on his feet, appeared magisterially
assured. In one letter to a friend he wrote, " I really
do not like making after-dinner speeches : though the
thoughts of them afterwards are sometimes rather
pleasant ". In another, when his reputation as an orator
was rivalled by few, he said : " Just now I'm in the

throes ! I've been asked to propose the Royal Academy at their dinner a fortnight hence : the toast of the year ! So send me helpful thoughts. You've no idea of how cold and miserable and forlorn I feel before I begin to speak ! "

One of his first speeches was at the dinner to celebrate the twenty-first birthday of the Bradford Golf Club. He replied for the guests. Though his speech was not reported in full, this little bit of it remains in the columns of an old newspaper :

" Sir Berkeley Moynihan acknowledged the toast in a racy speech. He declared that his capacities as a golfer were beneath contempt ; he had only just passed his third birthday. It was now generally accepted, he said, that the game of golf was very seriously detrimental to the health of many of those who played it. To any who were fortunate enough usually to win their matches he would put the question — ' Have you ever in your lives defeated men who were in fair — I will not say sound or robust — health ? ' He explained that when occasionally it had been his rare good fortune to inflict a bitter defeat on an opponent he generally found that that opponent was shaken in health, depressed in spirit, and that there was some very serious lack of co-ordination in his muscular and mental system."

Berkeley's style of speaking was warm and friendly but he never spoke with such informality as would deprive the whole effect of dignity. The humour of his speeches was mostly in the ingenuity of his allusions ; it was never, except affectionately, at the expense of others. He never told, either in public or private, an indelicate story and never made a jest in those terms. Neither did anyone tell him those stories ; his distaste for them was readily detected. He was not a prig. It was rather that such

humour was to him not humorous ; it had no funny
side, there was nothing to laugh at. Not smoking, drinking but little, and not dealing in the currency of doubtful
anecdotes, the club-room frankly bored him. Had it
amused him more, he might have understood some of
his fellow men better. But his ways were in accordance
with his character ; no doubt he gained, as well as lost,
by his avoidance of the ruder convivialities. As soon as
the after-dinner speeches were over he took his way home
and, long before the other guests had thought of moving,
was asleep in his bed.

He taught in the wards as he spoke on the platform —
with graceful reason and commanding interest. He was
neither portentous nor facetious. He invested his words
with a humour that betokened courage, not vain levity.
In his favourite attitude half-seated on a table — with
one leg swinging, the other resting on the floor — he
would discourse upon the case. He would embroider
the theme of his talk with a rich diversity of happy
illustrations. Curious incidents of his experiencing,
analogous examples, quotations pinning the subject down,
all flowed from his tongue in steady, mellifluous stream.
So lightly was his learning borne that not till the session
ended did its range strike home. While he talked the time
passed on so swiftly, so enthrallingly, that when he stopped
one was surprised to see how far the clock had moved.

In medicine, as in other spheres, there are many ways
of teaching. The categorical, listed method, taking the
various aspects of the case in sequent order one by one, is
very popular ; it relieves the lazy men of the necessity of
much text-book reading. Also much liked is that brusque
style that clothes a brutal, valid common sense in coarse
jocosity ; the points are rammed home and wedged in

place by the memory of a jest. But, as some think, best of all is the teaching habit that strives to stimulate, awakening in the listener a curiosity that sends him questing in his books with fresh enthusiasm. That is how Berkeley taught. If in the student there should be one spark of keenness, then Berkeley, with the infectious movement of his mind, fanned it into flame. He was a teacher of quiet fervour, proffering inspiration.

*   *   *   *   *

In 1906 he was advanced from the rank of Assistant Surgeon to that of Full Surgeon. His formal visits to the hospital were on Monday and Friday mornings, when he taught in his wards and examined cases, and on Tuesday and Friday afternoons, when he performed his operations. There were in addition visits for lectures and demonstration classes. In 1909 he was made Professor of Surgery in Leeds University. In 1912 he was elected to the Council — the governing body — of the Royal College of Surgeons. With characteristic vigour, and some lack of Northern caution, he put his hand to the College's affairs. At his very first committee meeting he energetically opposed the opinion of the President — and carried his point. Berkeley's neighbour expressed admiration for his zeal but doubts about his wisdom ; he considered that Berkeley had " dished his chance in the College ". The prophecy proved false : time was on Berkeley's side. But for the moment he was dismayed. For, being Berkeley, he had already set his eyes upon the Presidency.

In the few years before the war, perhaps encouraged by the academic dignity of his new Professorship, Berkeley undertook a project that had long been in his mind. It

had more far-reaching effects than anything else he did
at that period of his life. It was the pure expression of
his surgical enthusiasm. He tried to bind together in
amity the provincial surgeons of Great Britain.

London surgeons, collected together in a vast metro-
polis, had every facility for frequent meetings and exchange
of views ; without the waste of time, merely at will, they
could visit each other's hospitals ; the only implementa-
tion called for was their interest in their work. The
regular surgical meetings at the Royal Society of Medicine
gave them the chance to air their own researches and to
keep abreast of the surgical advances of the day. But the
provincial surgeons did not enjoy these benefits. Though
they might be members of the Royal Society of Medicine
they could not always spare the time to visit London for
its meetings — for meetings that as often as not were
uninspiring and productive of no new thought. In their
own towns, on the other hand, they knew the work of
their surgical colleagues so well that they had ceased to
find in it the stimulus of novelty.

Berkeley, taking a line from what he had seen in
America, had conceived the idea of forming a society
of provincial surgeons which would have as its object the
periodic refreshment of the surgical enthusiasm of its
members. Two or three surgeons from each big provincial centre would be members and the society would
be limited to a membership of about thirty. These
men would meet twice a year. On each occasion they
would be the guests of the members from a selected
town. It would be the duty of the hosts, for the two days
of each meeting, to arrange a series of surgical displays
and demonstration operations. Thus would an opportunity be provided, not only for the acquisition of new

learning and the rekindling of interest, but also for the making of friends amongst surgical contemporaries.

In July of 1909 Berkeley sent a letter to just under thirty provincial surgeons in which he put forward this proposition. He suggested the formation of ". . . a small and informal ' Society of Clinical Surgery '. . . . Such meetings should ensure closer friendship among us and make for better work." He invited them to come to Leeds to discuss the matter on a certain date and announced that it was his intention to show some operations and demonstrations at that time. The meeting took place, was well attended, and out of it Berkeley's society was born. It was the wish of the majority to call it the Surgical Club, but, as there was already a society of that name in existence in London, they compromised upon the Chirurgical Club.

The success of the Club, in the main due to Berkeley's solicitous nursing of it in its infancy, fulfilled even his high aspirations. But it did more than that. It was the model for the formation of other similar clubs in other branches of medicine by other men. It broke down many of the internal barriers of English medicine. From its loins sprang children, like the great Association of Surgeons of Great Britain and Ireland, that, feeding too on Berkeley's ardour, outstripped in importance the parent body. In the Chirurgical Club was sown a seed from which English surgery reaped a harvest. The rapid dissemination of new ideas and new techniques engendered by its meeting, and by all the similar meetings that followed it, had a wide effect upon the community. Patients throughout the land, treated by surgeons conversant with the latest thought, benefited by its foundation. It provided a milestone along the road of English surgery.

63, CLARENDON ROAD, LEEDS
Lord Moynihan's home from 1904 to 1914

On the Road to Success

As time went by the Chirurgical Club frequently spent one of its two yearly meetings at some foreign clinic, thus extending the scope of its original functions. When the Club adopted a motto in 1932 they took the words " Without Frontiers " — a title in which is implicit the surgical ideal. When Berkeley was elevated to the peerage, not the least happy of the felicitations that he received was the announcement that the Chirurgical Club had changed its name to the Moynihan Chirurgical Club.

*   *   *   *   *

By 1910 Berkeley was unshakably established. His position would have been at any time remarkable. If we remember that, having risen so far, he was still but forty-five, then we may fairly call his achievement phenomenal. All his early ambitions had been fulfilled and there were still many years to spare. Brilliant surgeon, with a now international reputation, author of the standard work on abdominal surgery, the accredited discoverer of the syndrome of duodenal ulcer, father of a surgical club full of high possibilities, and as a consulting surgeon everywhere in popular demand — with all these things his cup was full, even to brimming over. In bounding health, prosperous, happy with his wife and adoring his children with grateful pride, he strode towards the future.

I say his cup was full — better perhaps to say that the year 1912 saw it really filled. In that year King George V conferred a knighthood on him. He became Sir Berkeley. What a long way back it seemed now to the unhappy days at school, to the medical student days when he, his mother, and sisters, counted every penny, scrimping and saving ! And all such a little while ago — a bare quarter of a century ! How he wished his mother could still be here to share her boy's delight — now, and to the end of his life, no success could come his way without provoking in his mind affectionate thoughts of her. He never forgot how much he owed to her. By comparison how little to himself. Life had been very good to him.

In the early part of 1914 he sealed his success, prosperity, and family pride by moving into Carr Manor. This very beautiful house, standing in an extensive and lovely garden, was in the district of Meanwood, withdrawn by some distance from the noisy turmoil of Leeds. Here, in a house that he came to love dearly, Berkeley lived out his life.

But behind these scenes of happiness there was an ominous rumbling. A distant thunder as the clouds banked up. In September 1913 Berkeley received this letter :

" DEAR SIR BERKELEY MOYNIHAN,

" The Duke of Norfolk has promised to preside and Lord George Hamilton to speak, at a National Service League Meeting at Sheffield on the 21st November next. Would it be possible for you to be present on the occasion and say a few words from your Professional point of view ?

" Most people are, I think, agreed upon the physical advantages which would accrue from a system of Universal Military Training. And no one, I am sure, would drive home those advantages with greater cogency or better effect than yourself.

" I greatly hope that you may find it possible to render a real service to the Cause I have at heart, by taking part in the Sheffield Meeting.

" Believe me,
" Yours very truly,
" ROBERTS "

Lord Roberts, veteran soldier and passionate Briton, was stumping the realm trying to awake the drowsy lion. He saw the danger that lay in England's path ; he shouted the alarm ; but no one would heed his cry. Berkeley agreed to speak.

PART IV

THE SOLDIER

The Soldier

In 1914, just before the outbreak of war, Lord Roberts came to Leeds. His country, though now at the brink of overwhelming danger, was still lethargic — wilfully blind to the urgent need for preparation. " Bobs ", with irrepressible courage, was still raising his voice in the wilderness. He saw the German organisation rolling forward, with gathering impetus, towards the inevitable day of battle. He saw England, with its tiny standing army, spending the summer days in watching cricket ; he saw it engaged in pleasant speculation about Ascot and the Derby. When he spoke the news-sheets accused him of crying wolf — called him scaremonger, jingo, and militarist. He might well, having done what he could, have left the country to its fate. Weary in mind and shaken in physique, he might have withdrawn to the quietness of his home, to the shared retirement of his generation. But no — he struggled on dauntlessly, fluttering the nation's flag as it hung languid at the masthead.

It was with great pride that Berkeley and Isabel persuaded him to visit them at their new home. Carr Manor, a mansion ramblingly enlarged from a seventeenth-century farmhouse, invested in its dark walls of creepered stone a gracious loveliness. Berkeley, as he strolled about the flowing green lawns, let his eyes linger upon the house, and doing so, felt the peace of consummation. This home was his by right of his own unaided industry. Its dignity, he thought, accorded well with his station and reputation. For him and Isabel it was the reward for busy, laborious years. Now here they were, entertaining beneath its roof one of the great soldiers of the land.

Lord Roberts found in Berkeley a friend to warm his heart. Berkeley shared his passionate love of England ; like him was bravely upright ; with him felt the inspiration of a cause. Berkeley, still with his youthful love of soldiers in his heart, deeply admired the older man. From a locked drawer he brought forth his treasures to display before Lord Roberts. He showed him his father's sword and Victoria Cross. These, of all his possessions, were the things he prized the most. " Bobs " was much affected. He had not known of Berkeley's soldier ancestry, and now, discovering this, was more than ever drawn towards his host. But in friendly spirit he found fault with Berkeley. How could Berkeley have such fine heirlooms and keep them hidden away ? Surely he wanted all to know the man his father was ? The sword and medal should be set out, placed on a table for all to see ! In vain did Berkeley try to explain that, not diffidence, but fear of loss made him keep them both locked up. But Berkeley was touched. Deep down within him stirred the family spirit ; he was proud of his heritage. He would remember this day.

Talking with " Bobs " disturbed his mind. Successful, hedged about with duties on all sides, he had thought but little about the army in these past few years. Memories of his old ambition had flickered very low. But now, with the picture of adventurous sorties before his eyes and the silver note of bugles in his ears, his thoughts

flowed back to surge and eddy round his old ideal. All
nonsense — yes, no doubt — but if ever the chance came
his way again he would not say no. It seemed as if it
might. Lord Roberts talked of armies and politics, of
aggressive, jealous nationalism — of many things that a
hurried surgeon has little time to contemplate. But
would Berkeley really like that kind of life ? No, perhaps
not after all. The days of military glory were past —
gone for ever. War now meant only suffering and
tragedy.

For Berkeley, too, it would mean the end just when
success was sweetest. His fame, so great in America, was
beginning to lap the shores of his own land. Like other
pioneers in English medicine he owed his fullest recognition to foreigners. But now, in his own land also, his
name stood high. In surgery he was accepted as a leader
throughout the country. He was on the threshold of
great things. Yet now all plans and projects were per-
turbed. Confusing thoughts pressed in.

When, having seen his guest depart, he walked across
his hall, he could, had he so wished, have paused to gaze
upon his portrait where it hung above the stairs. It was
the Herkomer — painted in 1912. A forceful portrait,
it revealed Berkeley's character with penetrating insight.
Of Berkeley in his middle forties it was, for posterity, a
perpetual disclosure. The dark and firm assurance of
the figure breathed confident authority. The broad and
sloping shoulders told of latent strength. But most
impressive was the head ; its lightly balanced pallor
well contrasting with the sombre, massive frame. The
face was of a gentle and beautiful dignity. It expressed
a wisdom that transcended the foolishness of vanity.
The eyes beneath their overhanging brows were deep in

understanding, as if in lenient comprehension of the foibles of the one who looked at them. The set of the chin told not of arrogance or weakness, it spoke of profound self-reliance, securely pillared by tried experience. The mouth was straight, not hard, but firmly closed on a judgement measured, yet undelivered. But, though kindliness was everywhere about the painting, the whole was faintly tinged with aloof austerity — with the crystal light of moral principle, courageous and unashamed. It was a picture, unspoilt by the world, of a keen intellect and a noble heart. It was a picture of greatness, justly appraised.

Distinguished men, when they receive the praises of the world, have often over-topped their pinnacle. It is in the period that just precedes their fullest public fame that their desert is highest. At that earlier moment they are doing those things for which applause is later given. But when its sound is heard, new tasks and other engagements may enfold them. Berkeley's rewards and honours of the years to come were now bespoken. He was now at the height of his powers.

During the war his achievement was so great that it is hard to believe that peace activities could have more advanced his name. But, nevertheless, the four years of the war were taken out of his life when his potentialities were richest, when research most occupied his mind.

* * * * *

When war broke out Berkeley at once offered his services to the nation. He expressed himself willing to equip a full surgical team of doctors, students, and nurses, and to take it out to France. He was sincerely willing to sacrifice his practice, though he and his family were entirely dependent upon its earnings, and to be content

with a soldier's pay. He would have been happy — so
strong were the echoes of his youthful ambition, his pride
in his father, and his sense of duty — he would have been
happy to enrol in the army at once. But he had many
responsibilities at the hospital and many surgical calls
that could not be easily set aside. To go abroad was not
just a matter of being willing and at once setting off.
His offer could not, therefore, be at once accepted in the
form and manner in which he had proposed it.

But, though of necessity continuing in his customary
affairs during the first months of the war, he yet had
friends who tried to encompass his wishes for him. If it
was possible for him to serve, and his full usefulness not
be wasted, then there were those who would try to
arrange it.

In the autumn Sir Alfred Keogh, Director-General
of the Army Medical Services, received this letter :

" 3rd Nov. 1914
" DEAR KEOGH,
    " As I understand there is a great want of skilled
surgeons in France, may I bring to your notice Sir
Berkeley Moynihan, a surgeon who has a great name
throughout the North of England. I know him personally and of the good work he has done. I understand he
has offered to go to France and take with him a fully
equipped staff of doctors, dressers and nurses. . . .
            " Yours sincerely,
                " ROBERTS "

Its effect, in due course, was that Berkeley was given
a commission, with the rank of Major, in the Royal Army
Medical Corps. But this was yet to come.

In the meantime his practice, in spite of the war, was
growing amazingly. The nursing home in Hyde Terrace
was never without numerous wealthy and titled patients.

Stories of Berkeley's colossal fees were rife, not only in
Leeds but throughout the country. His documents, in this
respect, bring to light a not unilluminating incident.
Not long before the war Berkeley had operated on, in
Leeds, a great nobleman — wealthy, and though residing
mainly in the South, of great repute in every corner of
the land. The event made something of a stir in Leeds ;
there were paragraphs in the papers ; bulletins were
issued ; Berkeley was publicised. Leeds found in the
occasion proof that its son was now the master surgeon,
the chosen best. But it did not fail, quite humanly, to
discuss in detail Berkeley's prospective fee. With the
usual omniscience of gossip it told its friends the actual
fee. A bit steep ? — yes, but the patient was very rich.
Now the curious thing about this story is that, as the
records show, the fee that Berkeley really charged his
patient was less than one-third of that which the market-
place announced. In fact, though not small by ordinary
standards, it was sufficiently small to make the patient
feel that, to him, the treatment was worth a little more
in money than Berkeley had requested. When he sent
Berkeley a cheque in settlement of his debt, he enclosed
with it another, asking that Berkeley should accept the
sum for the Leeds Infirmary.

No account of Berkeley's life would be complete
without some mention of his fees. In medical circles they
were the source of endless talk ; some of it in jealous good-
humour, some of it in frank derogation. The news-
papers compared his earnings to those of first-rank
advocates ; the general public vulgarity admired what
they regarded as Berkeley's financial acumen, the " smart-
ness " of his business. The attitude of all was that
Berkeley was out to make " big money ". This, in the

middle period of his life, he certainly was not. It is even doubtful if he was towards the end. But now, in these 1914 days, he could have charged and obtained larger fees than he did demand. Of the days that immediately followed the war — of the economic heyday of English surgery — mention will be later made : that is the time when his fees were most debated. In that setting they may be best examined.

This nobleman — this provocation of all the talk — was not the only patient in the nursing home. At the same time there was also there a friend of Berkeley's — a family connection — one in poor circumstances. This person paid nothing for his operation, neither in service nor attendance. He stated that throughout the period of his illness, all the time he was in the home, at least a third of Berkeley's patients were paying Berkeley no fee. For some charitable reason or other he had operated on them all for nothing. He was not incapable of doing good by stealth.

Besides his practice and his work at the hospital Berkeley had, at this time, another great activity. He was in ubiquitous demand as a speaker at army recruiting meetings, at meetings that sought to collect war benevolent funds, and at all meetings where the infusion of a little patriotic fervour was the order of the day. Nor is this unkindly meant. On reading through these old newspaper cuttings, those crumbling yellow tombstones of dead and forgotten speeches, the most remarkable feature is the amateurish background that stood behind them all. It is clear with how little gravity many viewed the war. A few months would see it over — leave it to the regular soldiers, and don't disturb yourself : such was the general attitude. Berkeley, though he may have spoken the words

Berkeley Moynihan

of demagogy, yet weighed the true issues in his hand. In none of his orations did he at any time pretend that the struggle was going to be easy or the battle only brief. He presented the facts as he saw them, using every art to drive them home. The subject was wonderful stone on which to sharpen his oratory. A great race — facing its greatest hour. The speaker could not fling his words too high.

And yet what words they were! Hard to believe that Berkeley ever spoke them. A year ago so balanced, so level in judgement, the personification of reason — now so perfervid, so full of animus! If Berkeley, normally so stable, could be so swept away, then little wonder that lesser men should wax hysterical. England's peril, after the long quiet years, came with a vicious suddenness that overthrew good sense. Politicians and lawyers, divines and men of science, all gave tongue in an orgy of wild intemperance. With fanatic, startled eloquence they urged on the nation. Their speeches were the frenzied upshot of the dreadful moment; we, in our own day, by long expectancy prepared for war's impact, can extend an understanding tolerance to their wordy extravagance.

Berkeley, indeed, was better than the rest. He did not rant: he conjured an argument — one not unbased in fact. His favourite theme was Germany's scientific arrogance, her claims to discoveries that were not hers. She did, he said, by massive compilation of scientific literature give the impression that the major works were all her own:

"The new idea and the original inspiration take origin not in the German mind but elsewhere. But they are given 'eager hospitality' in Germany, and are analysed and discussed with untiring industry. Modifica-

tions of method and alteration of technical procedure
are developed and emphasised, and gradually the discovery is given a German dress and appears before the
world as a wholly German discovery. German writers —
by no means always in bad faith — take this position
for granted, and while their writings are industriously
crowded with references to the work of their fellow
countryman, the work of others is largely ignored. . . .
The impression they produce on those who consult them
is considerable, and undoubtedly they are the fruit of
great industry and are worthy of recognition. . . . The
German mark is placed on the whole of the enterprise,
and is widely accepted as a guide to the origin of the
whole undertaking. . . . Thus the German claim is
often allowed to pass without protest, and the industry
which is spent in elaboration and dissection receives the
credit which is due to the idea on which these virtues
are practised."

That seems to be good. Whether or not he would
have said it in times of peace is doubtful. But his sincerity
at the time is beyond question. He made the point in
many of his public addresses. The line of thought had
been engendered by the visit of a Scandinavian surgeon
to Berkeley's " arena " at the outset of the war. It was
the first time for many years, the visitor stated, that he
had not spent his holiday in study at German surgical
clinics : in coming to England he felt " disloyal " since, as
everybody knew, " all surgical advance in the last fifty
years has come from Germany ". Berkeley was furious.
It was his opinion that, though he recognised Germany's
contributions, other countries — America, France, Italy,
and England — had all made more fundamental discovery. He taxed his guest to provide evidence that
would maintain his sweeping contention. The reply
was that the Americans — the greatest travellers — all

held that view. This to Berkeley, with his enormous range of American friendships, was most of all distressing. He regarded it as a grave misinterpretation of the American mind : it was a misuse of the generous tributes paid by American surgeons to their hosts in the lands they visited : he could assure his visitor that Americans, when in England, spoke not in national but in international terms, they handed the surgical prize to no one land.

Subsequently Berkeley, seeking in his mind to find the basis for the Scandinavian's assertion, evolved the explanation above outlined. Having arrived at this conclusion, he firmly fastened on it. As was his habit when a subject gripped his mind, he used the theme not once but many times. Variously adorned with his oratory he employed it with telling effect. He tested and polished his case until he could expound it with most potent vehemence.

The force of his speeches lay in the happy combination of their emotional and intellectual content. He spoke best upon matters that lay closest to his heart. But he was never uncontrolled. With felicity he rode his eloquence on the light rein of reason. Acutely responsive to the feelings of his audience, he was quick to adapt his phrases to the moment's need. He was able to repeat success : not prolific in ideas, he would explore a prosperous vein on many platforms, only abandoning it when its relevance was done.

This particular vein was one that implicated his deep affections. It summoned his most persuasive language. He could not believe that the Scandinavian was rightly informed. Not so could his American friends Mayo and Murphy think. He with them admired German surgery ;

but they, surely, with him would not so casually dismiss Lister and his countrymen. So it was, with these matters foremost in his mind, that he said to his friend Harold Begbie, the author and journalist, " No nation is less materially minded than the American. It is a nation of idealists, a nation singing with enthusiasm for the highest and deepest things of life ".

In those days he was thinking a great deal about America. He believed that they too were thinking of him. He went on to say to Begbie that

" The one thing which can make atonement for all the agony and loss of this tremendous struggle is the new spirit in our midst which is just beginning to create the unity of the Anglo-Saxon race. This movement is far and away the greatest political event in the history of the world. Nothing can more dismay the Germans. Nothing should so encourage our Allies and reassure the small nations. It is an event literally of the most tre- mendous significance. It means the world triumph of democracy. But there is a danger. The politician must not meddle too materialistically in the matter. He must be told that he is on sacred ground. Only disappoint- ment can ensue from any attempt to base this *entente* on political or commercial interests. The basis is spiritual."

Those were his words just less than a quarter of a cen- tury ago. The trough of years that lies between has been shadowed with some sad misunderstandings. But the phrases had prescience : too much indeed did the meddlers intervene.

*   *   *   *   *

Is it fair to quote Berkeley's recruiting speeches ? Is it just to him to reawaken, for however brief a moment, expressions that were the instrument of immediate purpose

Berkeley Moynihan

and that were never intended for the calculated analysis
of posterity? I think it is. Those old words are so
characteristic of him — so like one aspect of himself —
that it would be a pity not to call them back again, to
let a whisper of them softly reverberate. Here is one of
those speeches — typical of them all — that finds preservation in the files. Who can deny that its truths have
enduring validity? The reader, as in quietude he travels
through it, will remember that it was spoken in the dusty
forum, in the rising passion of the hour.

"Sir Berkeley Moynihan, who presided, said that the
need for men was urgent. It must surely be apparent to
everybody that at the moment the British Empire and
everything that the Empire involved, all the most sacred
aspirations of Britons, were in the greatest peril in the
nation's history. When our people entered upon the
hideous and hateful war in which we are now engaged,
it was with the usual British spirit of gay unconcern.
War, after all, didn't appear to us to be a very serious
business. It was, perhaps, looked upon as a necessary
outlet for the bubbling youthful energy of the country —
something which would never interfere and had never
interfered with the main broad stream of our active
industrial life, or the even serenity of all our lives. Things
were very different now. We were at war with an
enemy that was ruthless, implacable, confident, and well
prepared. The strength of Germany lay not only in the
multitude of her people and the apparently inexhaustible
supplies of her munitions of war, but chiefly in the glowing
conviction that existed in every German mind that their
country was in the right. We could not deny that the
Germans had fought with great bravery, and at the same
time we knew that they had fought with the greatest
brutality and utmost bestiality. We had learnt from the
Germans new things about war. Ever since the time
of Frederick the Great the Germans had looked upon

182

war as organised pillage ; they had cast their covetous
eyes upon their neighbours' vineyards, and they had raided
them whenever they thought that they were strong
enough. They had derided the decencies of war and
had mocked at the restrictions that humanity had placed
upon war. (Applause.) Fortunately, Germany had
never fought with the fine, high, chivalrous spirit of our
army, and we could still claim for our own men that they
were the best soldiers in the world. (Applause.) ' I
have ', added Sir Berkeley, ' lived among them for many
months in France. I have seen them before they fought,
after they fought, when they were wounded, and when they
were dying. I know them from beginning to end, and a
braver, finer, more devoted, more highly inspired set
of men have never waged war on the face of the earth.'
(Loud applause.) ' I wish I had time to tell you what
has been told in full to me by those who played their
part in the first battle of Ypres in December of last year.
How our thin line, for which there was not a single man
or horse in reserve, was pounded for four days and four
nights incessantly ; how men, with eyes aching for want
of sleep and brains whirling, were attacked chiefly by
the Prussian Guard just after the latter had been reviewed
by the Kaiser and promised imperishable renown if they
broke their way through to Calais. They were sometimes
seventeen to one, and never less than four to one — four
fresh, eager, exultant Prussians to one weary, sleepy
Englishman. But the line held ! (Loud applause.)
Calais, the objective of the Germans, was saved, and
England was given time to make further preparation.'
(Applause.) "

Not much more than a year before — in the still days
of peace — one of the medical journals had printed this :

" The first speech — there were no formal papers
read — was delivered by Sir Berkeley Moynihan, and
was an intellectual treat of a very high order. This well-
known Leeds surgeon is the happy possessor of a capacity

for debate which would speedily make a great reputation in the House of Commons. He marshals his thoughts, without the aid of notes, in orderly logical development ; and he clothes them in language of crystal clearness and simplicity beyond the possibility of misunderstanding. His impromptu speech might be taken down word for word by a shorthand writer, and printed as a model of correct and graceful English composition, neither too rhetorical nor too bald, neither florid nor devoid of sparkle. He uses a naturally sonorous and pleasing voice with great skill ; the most perfect articulation and delivery enhancing the effect of the merits already described. He speaks without effort and almost without pause, yet in unhurried and steady regular flow. He has a playful wit and a mobile face. In a word, Sir Berkeley Moynihan is the most excellent of all the orators who addressed the Congress, and his oratory is exactly that type which appeals most to Englishmen."

* * * * *

The recruiting speech was made after Berkeley had been commissioned in the army and had been over to France on more than one occasion. On November 19th, 1914, he had received this telegram :

" Are you willing to proceed to France as a consulting surgeon with the rank and pay of a colonel R.A.M.C. * If so please call here to-morrow * Regard this as strictly confidential.

" Director General, Army Medical Department, " War Office."

Of course he went. The visit to the War Office proved to be the beginning of a great friendship, and the introduction to a chief whom Berkeley truly hero-worshipped. Berkeley, at the age of fifty, was capable of a young

man's intense devotion to an adored leader. Not many
months were to pass before his admiration for Sir Alfred
Keogh had become boundless.

On December 3rd, 1914, Berkeley set off for France.
He took with him as his A.D.C. Leonard Braithwaite,
who had been his assistant in the days before the war.
Before the journey Berkeley was promoted to the rank
of Colonel and Braithwaite was made a Captain. It
tickled Berkeley's fancy that they should enjoy these
relative ranks ; an official seal had, as it were, been
placed upon their five-year-old relationship of master
and man ; it gave him a secret pleasure, half humorous
and half self-satisfied. Now he would be able to keep
the young man in order !

On a day in 1910 Braithwaite had become both
Berkeley's private assistant and his Assistant Surgeon
at the Leeds Infirmary. For the next fifteen years,
apart only from the interruption of the war, he continued
to work in close association with Berkeley. Although
soon after the war he ceased to assist in Berkeley's private
work they remained together at the hospital until
Berkeley's retirement. Fifteen years is a long time. In
such a period even casual companions must learn much
about each other ; a working partnership so long maintained must tell a great deal more. And of all forms of
endeavour none is more intimate, nor more persistently
invested with the tense atmosphere that penetrates character, than surgery. In the hard and calculating light
of the operating theatre no weakness of heart or head or
hand can for long escape exposure ; it is a light that
compels the surgeon day by day to dissect his qualities
before his audience. On his easiest days the surgeon
bears the responsibility for his patients' well-being or

disablement, on his more frequent other ones the issues are life and death. His mistakes — whether they be of behaviour or policy — may not be remarked upon, he himself may remain in ignorance of them : but they do not go unobserved. In the minds of those who witness them they are stored up, remembered, and later used as evidence in that court of judgement which is the conclave of his colleagues ; the verdict exists only in the thoughts of these fellow surgeons, it suffers no statutory publication, but it invariably leaks out.

All surgeons make mistakes. That is a truism. What is important is the frequency with which these errors come, their origins, and the reactions to them of the man who makes them ; these things are only seen by the collaborator of long standing ; he alone can truly estimate the surgeon's powers — for he has seen the surgeon at work in a great variety of circumstances in different states of health, and in every passing mood. If after fifteen years of this the measured critic speaks in praise, the surgeon has won the approbation — and none other is wholly valid — of true authority. For so long, viewing each success and failure, did Braithwaite stand at Berkeley's side, and at the end he was able to say that they had been " years of the greatest pride in my association as well as years of perfect happiness ". Berkeley could not ask for more than that, and few surgeons would dare to expect as much.

From the first Braithwaite had been determined to learn as much as he possibly could from Berkeley. He came to know Berkeley better than any man had ever done. The relationship of these two men was of the perfect, unhurried sort ; it grew slowly, it steadily matured, and it only arrived at unreserved friendship when each had a supreme knowledge of the other's character. Each day Braithwaite watched every step of Berkeley's work ; each day he listened to every word that fell from Berkeley's mouth. In the early days Berkeley found this service almost too faithful. He had been accustomed to have his assistants go about their business when the operation was done. Here was Braithwaite following him everywhere, even to his conversation with the patient's relatives. One day, as after operation Berkeley descended the stairs at Hyde Terrace to talk to the family waiting down below, he turned on his assistant and said with some impatience, " Why do you always follow me ? " To which Braithwaite replied, " I told you, sir, when I came to you, that I wished to learn all I could from you. It isn't only the operation that matters. I want to learn how you talk to people." Berkeley frowned, and hesitated ; then suddenly that infinitely attractive smile lit up his face ; placing his arm around the shoulders of the younger man he said, " That's right. This is almost as important as the rest." Together they entered the room.

From that time onwards Berkeley, quite willingly, accepted the attentions of his assistant. Having once understood the other's point of view he was entirely reasonable ; he knew that in like circumstances he would have behaved as Braithwaite had. He loved to have devotion shown to him. He wanted to be the founder of a great school of surgery, to send all over the world disciples trained in the " Moynihan school ". He never quite fulfilled this wish. It is true that many young men acquired under Berkeley's tutelage a skill and knowledge the like of which no one but Berkeley could have given them. But more than that is required to make a school. To achieve the school of Berkeley's dreamings its leader must display a self-abnegatory dedication that Berkeley could not exhibit. He was too boyish, he had too many irons in the fire, and he loved success too dearly. These failings — if even such they are — should be forgivable ; Berkeley's fields of endeavour were large because his spirit was so eager, and his visions out-ran the time at his disposal to transform them into fact ; as to success, the penury of his childhood's home had scarred his attitude to wealth : when he was mean, it was, in spite of his acquirement of much money, because he never could forget how great had been the value of each penny in his poor mother's hard economy. Nevertheless, whatever school he might have made, he, its master, would never have turned out a better son than Braithwaite, nor one who so cherished his memory.

Berkeley and his assistant together solved a multitude of problems and brought to happy outcome as many operations of grave complexity ; together they stood at the foot of many a hundred beds. To the age-old question " Doctor, you will do your best for me, won't you ? " Braithwaite times without number heard Berkeley's invariable reply of " Money cannot buy my second best. I have but one quality of effort — that is my best." And out of all these labours shared they won to mutual respect and love. When the time came for them to part and Braithwaite wrote to tell his chief of the happiness, pride, and gratitude the years had left him with, Berkeley replied :

" Your letter was a source of the greatest joy to me. I could not answer it in haste : for I wanted to re-read and to treasure it. I have kept it in a secluded corner of my dressing-table : it has inspired and encouraged me in the mornings, and has been a comfort and a joy when the day's work was over.

" I have felt very sad at the thought of the severance of our official connexion. Fifteen years is a long time, and it is a great test of a man's character and attainments to associate with him all that time and not to suffer, at least sometimes, a disillusion. Throughout all these years I have had the greatest happiness in my association with you. Though perhaps I have helped to achieve the result, you are to-day unsurpassed in this country by any surgeon in your power of dealing safely and in the most con-summately skilful manner with any problem that an operation may present. And your loyalty and good faith have been without blemish. I have counted from the earliest days on your being the best man in our school in your day. Hope and expectation are becoming certainties. You have not yet fulfilled all my ambitions for you : they are set very high : but I am now more confident than ever in the future.

" In all these years I have grown so fond of you, and so proud of you that I cannot trust myself even to write what I feel — and I do not know whether I shall ever be able to tell you. But I believe you realise a little what your friendship has been to me. I want the world to hold of you the opinion I hold. I am sure no one will ever have a greater affection for you than I have. You are nearer to me than any man.

" With all my heart,
" Ever yours,
" BERKELEY MOYNIHAN "

There can be no manner in which two men can work together more pregnant with potential happiness than in the pursuit of surgery. It is for them to know not only the happiness of shared labours, for to that is richly added, making their cup flow over, the grateful thanks and happiness of those whose suffering they have relieved. Between the vast responsibilities they undertake and the spiritual rewards that come their way there is a just proportion. They toil under a high star, and when their task is done they know a double exaltation that has no parallel ; for them are the transcendental joy of the creative artist and the immaculate delight that comes from Christian service.

There stands in the hall of the Royal College of Surgeons in London a bust of Berkeley. The visitor may see it, give it a casual glance, and then walk on ; to him it may be just another bust — one amongst many. But it is more than that, far more. It is the durable memorial to fifteen years of mutual struggles, strivings, defeats, and victories. It is the memorial to all those things that Berkeley and Braithwaite did together, and to the emotions that they shared. It may be that some of those who read this book will, if ever they visit the College, seek out the bust and for an instant stand before it to remember these two men who faithfully served surgery and each other. Here is its story.

When Berkeley and Braithwaite had separated, Braithwaite sought about for some way in which he might give permanent expression to his devotion to his chief. He conceived the idea of presenting Berkeley with a bust in Berkeley's own likeness and in course of time the work was executed. The gift was dispatched to Berkeley and this is the reply that Braithwaite had :

" The marble bust has arrived and is unpacked.

" I cannot express my own opinion or expect it to be of any great value. But my pleasure in the possession of a bust given by you to me is very great and unalloyed. There is a new link added to very many now between us. It is my intention to give the bust in due time to the R.C.S. with a little inconspicuous brass plate saying

that it was your gift to me and mine to the College. So
we shall go down to posterity together."

This has been a long digression from the war. But
if the reader found its theme as pleasing as did the
writer, then he will perhaps extend indulgence towards it.

On their way to France Berkeley and Braithwaite
stopped in London to see Sir Alfred Keogh. Next day
they sailed for Boulogne. They travelled on a boat
reserved for Staff officers. As soon as they were on board
the two of them sat down on the deck and Berkeley
started to read *The Times*. As the other passengers walked
up and down before them Braithwaite noticed that all
the Army officers had the straps of their Sam Browne
belts crossing the opposite shoulder from that on which
he and Berkeley were wearing their own. He knew that
Berkeley was very proud of his uniform and would be
particularly sensitive to any criticism directed towards it ;
but after some delay he informed Berkeley that he thought
they were wearing their belts the wrong way round. " Not
a bit of it," said Berkeley, without looking up from his
newspaper, " I know how to put my uniform on." There
was a long pause during which Braithwaite again reviewed
the passers-by. Yes, there was no doubt about it, they
were alone in their glory. So he said to Berkeley, " Then,
sir, if we are right everybody else is wrong ". At which
Berkeley looked up, was horrified to discover that he was
not conforming to correct usage, and immediately dashed
downstairs — to reappear in a few moments correctly
dressed.

Nor was this Berkeley's only tribulation. At the outset
of the voyage he had inadvisedly announced that he was
a good sailor. Shortly after his return to the deck the
sea became very ugly indeed, and *The Times* was laid

aside. Yet again Berkeley went below — and this time he did not come back. He detested any form of physical weakness in himself. On all counts he loathed the memory of this voyage.

When they arrived in Boulogne the port was in a turmoil. No arrangements had been made for their accommodation nor could anyone give them any help. There was nothing for it but that they should fend for themselves. Braithwaite picked up the suitcases, and through the streets of Boulogne he and England's most famous surgeon trudged in search of lodgings. They finally came to rest in a place where the food was appalling, the beds as bad, and the general atmosphere even worse. This was their introduction to service in England's army on the continent of Europe.

But next day things looked up. They were moved to headquarters at Rouen and provided with a large red Daimler car in which to tour about and see the R.A.M.C. at work. Their chauffeur was Private Tupper, and he became the apple of Berkeley's eye. To Berkeley almost the best thing about the war — the finest thing that came his way — was Private Tupper. Here was a man of unfailing willingness, never tired, and always present when Berkeley wanted him. Perhaps Tupper already knows what Berkeley thought of him ; if he does not, these words may yet find their way to him.

Wherever Berkeley travelled he saw things that offended his surgical mind. He was full of energy and no less full of criticism. The A.D.M.S. at Rouen was Colonel Skinner, a man in vigour and enthusiasm not even surpassed by Berkeley himself. The two of them were off at eight each morning to set the army medical world to rights. And they effected a very great deal. The reports that Berkeley sent home profoundly influenced the reorganisation of the British medical service in France. Berkeley visited over a hundred hospitals and dressing-stations, and from the observations he dictated to Braithwaite on these tours his reports were prepared. He also supervised the construction of operating theatres in many new hospitals and even the construction of the hospitals themselves. But the thing that engaged his greatest attention, and that regularly made him furious, was the quality of the surgery that he saw. He continuously battled — as few could do like Berkeley — for its betterment. There is no question that its improvement was greatly due to him.

But the days were not all work. In the hotel at Rouen were living many famous men, distinguished in all walks of civil life. In the evenings they all engaged in tremendous discussions in the lounge. Berkeley, needless to say, was always to the front. From these war-time talks he garnered memories that never left him ; memories that he liked to resuscitate as later years went by.

Then there were visits to Paris. He and Braithwaite stayed at the Meurice Hotel and from there went out daily to visit the clinics in the town. No hours were more delightful to Berkeley than those he spent in the clinic of Dr. Crile. At the beginning of the war this famous American surgeon had with voluntary nobility come to France to assist in the care of the wounded. His surgical ability was outstanding and it gave Berkeley great pleasure to watch him at work. One in particular of Dr. Crile's habits gratified Berkeley : between operations Dr. Crile would discourse upon the case he had just done and the one he was going to do : he would invite those eminent surgeons that might be present to engage in the discussion. He and Berkeley had great admiration for each other, they sought out each other's opinions, and in so doing provided many an exciting surgical adventure for the doctors gathered round.

At the beginning of March 1915 Berkeley concluded any prolonged service he was to undertake in France. His later visits there did not extend to more than a few days at a time. He returned to England and resumed his regular work in Leeds.

From March 1915 onwards Berkeley was, in his own words, " sometimes in France, often in London, and occasionally in Leeds ". He continued to work at the Infirmary when possible ; he worked in the hospitals of the Northern Command in England, and he attended the meetings of the Army Medical Advisory Board and of the Council of Consultants. As inevitably happens in the medical hierarchy of the army, those in high places must give most of their time to organisation and little or none of it to clinical work. The result of this is often, in times of war, that great surgeons do but little surgery : they spend their time in administration. Though Berkeley was not entirely cut off from surgery he was compelled to give much of his time to office tasks, to the solution of many problems arising out of the conversion of a largely civilian medical profession into one predominantly military.

This alteration of his life was not as wasteful of great gifts as it might have been in the case of another man. Berkeley, versatile as ever, proved to have an enormous flair for his new duties. Solving problems, propounding schemes, encouraging workers in new fields, he pushed on with driving, relentless energy. His vitality made it possible for him to shoulder a multiplicity of duties that

SIR BERKELEY MOYNIHAN AND DR. G. H. CRILE
At the Lycée Pasteur, Paris, 1914

would have soon exhausted the average man.

But with all these responsibilities he found time to indulge his old love of forming medical societies in the causes of friendship and discussion. Even the disruptive blast of war could not deter him. This passage, taken from the *British Medical Journal*, pays homage to the faithful enthusiasm with which doctors at the war, in spite of all discouragements, followed their high vocation :

" The externals of outward calm and peaceful surroundings usually associated with the meetings of learned societies were commonly lacking at the gatherings of medical societies of the armies in France, for they were held in diverse structures — the Tarrant hut of a casualty clearing station, a partially demolished factory, or some school from which the customary occupants had been evicted. But noisy as the surroundings might be, from traffic over the pavé or artillery fire, the amicable feelings within, where each participator was concerned solely with relating his own observations and opinions, and not with ' crabbing ' some other speaker, were such as are sometimes lacking at home.

" To many who served out there the memory of these meetings will remain very delightful, and there is no doubt that they fostered clinical enthusiasm and did much to spread information. The first society to hold regular meetings was, we believe, formed at Rouen early in 1915, and owed much of its inception and success to Major-General (then Colonel) Bruce Skinner, C.B., C.M.G., D.D.M.S., and to Sir Berkeley Moynihan, the consulting surgeon at the base. . . . The membership consisted of field ambulance and regimental medical officers, with occasional visitors from neighbouring casualty clearing stations. The discussions dealt mainly with front-line problems, such as trench fever, trench feet, trench nephritis, surgery in a field ambulance, the ideal regimental aid post, abdominal wounds. . . . The knowledge gained, the friendship cemented, and the welcome opportunity for talking pure ' shop ', not to mention the tea served by the sisters when the meeting took place at a casualty clearing station, combine to form a memory which will be lasting with many."

During his days in Leeds, too, Berkeley found time to nourish surgical interest and friendship. Amongst his many operations were some that inevitably — for public interest, not always of his own seeking, pursued him everywhere — found their way into the columns of the press. Since all surgical attacks upon the heart have for a long time had a fascination for the lay reader, it is not surprising to read that

" A delicate, though not unique, surgical operation which has recently been performed in Leeds, has aroused considerable interest in the medical profession. The operation, performed by a Leeds surgeon (Surgeon-General Sir Berkeley Moynihan), consisted in the removal of a bullet which had lodged in dangerous proximity to the heart. The patient is a discharged soldier. . . . He was wounded at Loos. A shrapnel bullet entered his shoulder, passed through the collar-bone and lodged in the muscle of the heart. Recently it was discovered that the bullet had moved slightly, and —— entered Leeds infirmary where it was successfully removed."

Berkeley was much absorbed by the surgical problems presented by wounds of the chest. Before the war all surgeons had been very chary of undertaking operations upon the lungs ; they felt that the risks outweighed the advantages that might be gained. But in peace-time surgery of the chest is limited ; its occasions do not frequently obtrude. In war, however, wounds of the chest were of high incidence ; the surgical issue was paramount. Berkeley through his experience became convinced that the dangers of chest surgery were exaggerated. He considered that, given skilful hands and a good technique, the lung could be explored both with impunity and profit. He worked hard, as he always did when his mind was once made up, to propagate this view. He neglected no occasion that gave him opportunity to persuade his fellow surgeons that his estimate was right. Time has established his case. Surgery of the lung has advanced far since those days and its initial progress was due to the fact that surgeons had rid themselves of the fear of opening the chest.

*   *   *   *   *

In spite of war's disturbances men still pursued some of the pleasurable activities of peace. In October of 1915 a dinner was given at the Leeds Club in honour of Sir William Osler. Berkeley was to receive the guest. Osler, one of the greatest physicians of all time, was then Regius Professor of Medicine at Oxford ; he was at the height of his fame ; he had come to England bearing the laurels of his work during the early days of the Johns Hopkins Hospital in Baltimore. Berkeley profoundly respected and much loved this man ; two things he greatly shared with him — love of the profession and love of friends. Osler had a genius for friendship and his modesty made him universally loved. This little card, written to Berkeley before the war, was entirely characteristic of him :

" Many thanks for your papers — *Carnifex maximus !* I wish you had been at my section of the Congress to have heard the sweet things somebody said of you. He probably has a duodenal ulcer !

" W. Osler "

But Berkeley's part at the dinner was not fulfilled. On

the back of his menu card is written, " I couldn't go to the dinner, though I was host ! I had to go to Reading to see Pat (his son) who had an attack of appendicitis. M." It was a great disappointment to him. It would have been a proud moment in which he welcomed " Willie " to Leeds.

It is doubtful whether any writer, no matter how superlative his gifts, can bring to the lay reader the wonderful man that was William Osler. Perhaps no doctor born to the English tongue has ever been so loved. It is not possible to write of him without being carried away upon a stream of words that, to those who did not know him, must seem extravagant. He was a man beyond the scope of ordinary terms : he is not to be described in the language of restraint. He had a character most beautifully compounded : wisdom, patience, gentle humour, and the largest heart in the world — all these were his. And they were all engulfed in the tragedy of war. When his son was killed his spirit died ; his body struggled on for a little while and then, cold from the lack of inner fire, itself declined and died. Name what disease we will — we know that war it was that took Willie Osler's life.

After Osler's death Berkeley wrote for the press a brief memorial note. It is now almost forgotten. Unless revitalised by another printing it will, I fear, before long be lost for ever. It would be a pity if so fine a tribute were never to be read again. Nowhere has Berkeley expressed himself so completely without vanity ; nowhere are his words so disembarrassed of the striving for effect : the phrases are free from his too frequent mannerisms and instead are imbued with the grace of an unself- conscious sincerity. Many of the thoughts mirror the best in Berkeley himself — of him, too, they could not untruly be said. Here to write the sentences again cannot be wholly irrelevant to the account of Berkeley's life ; the native Berkeley is embalmed in them. Here, then, they are :

" Many medical men over the whole world will hear to-day of the death of Sir William Osler with a sharp pang of grief, and with a heavy sense of personal loss.

" Osler was, of course, a deeply learned and most cultured physician. He probably knew more of the history of medicine in all ages than any living man. He certainly was unrivalled in his knowledge of the new work being done in all countries. He was the friend of many who were carrying on the newest researches, and not a few of them looked to him for guidance, inspiration, and encouragement. His mind, therefore, ranged at ease over the whole field of medicine in all ages.

" It was a delight to make an unprovoked intellectual assault upon him, and to test his knowledge of a perhaps recondite medical subject which much labour had just made one's own. He was never found lacking in knowledge, and often his replies had that note of personal and intimate acquaintance with his subject that made his hearers believe it had been his special and favourite study.

" He wrote much upon medical topics and upon philosophy. His text-book, which ran through nine editions, was the best in any language. His casual papers, introductory addresses, and such-like, had about them something of the charm, and all the exquisite expression of *The Autocrat at the Breakfast Table* and the others of that series.

" To the weary practitioner no books were so unceasingly helpful as his. He seemed to understand the harrassing difficulties, the discouragements, the disappointments that come sometimes even to the most successful.

" He had a word of understanding, of solace, and of

cheer for everyone. He made one feel anxious to do better work and to be capable of greater effort. He created a desire to be worthy of a profession the tradition and the practice of which are so noble.

" But, above all, Osler had personality. He radiated friendship. Almost all who knew him loved him, and hundreds of men in all countries looked upon him as their own particular friend.

" He kept up a gigantic correspondence, and in every letter there was a note of cordial intimacy and affection, now to one member of the family, now to another ; so that it seemed as though he were spiritually in closest touch with all. He possessed in a degree rarely seen the power of attracting good men, and of getting out of all men, able or otherwise, the very best work it was possible for them to give.

" His good-humour, his cheeriness, his aptness of phrase and illustration, his loyalty, his integrity, made him one of the most lovable of all men.

" Many of us to-day will feel with acute distress that we have lost a staunch, true friend, a prince among men. And the world is the poorer for the loss of one of the very greatest physicians it has ever possessed."

Yes, Berkeley has never so beautifully conveyed true meaning, and his own emotion. He was great in his perception of greatness in others ; he could be humble before a noble mind.

*   *   *   *   *

Berkeley did vastly enjoy the war — or rather, he enjoyed his part in it. He was not insensitive to the sufferings and the loss of others ; his kindness supported many in their grief. But he delighted in the tasks imposed upon him, in the opportunities to make new friends, and in the exercise of his powers behind the scenes of war. Above all he loved the fact that he was a soldier. In the maintenance of family tradition, albeit only by chance, he took incalculable pleasure. It was with the thrill of a boy's heart that, when promotion came, he signed himself " Major-General ".

In January of 1917 Berkeley was appointed by the King a Companion of the Bath. At the same time his chief, Sir Alfred Keogh, was promoted to the very high honour of Knight Grand Cross of the Bath. Berkeley wrote from Leeds :

" DEAR SIR ALFRED,
" The news which I have just read in the morning paper, of your decoration with the G.C.B., has given me a greater pleasure than I could make you realise. I write at once, and away from reference, but I feel certain that this is the first G.C.B. ever conferred on a medical man. Of your deserts it would be improper for me now to say anything. One fact however is common knowledge, that you have received an unstinted degree of trust, respect, and affection, by every medical man who has had the high privilege of working under you. The representatives of the Profession may some day be able to speak without restraint, and to act in accord with their opinions. Then, I hope, other honours await you. Meanwhile your honour and success are ours. You have exalted our calling in the eyes of the world, and there is nothing greater than that, that any man can do.
" In profound respect and content with your leadership,
" I am,
" Yours,
" BERKELEY MOYNIHAN "

And a few weeks later he also wrote :

" DEAR SIR ALFRED,
" You have set up in the sight of all men in our Profession a nobler and more exalted standard of virtue, integrity, and efficiency than any medical man of our

day. My association with you in your work, slender
though it has been, has been a greater inspiration to me
than any influence that ever came to me in my life. I
can never forget your kindness, and nothing can diminish
my personal devotion to you, and my unbounded admiration for all that you have done for your country in the
hour of her trial. For me you will always remain the
supreme and most perfect example I have ever known
of the great public servant.

" With all gratitude and affection,

" Yours,

" BERKELEY MOYNIHAN "

Many of Berkeley's contacts with Sir Alfred were
through his work on the Army Medical Advisory Board.
This Board was a small group of about half a dozen
doctors — all famous either in civil or army life — who
advised on the personnel and policy of the army medical
service. Berkeley had two great friends upon this Board ;
one an old one from the days of peace, the other a new
one with whom his friendship blossomed during the years
of war. The former was Sir Robert Jones, famous ortho-
paedic surgeon from Liverpool ; he was a man like
Osler — a doctor most gentle and lovable. The latter,
whom he came to know later on, was Colonel (late
General Sir John) Goodwin ; he had been in the army
since the days of his qualification and, like Berkeley,
dearly loved his profession. With these men, as always
in the company of those of whom he was fond, Berkeley
was at his best. His affectionate humour and cheerful
spirit never failed him — or them — even in the war's
most dreary days.

Berkeley and Sir Robert, when in London together,
used to stay at the Royal Automobile Club in Pall Mall.
They had some good times there. Berkeley's great joy

was the swimming-pool ; hardly a day went by in which
he did not find time to use it. Whenever possible, no
matter how cold the weather, he would inveigle one of
his friends to bathe with him. In later years he used
the Royal Automobile Club less ; perhaps he desired
more quiet, perhaps in its swarming membership he felt
himself lost ; but in the war years he was often there.

The place that, of unavoidable necessity, he was least
often in was his home. His affairs and travels left him
with little time in which to idle there ; they deprived
him of those hours of play in which a father comes to
know his child. When the war was over, Berkeley, by
then habituated to a day of ceaseless work, spent little
time in fireside play. He was intensely fond of his children — proud of them too — but, robbed of the hours
of intimacy that he should have had with them, did not
always understand their point of view. Strangely, but
understandably, he knew his children best of all at the
end of his life. Only then did he have the leisure to
get to know them well. There is a sadness about those
partially wasted years. Though they were no one's
fault, they were the whole family's loss. Berkeley and his
children missed some of the mutual happiness that only
long hours of companionship can bring.

During the war Dorothy was old enough to assist her
father in his operating theatre. This delighted Berkeley.
But Shelagh and Pat were children ; such time as he
had with them was stolen in minutes from the over-
crowded days. To them he was magnificent — but
remote : one who at intervals descended from the home
of the gods for a too brief hour of glorious play, returning
then to the mysterious world of darkly important comings
and goings. They were left alone with their mother —

and even she seemed to them much preoccupied.

And so she was. Upon Berkeley she had come to rely in almost everything, and now his help was rarely there. And even when he was at home his assistance was sometimes withheld. For he had a failing that, discovered in one so imaginative, comes as a mild surprise. He, so utterly self-reliant, little understood that others lacked his own internal strength : that, often seeking no aid, they yet longed for a patient listener to whom they might recount their woes. Berkeley looked on his home as above all his place of rest and refreshment. Whenever possible he wanted no troubles there. He would sometimes say to Isabel, " When I come in through the front door I leave my troubles on the mat outside ; when I go out next morning I take up my burden again. I expect you to do the same." In saying so he forgot the many opportunities that came his way each day for him to throw off his own worries. Amongst the many who shared his daily work he could, by casting off a trouble here and there, free his mind of nearly all its doubts. Having many to console himself he forgot, in perfect innocence, that he was his wife's sole comfort. Not in his consciousness did he realise how much he relied upon her. Nor, vexed by so many problems of the world beyond his home, did he remember always that, to those who have to deal with them, domestic problems too may be seemingly as grave.

But, allowing for a human weakness here and there, his character was never more splendid than now. Though having just cause for vanity he yet remained humble. His judgement was unimpaired, for there was no exaggeration of his self-esteem. In time to come he did indeed fall victim to a satisfaction with himself that, however much we may condemn it, irresistibly coloured his view. But now his vision was perfect. It had a clarity and penetration entirely beyond that encountered in normal experience ; it many times newly amazed even those who knew him well. Persons, for some time separated from him, came to think in retrospect that, in his presence, they had been spell-bound by his influence ; that in fact his mind had not the piercing quality that, at their last meeting, they had granted it. In relegating him to the general level of their acquaintance they restored their conceit of themselves. But, on encountering him again, the wonder of his intellectual power broke over them afresh. With rational logicality he could dispel the miasmic vapours that enshrouded — as they do in the case of most of us — their daily thoughts. About his conclusions there was not that spurious, evanescent rectitude that comes from the impact upon us of mere forceful personality alone ; they were right for the right reasons, and he had the power to drive them home. His intellect ranged out beyond the country of cold understanding ; carried forward by the warm friendly emotion of his love for his fellow beings, it reached into spiritual uplands. From those heights it brought down strength that it passed on to others. In the mountains of hope it scored channels down which poured rivers of encouragement.

Those who never knew him will perhaps doubt these words. That doubt is the measure of the words' inherent truth. But those who did know him — so remarkable was his character — may say that what is written here, conveying less than the man's full stature, is understatement.

*   *   *   *   *

In July of 1917, from the headquarters of the Advisory Commission of the Council of National Defence of America, Berkeley received this letter :

" MY DEAR SIR BERKELEY,

" It gives me pleasure most heartily to endorse the invitation extended to you by the Surgeon-General, W. C. Gorgas, U.S.A., through the Surgeon-General, Sir Alfred Keogh, R.A.M.C.

" In addition to details thus conveyed to you, let me emphasise, first, that we need you. The fact is that the service you can render both to your country and to ours here next October is not to be estimated. We shall be delighted to welcome you and to make all arrangements that you meet the profession on this side to the best advantage.

" Second, our plan for the week in Chicago beginning October 22, is that on Wednesday evening you address the members of the Clinical Congress of Surgeons, your subject being such experience drawn from the War as you may determine to be of greatest usefulness. On Friday evening of the same week we desire that you deliver the Sixth Convocation address of the College. On that occasion you have as splendid and as dignified an audience as this continent affords. It is our custom to publish the address and to give it in this form wide distribution.

" As for details . . .

" I am,

" Faithfully yours,

" FRANKLIN MARTIN
" Member of the Advisory Commission and Secretary of American College of Surgeons "

The General Officer in charge of the R.A.M.C. section of the Northern Command was informed that Berkeley, who was under his orders, had been " selected to proceed to America on a Special Mission " and that he was to be " warned accordingly ".

In the autumn of 1917 the following announcement appeared in the American press :

"Sir Berkeley Moynihan, who has been assigned by the British Government to advise the United States Army Medical Corps in its preparations, arrived here to-day. Sir Berkeley Moynihan is Professor of Clinical Surgery at Leeds University and an authority on abdominal operations. During the war he has been serving with the rank of Major (temporary Lieutenant-Colonel) with the Second General Northern Hospital at Leeds.—*Reuter*."

Berkeley remained in America for less than a month ; but, during those few weeks, he had such a reception and such a triumph as even in his wildest fancy he could hardly have anticipated. At each one of his many public addresses in Washington, Chicago, and New York, he received an ovation. He was lauded in the press — which recorded his every utterance. He was the guest of Dr. George W. Crile, President of the American College of Surgeons, and many receptions were given in his honour. And, final felicity, his companion throughout the tour — his colleague upon the special mission — was his great friend Colonel Goodwin.

Berkeley's American speeches fell into two classes : those of strictly surgical interest and those upon the general aspects of the war. The surgical ones were concerned with operations upon wounds of the chest, the antiseptic and disinfectant treatment of wounds, the importance of bringing the wounded quickly to the hands of the surgeon, and with the amazing success that had attended efforts to control the spread of epidemic infection in the modern army. When speaking to lay audiences he repeated, in various forms, the recruiting speech that here occurs on an earlier page : he delivered it with tremendous effect.

Apart from these subjects he employed one other theme as well — the causes that had led up to the war, and the issues it had placed at stake — when he spoke at the Convocation of the American College of Surgeons. Before this Fellowship Address Berkeley and Colonel Goodwin had the honour of being made Honorary Fellows of the College. Berkeley was introduced by his dear friend of pre-war days, Dr. William J. Mayo, who said before the assembly :

" Mr. President : I have the very great pleasure and privilege of presenting to you for Honorary Fellowship in the American College of Surgeons, Sir Berkeley Moynihan of England, Colonel in the British Army Medical Service, Professor of Surgery in the University of Leeds, Master Surgeon, Author, Teacher, a kindly gentleman and friend to Americans. Sir Berkeley holds a place in the minds and in the hearts of the English Medical Profession which but one man in my time has ever held in the American Medical Profession. That man was the late Dr. John B. Murphy. And more than that, no man can say."

Berkeley was deeply affected by the generosity of these words. When introduced by the President to give his Address he said first :

" May I, before I deliver my address, break silence with regard to the dignity that you have recently conferred upon me ?

" No honours ever come to a member of our profession which he holds in higher esteem than those that are conferred by members of his own body. And to-day you have conferred upon me an honour which I would not change for any other that could be given by any body of medical men in all this world. And you have surrounded that gift to me with every circumstance of honour.

" Your President to-day, Dr. Crile, is one who for many years — more years than either he or I should care to remember — has been a constant incentive to me in my work, a constant inspiration to me and an unceasing stimulus for me to seek out in surgery the better way.

" You have heard me presented to the President by Dr. Mayo, and I think that in speaking both of your President and of Dr. Mayo, I really should have adopted for their comfort the practice of anoci - association, surrounding them both with an impenetrable barrier through which no sensation could pass. [An ingenious witticism based upon some research work of Dr. Crile's — in which ' anoci-association ' was the central feature.]

" Of Dr. Mayo it is impossible for me to speak in terms which would fully express my unceasing admiration for everything which he has done for surgery and for surgeons all the world over. I, who have worked in a very similar field to that which he has made famous, desire to express to him my boundless admiration, and to say that I feel under the greatest obligation which one surgeon can possibly owe to another.

" Finally, you have conferred upon me this Honorary Fellowship in a city which for all time is made not only memorable but sacred for surgeons in all parts of the world as the home of Dr. Murphy. My debt to John B. Murphy was a debt that I could only pay in his lifetime by lip homage, and by carrying out the lessons which I learned from hearing him — and you all know what an inspiration that was — and from reading, I hope and believe, every word he ever wrote on any surgical topic. No man more often in difficult moments stood by my side in spirit at the operating table and guided my hand and directed my judgement. To the sacred and illustrious memory of John B. Murphy I offer a heartfelt tribute."

Berkeley's Fellowship Address was entitled *The Causes*

of the War. It is too long to reprint here ; it illustrates more the times than Berkeley's character ; and, for those who wish to read it, there exists a full reproduction elsewhere.

In substance the speech was an analysis, enquiring rather than dogmatic, of the underlying motives that caused Germany to wage war. " No doubt ", he said, " many answers, each conflicting with the rest, and yet each containing some small grain of truth, may be given to these questions." He considered that two answers stood out above the rest :

" No one can doubt who reads history with an un-biased mind that Prussia has increased often, if not always, at the expense of other states by acts of sudden and unprovoked aggression. . . . War is the national industry of Prussia ; it is her means of acquiring wealth. It is by her military successes that she has enlarged her borders, added to her own infertile lands, solidified her gains, and been able to prepare for a still further attack upon her next chosen victim. . . . No state in history can compare with Prussia in its exploitation of the doctrine of plunder ; the doctrine of taking because it has the power, and of keeping because it has the strength to do so. . . . From her point of view she had every reason to think her methods were right. Not for one instant, of course, did she call in question the principles or doubt the ideals which underlie her action."

Then, further on, he continues :

" Or, we may answer the question differently. We may say that Germany had grounds for her belief that she was a nation encircled by hostile powers, jealous of her splendid growth, of her swift acquisition of wealth, of that armed strength afloat and ashore to which she added daily. . . . We can understand Germany, though we cannot for one instant agree with her, when she says

that for her this is a war of defence, that she is fighting
for a way out of the strong iron bastion that has been
built up round her frontiers. . . . The motive of war,
if this answer were true, would be Germany's fear —
fear — the black godmother of cruelty."

Then he comes to his main thesis :

" But anyone who has given thought to the matter
(and who has not ?) must agree that whatever else this
ghastly conflict now is, it is in simple truth not a clash
of merely material interest. This is a moral war. It is
a holy war if ever there was one. It is deep down
a war between conflicting and discordant and uncom-
formable moral systems. It is a war, therefore, in which
a real peace cannot come by compromise ; for you
cannot come to any terms but one, with that which you
feel to be a principle of evil, with that which you feel in
your innermost soul to be the deadliest enemy of mankind,
and the most menacing blight with which civilisation
has ever been threatened. What, then, are the issues at
stake ? . . . The principle ground into the very fibre
of the German peoples, accepted by them, gloried in
by them, worshipped by them, inspiring them, is the
principle of TYRANNY. What exactly is meant by that ?
It implies a complete surrender of individual rights and
liberties, and an unquestioning submission of them to
a power exercised exclusively from without. . . . It is
something outside and above the individual, uncontrolled
by him, owing no allegiance to him, but directing him
and ordering all his actions in a manner and in a direction which he is told is for the benefit not only of the
paramount authority, but incidentally or consecutively
of himself. Tyranny, that is to say, is the power exercised
by an irresponsible autocracy ; it is the supremacy of the
state carried to its ultimate expression ; and it is by
implication an attribute of every individual in the state.
This is no ignoble creed, and Prussia, let us tell it to her
credit, has made a robust philosophy of it, and has gained

the staunch and willing adhesion to it of almost every man in her nation.

" Over against this what have we set up, on our side, as our standard ? What is the principle by which we are sustained ; whence do we derive our soul's refreshment ? It is hard to find the precise word, but none fits so well as ' Liberty '. And by liberty we mean here the inalienable and indestructible right of every human being to express himself, to be himself, to develop from within. . . . The laws which govern and control him are laws which he himself has helped to make, and to which he, with others like him, willingly conforms, not so much because the laws are good, but because they are laws which he and those who have gone before him have in freedom imposed upon themselves. This is democracy. To us as surgeons practising a scientific profession, the conflict between these irreconcilable principles is of deep significance."

He then goes on to a careful examination of the effects and practice of tyranny. He discovers how, in the end, all forms of education in the state become prejudiced and their truth contaminated ; how all the holders of professorial posts become the timorous servants of the state ; and how the national stamp, eliminating individuality, is placed on every man. He then anatomises liberty and, in the process, uses these words :

" The system of liberty desires rather to develop and strengthen the character of the future citizen ; the system of tyranny seeks to train and stamp the intellect with a certain quality. It is free natural growth on the one hand ; it is repressive and specific culture on the other."

He continues then, towards the end :

" Tyranny means at last intellectual sterility and death. How impossible it is for a nation held in the grip of tyranny to give its citizens intellectual freedom, great though its desire may be to do so ! Progress in science must, first and last, depend upon the unrestrained freedom of exercise of all the faculties of the human mind. Of these imagination is perhaps the chief. Imagination is the mother of fact. Or, one may say, it is the scaffold upon which one stands to build the structure of truth. Imagination, as Keats tells us, may be compared to Adam's dream — he awoke and found it truth. It cannot surely live in the narrow restrictions and in the dank and stifling air where the noxious weed of tyranny thrives. For, hamper it as you will, thought in the long run must have its way, which is the way of challenge and enquiry. . . . Tyranny is not a force to set ideas in motion. Under a system of tyranny intellectual salvation can only come from revolt. How else can we account for the eternal freshness of the Jewish mind, and for the splendid achievements of that race, which, tyrannized by every power, has kept its own religion, and lived its own intellectual life, not by submission but by resistance to those who held its men in bondage ?

" In this war, as I see it, we are fighting, therefore, for liberty. Of the two discordant systems of morals one only must triumph and survive. If we compromise with that which we believe to be a principle of evil, a precursor of moral and intellectual death and dissolution, we are false to those who have given their most precious lives that truth might conquer at the last ; but more than this, we are false to those who come after ; we are shackling for generations to come the minds and the souls of men ; we are failing in our plain duty to humanity."

With these words he concluded a masterly speech. In the dignity and penetration of its intellectual power it was as good as any he ever made. It was entirely free from any Irish exaggeration of sentiments ; the persuasive charms of rhetoric were courageously forgone.

From start to finish it displays the crystal beauty of Berkeley's mind during this period of his life.

*   *   *   *   *

No sooner was the surgical convocation over than Berkeley was swept on to other meetings and other duties — and however arduous they were, his amazing zest remained supreme. He was so busy that there was almost no time for letter-writing. But in Washington he stole an instant to write to his wife, telling of one of the better moments — and how he loved them when they came ! — saying to her :

" MY VERY OWN LITTLE TINY,

" This has been a great day. I heard this morning that President Wilson would like to see me, so after lunch we went to the White House, and I had a short interview 8 or 10 minutes with him : talking hard all the time. He is like his photographs except about the mouth, which is much nicer than in any of his pictures. He was very charming and agreeable, asked about all the work we were doing, and how I had enjoyed the trip. The White House is very like an English Country House ; the decorations are quite beautiful.

" In the afternoon I had to go to a meeting of the Cabinet and spoke to them for about half an hour. They gave me a very warm welcome and said all sorts of nice things. To-morrow I go to Philadelphia for one day. . . . Then I go to New York to await the boat. At each place I have to speak to very large audiences, over 2000. . . . I have only had two letters from you so far ! They are so slow in coming nowadays. I send you all my very best love.

" Ever your very own,

" B."

After Berkeley's one day in Philadelphia his wife

received, too, another letter — from an old friend of hers there :

" My dear Lady Moynihan,

"I cannot resist sending you a little note just to tell you how delighted and honoured we have been by Sir Berkeley's all too short visit.

"I am sure he will be too modest to tell you himself how enthusiastically he has been received everywhere and what an inspiration he has been to all in his masterly handling of the subject nearest to all our hearts to-day.

" Men whose opinions count for much in this country, have told me that in these short weeks, Sir Berkeley has done more to open the drowsy eyes of the public to what is required of us than anyone else so far and that there is no doubt that he has firmly cemented the friendship and good-fellowship between England and the States by his generous and tactful public speeches. — That is big praise for a man, and the best part of it is that it is deserved.

"I heard Sir Berkeley only once — at the Waldorf last Thursday night, and I have told him that my thoughts travelled to you, wishing that you could have been with us to see the welcome a wholly American audience gave him and to hear the thunder of applause and cheers ! Sir Berkeley spoke, in that golden voice of his, for a full hour and at the end they wanted more ! He had simply held everyone tense with interest.

"I know that all this will please you and it gives me great pleasure to write you of Sir Berkeley's great triumph here. . . .

" Cordially yours,
" ____ "

And after the New York visit there came to Isabel this letter from Berkeley's old friend Dr. W. B. Coley :

My dear Lady Moynihan,

We cannot begin to tell you the joy that Sir Berkeley has given our household by his all too brief visit. The only thing lacking was your presence. When this long and terrible war is over you must both come over for a long rest and a warm welcome we will give you. I wish I could give you some idea of the splendid reception given Sir Berkeley everywhere he has been. I did not want to lose any of his visit and went to meetings and speeches four days with him and listened to two addresses a day, so much more wonderful and inspiring than the ones that came before. . . .

" We are just starting for the steamer to say good-bye. How we wish the visit might be longer, but I know that you are anxiously awaiting his return and that he is greatly needed at the front. . . .

" With much love from all,

" Faithfully yours,

" W. B. COLEY "

Once more upon the Atlantic, homeward bound, Berkeley had time to order the impressions made upon him by his trip. He had time — both in reading and in writing — to deal with his accumulated correspondence. From every place that he had visited had come to him letters of praise, gratitude, and affection. Here are two of them — speaking in the same voice as the many that we cannot print :

[From Rochester, Minnesota]

" MY DEAR SIR BERKELEY,

" I do not feel that I can close the day until I have expressed to you the profound impression your splendid address made upon me this evening.

" No hymn of hate, no ' strafing ' ! but a noble beautiful and spiritual effort that painted our duty to civilization and which anticipated the rapture of that duty well performed, the emancipation of the human race for ever and for all time. You almost breathed a merciful prayer of pity for those who blindly, ruthlessly defy every law human and divine. It was a very moving

216

and impressive effort and had a profound effect upon your audience.

"With best wishes for a great success in all your undertakings,

"I am, my dear Sir Berkeley,

"Very sincerely yours,

"H—— "

From Philadelphia came a letter from the daughter of an old surgical friend of his, who had but lately died :

" DEAR SIR BERKELEY,

" I wrote my mother as nearly as I could remember all of the beautiful things you said about Father, and about your speech and how the people leaped to their feet to greet you (I have never seen that before in Philadelphia) and what an inspiration it was to hear you and above all what a joy it was to me to see you again. . . .

" I am sure you don't realize how wonderfully you spoke the other night, it was a great experience for everyone who heard you, and something that I shall always treasure as a very dear memory.

" I shall pray very hard that you may get home in safety and that it won't be very long before we see you again either here or in England, that land that such men as you are making us feel is the home of the finest and most *glorious* people in the world.

" Believe me always to be affectionately yours,

" E—— "

With these letters, and all the others like them, came a very special one. It was from Dr. Crile, who had travelled everywhere with Berkeley during the weeks gone by :

" MY DEAR OLD EMPIRE,

" With neither Sousa nor Susie nor the footlights in contemplation to-day I am conscious of a slight feeling of loneliness. However, the wonderful three weeks are ours ! How much has been accomplished will probably surprise you some day : but of this I am certain that to me it has been priceless : nothing will I cherish more than this campaign with you and all the wonderful things it brought and included — and which I now place in the sanctuary of my memories.

"Good luck ! Now and always,
"G. W. C."

At last — rested by the peace of the ship, refreshed by the hours of absence from noise and hurry — Berkeley sat down to write the story of his travels. By a happy choice, for in less than six months she was to die, it was to his sister Eva that he dedicated the letter. The thought that he had given her this great pleasure must have comforted him in the days that lay ahead. His love for his two sisters was passionate ; from them he drew an understanding sympathy that others could never give him. They had shared with him the isolated intimacy of poverty and struggle ; they alone knew the adversity out of which his career was born. When Eva went, so too went part of Berkeley ; to her loss he never was reconciled.

"U.S.M.S. *St. Louis*
18.11.1917

" BELOVED,
" This is the story of my visit to America ! I arrived Oct. 18th, and drove straight to Dr. Coley's house. He is an old friend and I had promised to stay with him. Then I learnt that Dr. W. J. Mayo was to give the ' Carpenter ' address at the N.Y. Academy of Medicine that evening and that I was to dine with him, hear the Lecture and speak afterwards. All these I did. They gave me a quite wonderful reception. The Chairman, Dr. James said, ' Mayo is the M—— of America and M—— is the Mayo of England '.

" After the meeting I talked for an hour to Dr. Mayo about the organisation of the U.S. Medical Department and at his request went on the 20th to Washington to pick up General Gorgas (of Panama Canal fame) on my way to Chicago. We passed Harper's Ferry and other places famous in the Civil War on the way, and saw such Autumn colouring as I have never seen before, glorious beyond words. We travelled all night and I had my talks to Gen. Gorgas and told him all about our medical arrangements in France and England.

"We arrived at Chicago on Sunday an hour late. I was met at the station and taken direct to an Hotel where a meeting was being held. They all rose and gave me a tremendous reception as I came in. I had to speak at once for about 20 minutes and again at a special meeting in the afternoon. On Monday I was told that there was to be a great patriotic Meeting at 'Orchestra Hall' 8 p.m. and I was asked to make a 'rousing patriotic speech'. I demurred, being an Englishman, but it was no good. The Hall held between 5,000 and 6,000 people and was packed to the doors. Sousa's Band was there and the Secretary of State for the Navy spoke also. I spoke for 50 minutes and you will see what the papers say — 'women sobbed, women smiled, just as he made them'. After I had finished the whole audience rose and cheered like billyho for about two minutes and Sousa played 'God save the King'.

"I had only about half an hour to prepare the speech and I had only half a sheet of notes, but it seemed easy enough. When I told of Ypres you could really hear the sobs all over the place, and the deafening cheers when I said 'But our thin line held'.

"On Monday I gave two addresses, one to 2,500 and one to about 1,100 overflow on 'Gunshot Wounds'.

"On Wednesday I gave an Address to the Chicago Medical Society to about 1,500. On Thursday to about 2,500 on 'Injuries to Lungs' and on Friday I gave the Convocation address at the Annual Meeting of the American College of Surgeons and was made an Honorary Fellow thereof.

"Every time my reception was almost overpowering.

They always stood up and cheered the roof off—bless them.

" The same night I went to Rochester with Dr. Mayo and spent Saturday and Sunday on the Mississippi on his boat. It was snowing all the time, but quite lovely and very jolly on the old type of boat, with wheels astern. Then I had a week of Surgery at Rochester and went from there to Washington where I saw the President and had quite a long talk to him at the White House. His A.D.C. came to me afterwards and said he had been asked to tell me that the President had enjoyed his talk with me very much indeed, and was going to give me his signed photograph.

" Later in the day I went for two hours to a meeting of the Cabinet and spoke at great length, and answered all sorts of questions. Afterwards many of them complimented me on my ' splendid speech '. The Secretary of State for War, Mr. Baker (they told me he was a famous orator), was there and spoke, but they said, ' I guess he took the back seat to-day '.

" The next day I was given a big Dinner. The health of the King was drunk and I was asked all at once to propose the President. I got up and on the spur of the moment said — ' I rise to propose the health of one who is prudent in counsel, wise in action, eloquent in speech, a man among Kings, a King among men, the President of the U.S.A.' When I sat down with the rest after we had drunk the toast, everyone was dead silent and the Chairman said, ' I guess the Dinner ought to stop right now '. The aforesaid A.D.C. who was there, Admiral Gregson, came up and asked me to write it on the back of my visiting card, for the President himself.

" On the next day Wednesday I spoke at Philadelphia to about 2,000, and on Thursday at the Waldorf Hotel in N.Y. to about 3,000.

" At both places I had an immense reception — at the latter I said, ' I have been asked by many people in many places when this war will end. May I say most respectfully that for America this War will begin when

SIR BERKELEY MOYNIHAN
Chicago, October, 1917

every man of military age has offered his services and is
prepared to sacrifice his life for his country. When in the
Temple of Freedom and upon the High Altar of your
Patriotism you have offered up your wealth, your souls,
your honour. When you have mourned your illustrious
dead in thousands and in hundreds of thousands, and
have realised that they have died nobly in support of the
worthiest cause for which the sword was ever drawn.'
That sent a wail and a sob all over the Hall. Finally, I
said that America had waged three wars under three
great men. In the first, under Washington, she had fought
not the English people but the same stupid Prussian
autocracy as we were fighting together now, and in the
second, under Lincoln (whom I quoted), she had fought
to decide who should rule in her own house. Now she
fought with us. In her first war she had gained liberty
for America, in her second, liberty *in* America, and in
her third with us she must win liberty for the World. I
was going to add then ' Our eyes shall see the coming of
the glory of the Lord ' and finish, but I could say no more.
The whole house rose and shouted with delight and
cheered whilst I walked back to my seat. Even Gladstone
in Midlothian could never have had a fiercer cheer than
I got then. I could not have said another word to save
my life. After it was over they crowded all over me to
shake hands. It was terrific and I had spoken for an
hour and ten minutes. It seemed like half an hour.

" So this is the story of my happy visit. I was overwhelmed on all hands with kindness.

" Now I am on the *St. Louis* coming home. We have
had one very bad day but the others have been tolerable.
I am longing to be home though. I have enjoyed every
minute of my time. America is just beginning to realise
that the War will be a big business and a long one. They
are going to be in it for all they are worth.

" My best love to you,

" Ever thine,

" B."

* * * * *

Berkeley left Colonel Goodwin behind him in America, where the Colonel had further work to do. They had become close friends and their intimate companionship had engendered in Berkeley a great admiration for one who had been both doctor and soldier all his life. Immediately on his return to Leeds Berkeley wrote to his friend :

" MY DEAR GOODWIN,

" My first letter must be to you. We had a quite uneventful crossing, except for the extreme turbulence of the waters on one day, when I kept in my bunk and slept soundly till 6.0 P.M. The most interesting passenger was Raemakers, with whom I had several very interesting talks.

" We arrived on Thursday last, and on Friday I had a long interview with Sir Alfred, and left your letter to me with him. I told him of all our doings, of our rhetorical campaign, and of the good effects which I felt certain had already followed, and which would be increasingly evident as time passed. I entered into the fullest details of all you had done before I arrived, and of what we did together, and of the final rally in New York. That I think was the most wonderful reception of all. The audience was magnificent. The D.G. was delighted with all I had to tell him, and he was most deeply and acutely appreciative of all the splendid work you have done since you went out to America. In my opinion, as I told him, the value of your work could not be exaggerated. You have done incredibly well in the most trying and difficult situations. The Country is fortunate in having had a man of your character and attainments to serve it in a very critical period. Keogh is full of gratitude to you. No reward could be too great for you. . . .

" To me the chance of meeting you and making friends with you has been most memorable and I count this as one of the happiest of the many happy results of my visit. . . .

> " With warmest regards,
> " Yours very sincerely,
> " BERKELEY MOYNIHAN "

In the meantime Sir Alfred Keogh had received a letter from America. Dr. Franklin H. Martin of the Advisory Commission of the Council of National Defence had written :

" DEAR SIR,

" I wish to thank you on behalf of the medical profession of America, the medical departments of the United States Army and Navy, and the Council of National Defense for detailing Colonel Sir Berkeley Moynihan ostensibly to deliver a convocation address to the American College of Surgeons, but in reality by his eloquence to effect one more strong link between England and us.

" May I briefly recite to you his services to us in the short three weeks he was here ? . . . [Here follows a record of the movements already recounted in Berkeley's own letter.] . . . Sir Berkeley was one of the principal speakers at the opening of the Clinical Congress of Surgeons. . . . The address easily made Sir Berkeley the hero of our great meeting. . . . Since I am the responsible one in our war council for the maintenance of our Sanitary and Medical Corps personnel, I cannot emphasise too strongly the importance of Sir Berkeley's vivid presentation of our problems to that group of my confreres and responsible heads of department of our government. His influence will be of incalculable aid to me. Following Sir Berkeley's visit to Washington, two large meetings followed, one in Philadelphia where two thousand medical men were present and one in New York which was attended by thirty-five hundred medical men and their wives. These were patriotic meetings at which the principal addresses were made by Sir Berkeley and Major George W. Crile.

" The effect wrought by the presence of Sir Berkeley and Major Crile, was, first to stir the members of our lay medical profession so that they would understand the importance of offering their services to their country, and second, to strengthen the friendship and comradeship between the people of our country and yours. We feel that our desires were abundantly fulfilled in these important meetings.

" May I again express the thanks of the Council of National Defence and my personal thanks to you for making it possible for us to receive Sir Berkeley Moynihan.

" Yours very truly,

" FRANKLIN H. MARTIN "

Sir Alfred Keogh in his letter of reply to Dr. Martin said :

". . . I know that Sir Berkeley himself feels very deeply all the kindness which was extended to him in America. I am glad indeed to think that his experience of Army Medical Organisation as well as of War Surgery has been of so great utility to the authorities in the United States. . . . It is only of recent years that the relation of medical science to Armies in the Field has begun to be appreciated. I think in that respect — and I speak from some personal experience — the Regular Service of the United States Army has been in some degree ahead of us, and indeed Sir Berkeley's mission in England at the present time is not dissimilar from that which he has just fulfilled in the United States. There is still much room everywhere for improvement in this respect. . . .

" Yours faithfully,

"A. KEOGH "

From Sir Alfred Keogh himself Berkeley heard of the

good American opinions he had won. He was deeply moved. The extent of his admiration for Sir Alfred and the strength of his devotion to his chief are portrayed in this letter written in December of 1917. In it is revealed Berkeley's capacity for passionate feeling towards one who could touch his heart.

" DEAR SIR ALFRED,
      " Your letter has stirred me to the depths. It shall be among the most treasured possessions, and pass some day to my son. I can most truthfully say that no letter I have ever had has so powerfully affected me. It has always been, and it still must be, impossible for me to tell you my opinion of your work since the war began : though at times it has been difficult to keep silent. Ever since the day in November 1914 when I called on you before going to France I have come by degrees to realise the immensity, difficulty and intricacy of the task confronting you. From that day to this I have become strengthened in my belief, indeed in my most confident conviction, that your services to the Army and Nation and our Profession were incredible, not only in their magnitude but in their swift and easy accomplishment. Your sagacity, insight, resolution, and courage have achieved results that no one could have believed possible. And the warmth of your heart towards every soldier who is suffering has been an incentive and example to us all. . . . I do not speak for myself alone but for every man who loves his country and his calling when I say that our profession never had so able or so revered a leader. Every man who has served under you or near you is ready to say that you have inspired, guided and directed us in a manner which has aroused our highest admiration for your work and character and our warm and undying affection. I cannot re-read this letter : it cannot express what I feel, it cannot pay my debt to you ; it can only offer a tribute of unshakable loyalty and devotion to one whom I believe to be the noblest

servant of the State.   The whole Nation should thank God for you.

"Ever yours,

"BERKELEY MOYNIHAN"

*   *   *   *   *

From the posting of that letter Berkeley turned to give once again all his thoughts to Europe.   Even though he had been absent from England for but a few weeks, an accumulation of many important affairs awaited him. As if untired by more than three years of war's enormous strain he attacked them with the old enthusiasm.   All were astonished by a vitality that remained undiminished after such vast exertions.   His courage never failed. Assaulted by the dark spring of 1918, when the chill wind of faltering hope drove through the English trees, his spirits never trembled in fear.   He could out-brave his worst imaginings.

On the King's Birthday in June 1918 he was made a K.C.M.G. — Knight Commander of St. Michael and St. George.   It was a reward — though in his heart he needed none — for his services at home, in France, and in America.   Upon his desk the letters piled up — the many congratulations of his friends.   Felicitations of this sort, with but the slightest variation, all read alike.   For their recipient, kindling as they do the fires of olden friendships, they have the power to revive memories ; for others their interest is limited, in that it may be a famous one, to the sender's name.

But, forgoing a catalogue of Berkeley's distinguished friends, there yet remain two of these letters that, because of their accompanying sentiments, still have surviving interest.   In the same Honours List as Berkeley had appeared the name of another Leeds surgeon, an old friend of Berkeley's. This man's wife wrote :

" I was so pleased to see your name in the paper and know how proud Lady Moynihan will be feeling, for like me, we have each of us got husbands to be proud of. I know how pleased you will be over H.'s C.M.G., it does help a little to compensate for the four years of separation we have had, but not altogether, nothing can ever really do that, except that we may be spared to each other for many years to come. . . ."

Those sentences tell of the women's war — of the irreplaceable, stolen years — and are a just estimate of a soldier's glory. There is no whining, there are no tears : but not by a piece of coloured ribbon before her eyes is a wise woman's mind bemused.

From behind the lines in France came a letter from a doctor in the field. Even the scars of battle could not efface a humorous and gentle recollection of the almost forgotten days of peace — when surgery was an adventure, and not the sweeping of a butcher's shop. After congratulations, the writer says :

" The news to-day is good and we are holding and punishing the Bosch in his latest effort. The situation on the whole rather appears to one like the physician's attempt to treat duodenal ulcer, and, one must look forward to America, in the form of the scalpel, eventually destroying the ulcer. . . ."

With the end of the war Berkeley's army work gradually declined. But not until the autumn of 1919 were his services so little needed that he could resign his commission. When the time came for him to return to civil life he did so gladly. He had seen enough of tragedy and vain suffering. He knew that throughout the terrible years he had been one of the lucky ones — fortunate in his work, called to inspiring duties, and spared the misery that had fallen to the lot of other men. But he ever remained grateful for the friendships he had made and was proud that, like his fathers before him, he had been called to noble service in the name of England.

In the leadership of the Royal Army Medical Corps Sir John Goodwin succeeded Sir Alfred Keogh. In a letter to Sir John, written a year after the Armistice, Berkeley placed the postscript to what had been a tremendous phase in his life :

" MY DEAR GOODWIN,

" Your letter has given me exquisite pleasure. The time has certainly come for me to be demobilised. For the last three or four months activities in all parts of the Northern Command have been dwindling. The hospitals that remain are now running automatically. I have completed an inspection of them this week, and everywhere the surgery is good : principles are well-established and the practice would satisfy a cold stern critic. I sent a brief note to my D.D.M.S. on Thursday and told him that there was little left now for me to do, and offering to go anywhere in the Command to see a case or cases in my civilian capacity.

" My work for the Army has been the greatest delight of my life and I shall look back on it not only with supreme happiness, but with thankfulness that I was permitted to serve in so many congenial posts. On all occasions, in every rank I have held, and wherever I have been sent my lot has been made easy by the consideration and overflowing kindness and help and encouragement offered by everyone. I have had wonderful support on all sides. In the Northern Command I have been backed by the most splendid loyal men that anyone ever had in a team.

" But my chief memory will be of my good fortune in

having served two Chiefs for whom I felt the greatest admiration and warm affection. When all the work of the A.M.S. is coldly reviewed in the future it will be recognised how miraculously fortunate we were in having Keogh and yourself, each in your own time and by your own methods, to lead us, and to overcome the grave problems which confronted each of you. The work of one was the corollary and completion of the other : and in the whole profession inside the Army or out, not two better men, each appropriate in his own time and task, could have been found. Of Keogh's kindness to me and of his over-generous recognition of the little I did I shall carry an imperishable recollection.

"My first meeting with you was in Chicago when your card was passed on to me and I looked up across the room and saw you. From that moment onwards you have not only been a friend and helper beyond praise, but you have been a counsellor of rarest wisdom and tact. I cannot tell you till you leave your office all that is in my mind and heart : but it is the simple truth to say that to many of us you have put a new complexion on the old virtues, efficiency, devotion, loyalty. Your work for the A.M.S. is happily only well begun : but when it is over I know what the verdict will be. And the country must then realise your worth and keep you in some high post where your great gifts and wise guidance can be used for the common good for many years.

"My best wishes, as you know, will always be yours,
      "With my kindest regards and warmest thanks,
            " Yours ever,
                  " BERKELEY MOYNIHAN "

PART V

THE BUSY YEARS

The Busy Years

THE practice of a consulting surgeon mirrors the prosperity of the times. There are many operations which, though serviceable, may be neither urgent nor necessitated by immediate pain. It is from the performance of these procedures that the better part of the surgeon's income is derived. Emergency operations are relatively infrequent and, though more steady in their flow, are not the most important constituent of the surgeon's livelihood. For one patient whose perforated duodenal ulcer calls for immediate operation if life is to be preserved, there are many whose duodenal ulcers, chronically painful as they may be, are yet not the occasion for undelayed surgical intervention. In this latter group, if operation there is to be, its day and time may be chosen by the patient to suit his own convenience. When money is close, as in periods of economic depression — and most of all in times of war — the operation is postponed as long as possible. But at the turn of the financial tide the consulting-rooms again fill up ; then many come in search of relief from their neglected or untended maladies ; and the surgeon — prosperity's weather-vane — is as busy as he was idle but a little while ago.

During the years of the war the consulting surgeon's practice dwindled to almost nothing. Pressed by taxation and rising prices it was with difficulty that he maintained his solvency. But with ironic humour he struggled against adversity. Berkeley reflected the times in his story of the surgeon who, informed by a patient that the latter feared he could not afford the surgeon's fee, replied, " My dear sir, no coin has yet been minted so small that I should scorn it as remuneration ". The glory had departed from Harley Street.

But after the war the accumulated ailments of four years came for attention. Hospitals, emptied of the wounded, filled up with civilian patients ; no nursing home was capacious enough to hold those who sought to occupy its rooms. For the next few years the private practice of surgery knew the greatest boom it had ever enjoyed. Even the humblest, least fashionable, surgeon found his employment profitable. It was the great heyday of the man with the scalpel in his hand. Though he might come without credentials and though his skill might be mean — yet a rich traffic awaited him.

If the unknown surgeon could thrive like this it can well be imagined how mightily must have flourished surgeons of repute. Patients flocked to the doors that bore the plates of titled men. To Berkeley's door came patients from all over the country — more than that, from all over the world. From India, South Africa, and America they came ; royalty and wealth from many lands passed through his rooms. He could not leave Leeds for any undeclared mission without paragraphs appearing in the papers to engage their readers' speculation as to what great personage he was off to see. If he went away with his wife for a few days there would be seen in the press :

" *In London Now.*

" Sir Berkeley Moynihan and Lady Moynihan are staying for a few days in London — a fact that always

arouses a good deal of curiosity lest some very distinguished invalid should be the object of the visit. Sir
Berkeley, who is among our most famous surgeons, is
continually being asked to settle in London."

He was asked to do more surgical work than, perhaps,
had ever been offered to an English surgeon before. How
remarkable is that fact is unlikely to be completely
appreciated at sight by those outside the medical profession. It is, at any time, an unusual thing for patients
to leave London to see provincial doctors. The faith is
widely held, and not easily destroyed, that London
doctors are the best. There are many obstacles in the
path of a patient who leaves London to consult a doctor
somewhere else — the criticism of his unemancipated
friends, the frowns of the smaller-minded London
specialists, and all those factors, multifarious and tedious
to define, that go to make up the potent metropolitan
snobbery. If disaster should attend the excursion, how
little sympathy awaits the patient ! — if all goes well,
then friends will frankly say that London could have
done the work as well ! Only a doctor of supreme
authority could steadily withdraw from London those
who sought the best.

Berkeley proffered the best. A narrow margin of
superiority over his fellow surgeons would not have been
enough to attract the crowds to Leeds ; it was the considerable measure of his uncontestable primacy that drew
them there. He was the greatest abdominal surgeon of
the day ; a fact which some might resent but which all
were compelled to recognise. In no man were so combined skill and learning ; no surgeon, so gifted with
facility, presumed less on his gift.

That, in these circumstances, Berkeley should amass

a fortune was inevitable. His services were demanded by the very rich and they were willing to pay heavily for any inconvenience to which they put him. More work came to him than he was able to manage. In self-defence he raised his fees, then raised them again. In so doing he was accused of being mercenary. But had he not done so he would have been accused of giving preferential treatment to some of his patients over others. The matter is not one to be lightly set aside, for because of it Berkeley's honour was many times impugned. With what justice it is difficult to see. Admittedly, when his patients were exceedingly rich he charged them very high fees ; but why should he not do so ? He was providing something that was of almost immeasurable value to them, and they, being so wealthy, would not be incommoded by the fee. He had been very poor ; in hardship he had worked prodigiously to cultivate his powers ; he was entitled to choose his ground. Why should he, who had sacrificed his leisure to the perfection of his hand, be now the patronised servant of those rich persons who, having never known such self-denial, now sought to buy that dexterous hand ?

Criticism would be valid had his affluence been attained by extortionate practice. But it was not. To those in the Leeds environment, to those patients sent to him by practitioners who had supported him from the early days, and to those necessitous people who came to him with some substantial claim, he was most generous ; when with propriety he could have asked for more than the average fee he often proved himself satisfied with less. Instances of his charity are many ; though they do not appear to be as many as those who have never heard of them. Here is one — chosen from a group of many like examples.

A business man, in modest circumstances, to consult Berkeley travelled fifty miles from Lancashire. This man, suffering from gall-stones, had been advised by his own doctor that he needed an operation. Surgeons had been discussed and the patient announced his wish to visit Moynihan. The doctor, knowing how high the fee would be, rightly informed his patient that another surgeon would do the operation for a lower charge than Berkeley and with sufficient skill. The patient was adamant and insisted on going to Leeds. Berkeley confirmed the diagnosis and agreed that an operation would be necessary. When asked his fee he announced that it would be a hundred guineas. The patient went home to think it over — he was not at all resentful, but the fee certainly had been much higher than he had expected. He informed his doctor that it was one he could not afford and that he would therefore submit to the hand of another surgeon. The doctor wrote to Berkeley to tell him of these things ; he told Berkeley that he and the patient were going elsewhere — and this quite without dissatisfaction, for neither he nor the patient had any special claim upon Berkeley's kindness. By return of post a letter came from Berkeley : " Do not worry about the fee, send Mr. —— along. We'll fix up something satisfactory." The operation took place and the patient paid a bill that he could well afford.

The people of the North Country had been faithful to Berkeley when he needed faith ; he, when success was abundant, always remained faithful to them. Like them he knew the value of money. To a Southerner he may have appeared over-thoughtful where money was concerned ; but, as those in Leeds are well aware, there is a vast difference between being careful and being acquisitive — though moneyed folk may not perceive it. No one suffered because Berkeley grew rich. Of all surgeons the same cannot be said.

*   *   *   *   *

In Berkeley's physical aspect the war had brought a change. His hair, though no less thick, was fast becoming grey. His figure had filled out ; he was now thick-set. The expression on his face — tempered by security — was gentler, though no less keen. He was less pale than he had been in youth : there was a pinkness about his cheeks. Indeed he was one of those men that are more handsome in middle-age than in young manhood. There was now outstanding authority — even greatness — in his appearance. He looked like a famous man. He was as meticulous as ever in his cleanliness : however busy he was he never looked other than if he had but recently come from his bath. There was always a glow about him ; a fragrant freshness. To these cleanly habits he was provoked both by pride in his person and by his anxious avoidance of all infection. After one patient had left his room and before he saw the next, he would retire and wash his mouth out with an effervescent antiseptic. He took every care to avoid transmitting or acquiring infection. His linen was always fresh and his clothes most carefully brushed and pressed. If he was vain about his appearance it was at least hygienic vanity.

It can hardly be doubted that he knew what a fine figure he presented. He was far too intelligent to preen himself or to indulge in pompous affectations ; but he left the onlooker with the impression that he was acutely self-aware. He was confident — and his presence sustained and amplified this confidence. He had, as we should both permit and forgive, no more than a " proper pride ". Some thought him to be assertive, but he was not ; it would be more correct to observe that he could not help being dominant. He was better understood by persons more tolerant, by those who allow for a little human frailty in each mind. On a public occasion in London Berkeley once stated, " My ideal surgeon is a very handsome man of distinguished presence, a man of wide knowledge and general culture, a man of great technical skill and sound judgement, and a man of compassionate heart " : to which Sir Arthur Stanley, with kind percipience, replied, " It is not given to many people to know themselves so accurately and so well as Sir Berkeley evidently knows himself ". But it is true to say that Berkeley's remark was just as genuine as Sir Arthur's was penetrating.

As in his early days in practice, Berkeley still took great care of his physical health. He was not cranky about it ; he merely applied to it the reasoned logicality that he brought to surgery. He was abstemious in his habits. He loved good food of every variety, but at dinner he would eat sparingly of each well-cooked dish, drinking as always but a single glass of wine. He was a great drinker of water and believed in eating a lot of fruit. If busy he would often lunch in his consulting-room ; on these occasions he never took more than a few sandwiches, some fruit, and a glass of water. He loved cherries. He often arrived at Park Square at the end of the morning, having walked down from the hospital with a paper bag full of cherries that he had purchased from a street vendor on the way. Upon these he and his secretary would lunch. He ate nothing in the course of the afternoon, but he liked to drink a cup of weak tea at four o'clock.

He continued to rise betweeen six and seven and to work at his desk until eight. He would then breakfast in his dressing-gown, as he preferred, once washed and dressed, to go straight off to work. In the summer he loved to swim whenever possible. At his direction a swimming-pool had been built at the bottom of his garden ; here he loved to spend sunny afternoons with his family. Busy as he was, these occasions were infrequent ; but in the summer he would find time for a little while at the pool before going in to dress for dinner. He enjoyed tennis too : his wife was still a fair player and he himself was a good one. But he played for fun and exercise, and not to win ; he took it seriously enough for pleasure, but not so seriously as to turn himself into a bad loser. At this time of his life he managed to play golf regularly at each week-end. He approached it as he approached his tennis — he played for his own delight. He was not bad at the game but he never excelled ; he was a steady middle-handicap performer. He usually played with his old friend Mr. Oldfield, and with him was never so happy as when their golf was interspersed with bantering talk. Mr. Oldfield tells the story of how, when they were accompanied on their round by a fellow doctor, the latter remarked that they did a great deal of talking ; to which Berkeley replied, " Oh yes, you mustn't think that we come here just to play golf. We settle the affairs of the universe while we are playing."

As Berkeley grew older he found increasing consolation in the beauties of his garden. He was not a gardener himself ; he preferred to appreciate rather than to create. After his occupation of Carr Manor, he had placed the ground in the hands of Mrs. Martineau — one of the most famous garden-designers of the day — who had evolved for him one of the most beautiful gardens in Yorkshire. The terrace that ran before the house gave a glorious view of the lawns as they swept down to the distant meadows ; here Berkeley would stroll in restful contemplation when his day's work was done. It was to be his fate, in the years to come, to spend several days of each week in London. He enjoyed being there. But he always hurried home at the week's end to spend as much of Saturday and Sunday as he was able amidst his own flowers and trees. In the quietness of his garden he composed many of his speeches and in its stillness he rested his mind.

Though Berkeley loved company he and Isabel, after the war, did not do much entertaining. The delicacy of Isabel's health and the sad affliction of her increasing deafness found her easily tired by numerous company. The two of them gave garden parties for their friends, for the nurses from the hospital, and for charitable organisations of many kinds ; but within the house only their closest friends were often seen. Isabel was proud of her house and took efficient pleasure in the affairs of its management ; she had enjoyed most of all the days of housekeeping when they were first married and before prosperity had enlarged her staff. She had been happy in the knowledge that it was the work of her own hands that made Berkeley comfortable.

But when they did have friends to dinner their guests were entertained with gracious perfection. A black silk cloth covered the dining-table : upon it, in the soft warm light, the glass and silver gleamed most beautifully. The wines were good, and Berkeley's philosophic wit

R

matched their elusive bouquet. He was an admirable host ; and if he bestrode the conversation — as indeed he often did — he was justified in doing so because all found charming the diversions of his talk. He would draw everyone into the conversation ; he would dispel diffidence and make each individual feel at his or her own best ; and he had a thoughtful way of deferring to his wife. His general information exceeded Isabel's and his reading was far more wide, but all present felt that he sought her opinion upon any subject that was being discussed. And so he did. He had a profound faith in her as a touchstone of men's characters and their thoughts ; to her he would bring people for measurement and upon her estimate of them he would act ; when he and Isabel disagreed in their judgements of men it was usually upon hers and not his own that he would act.

He liked to keep the talk upon general topics. He was never interested in trivialities. Philosophy, books, and the great broad issues were the themes he liked the best. His beloved Shakespeare and his Kipling — whose books stood beside his bed — he would quote and examine with a lover's tongue. He was full of apt reference from the Bible ; he contended that in his allusion to it his memory was more precise than that of the Archbishop of Canterbury. His knowledge of the dead languages was not great. It was in fact meagre. When these were used in argument against him he would, in clever self-defence, quote the words of rough John Hunter — tremendous surgeon and anatomist in days of old — who, when taunted by Dr. Foot with his ignorance of the classics, replied, " Jesse Foot accuses me of not understanding the dead languages, but I could teach him that on the dead body which he never knew in any language dead or living ". But in his heart Berkeley, jealous that any should be more learned than himself, wished that with the careless ease of the scholar he could sprinkle his talk with Greek and Latin.

Reasonable as he was in general conversation, Berkeley was yet given to dogmatic asseveration. Having made a certain statement he would not yield. The talk might be about modern writers and he would give it as his opinion that " Winston Churchill is the greatest living writer of English prose " ; after which, no matter what others might say, he would not give an inch. But he was entirely good-humoured about it ; he was not put out when others declared him wrong. He detested the introduction of acrimony into the argument ; if bitter words were spoken he changed the matter of the talk. He never again thought so well of any man after he had once heard him display ill-temper in the verbal transactions of the dinner-table. Nor would he tolerate gossip ; petty personalities were anathema to him. He hardly ever spoke unkindly of any man ; and of those he held in poor opinion he would never speak at all. He truly took a " noble " view of all the affairs of life. He could show sympathetic understanding for man's failings without weakly condoning them.

Sometimes his guests went with him to the theatre. He himself went regularly there. For a number of years, like his loved father-in-law " Mr.", he had a box at the theatre every Friday night. There with his family, surrounded by the people of Leeds, he delighted to sit. He was easily amused and with the spontaneity of a child would laugh uproariously at the simplest jokes. He liked, too, plays that pursued a line of thought, plays that gave him something to argue about. He had a great affection

for pantomimes ; through the winter season he would go
to them many times.   He enormously admired the plays
of Noel Coward.   After he had seen several of them his
work brought him into contact with their author.   This
made him admire them more.   He liked Coward ;   he
enjoyed his company ;   and he never failed to praise his
intelligence and gentleness of nature when his name was
brought into talk.   But Berkeley's pleasure in Coward's
plays did not dispel his liking for less sophisticated things.
He went to a great many thrillers.   Though he had no
real ear for music, he went often to musical plays.   He
would sometimes go to Stratford-on-Avon to see the
plays ;   that was a favourite jaunt.   Indeed, just to be in
the theatre was his pleasure ;   to have about him the
sounds and smell of it.   In this he was happy in his
family, for his daughters Dorothy and Shelagh, and his
son Pat, had a passion for the theatre too.

After the war his extra-mural reading, always considerable, became of even greater range.   It was a marvel
how he found time to read so much.   He was so busy that
he was rarely seen sitting with a book in hand.   He was
a quick reader and mostly read in bed.   He retired early :
usually he had gone up to bed by ten.   This perhaps is
the secret, for such there appeared to be, of how he
managed to master so many books.   As in his student days,
he had only to read a book once to be able to remember
it in detail ;   even being able to give direct quotations
from it, for many years to come.   He loved books ;   not
with the devotion of the bibliophile, but with the ardour
of the collector of ideas, of one with insatiable curiosity
about his fellow men, and of one for whom the words of
the English language were a string of priceless jewels.

He was always alert to, and easily infected by, the

interests of others. Much of his reading was inspired by the incidents of conversation. His extensive reading in Egyptology was the result of casual talk with Mr. Howard Carter, the famous Egyptologist. With the enthusiasm of a schoolboy he dug into the subject, visited Egypt, and after but a little while could hold his own with any expert Egyptologist. With many other subjects he did the same ; he learnt with rapidity because his interest was perpetually fresh. His knowledge of them all was not, nor could it be, as deep as that of those who had restricted their enquiry to certain fields. Such people sometimes spoke of him contemptuously because they had detected in his learning a facile superficiality ; they accused him of trying to impress. That is not wholly fair ; he spoke with the eager arrogance of a boy because, like a boy, he was impatient to tell others of the new discoveries that had recently excited him. Even if he did not always delve far down he made up for that fact by covering a vast amount of ground ; there were few aspects of man's endeavour concerning which the words of the specialist were not comprehensible to him.

He had a lively interest in the history of surgery. Before the war this was not so. He might never have developed it had he not been called upon, as he was now, to speak before so many medical communities. His researches into the matter of these speeches quickened his interest. He found adventure in a subject that had been at first sight arid. The evolution of surgery attracted him, but, characteristically, it was the old-time surgeons themselves that held his mind in thrall. These had a fascination for him. He saw them, a great procession of man's benefactors, marching down the years. He felt the glory of history and saw himself, no longer standing

alone in the false vanity of isolation, but taking his place
in the long line, and — as he did so — turning to hold
his hand out to those who came behind.

This sentiment made even stronger his affection for
his students. To them he tried to communicate these
feelings. It is an explicable paradox that, with the years,
though he developed some vanity his surgical humility
increased ; as a man of ever-growing achievement he
had more and more to be vain about, but, as a surgeon,
in historical perspective he had an increasing realisation
of his modest place. He was one in a great line and,
when he stepped forward, he wanted another to take his
vacant place. He strove to convey his sense of these
things to his students. In pursuance of this end he gave
his best teaching — and was successful. As time went
by there came to him little tributes to the generous influence he had been : letters from the pupils he had taught.
There are many of them ; too many to set down here.
From the early nineteen-twenties here are some :

" Thank you so much for the testimonial you so
kindly wrote to me. I feel it is far above my deserts,
and I am most grateful. Thank you also for the privilege
of working under you for four months. To have done so
is a great honour, and your teaching will always inspire
me to do my best — in however humble a sphere of the
profession ! "

" I venture to lay before you my sincere thanks for all
I have received from you in my Student days — so many
things spiritual and material, so many thoughtful lessons
and so much help and inspiration."

And from one who had assisted him for several years :

". . . it has been a wonderful experience for me, and
I have thoroughly enjoyed being a member of what I am
sure was the most competent team in the world ".

A sentence that Braithwaite wrote to Berkeley I have already quoted. The letter in which it came touched Berkeley's heart and moved him to an affectionate reply of rare outspokenness. This is the rest of what Braithwaite wrote :

". . . I want you to know that the fifteen years I have been so closely associated with you have been years of the greatest pride in my association as well as years of perfect happiness. You have given me absolute freedom in every way. . . . You have stimulated me to do things I could never have done otherwise and you have set before me an example in devotion to work and to school which I shall hope to follow as far as I can — and I want to thank you for all these things. . . . When I look back as I must some day on my career, believe me you will fill the greater and the better part of the picture. I cannot tell you how proud I have been to have been near you all these years and to have shared a little in your glory."

In the success that Braithwaite won, Berkeley, when it came, must have been happy. He must have been pleased to see his teaching fully justified. But not in precept alone did he help his students : he helped too in other ways. There are those who say that Berkeley was mean — and he did indulge in some seemingly unnecessary economies — but there are letters that speak of hidden, generous things :

" Please accept this first instalment of the debt I owe you, with my heartfelt thanks to you for your kindness and my apologies for being so remiss in showing my gratitude in a more tangible form. . . ."

" At last I send the remaining twenty pounds of the money you so kindly lent me when I was a student. The memory of your kindness will always be with me and I shall never be out of your debt. It has worried me a

little not to have paid any interest on your loan —
although you never treated it as a business transaction.
Perhaps, when I am better off, you will accept a donation
towards your Lame Dog Fund ? "

In these years Berkeley transmitted his faith not only
to those who regularly worked with him but also to many
surgeons who came to see him work ; and, as this next
letter shows, to the humble as well as the famous he
offered his best :

". . . It is impossible for me to attempt to describe
my gratitude to yourself and to the other member of the
Infirmary Staff, for all the kindness which has been
shown to me, a totally unknown and junior surgeon ; I
have never experienced even the half of what I may
describe as ' the surgical hospitality ' that I have received
in Leeds, in any other centre. . . . It is an impertinence
for me to express any opinion with regard to such an
unrivalled master of the art as yourself, and I refrain
from so doing, except (very indirectly) thus — I have
now an ideal far higher than I possessed forty-eight hours
ago."

These letters tell of the impression Berkeley made on
those who came in contact with him. No less instructive
are his own letters about the surgical life. He is here
writing to a lady who is about to marry a surgeon ; in
this letter is his interpretation of the journey that lies
ahead of a young surgeon and his wife :

" A great trust is to be in your hands. —— has all
the capacity to be the greatest surgeon in this country.
The ascent of such pinnacles is an arduous task and it
calls not only for unswerving diligence, but for surrender.
So many things upon which a man may set his heart
have quietly but unfalteringly to be set aside. The eyes
must be fixed unwaveringly upon the summit, and nothing
else outside the home may intrude to prove a handicap.

You are young, made for happiness, and some sacrifice will be yours also. But you must not mind. The greatest work lies in service, and —— can serve not only his own people here, but all humanity, by the gifts he can bestow upon the cause to which he devotes his life. I have the very highest admiration for him and great affection for you both. And I want, above most things, to see him fulfil a great destiny, and to rest secure upon the heights. Help him all you can, my dear, especially when it is hard to do so, and some day, not far distant, the greatest of all rewards will come, the gratitude and benediction of all mankind."

This was not only advice, it was retrospect as well ; that was the road Berkeley himself and Isabel had travelled. And Berkeley did now enjoy the gratitude of many men. He would be a poor surgeon who did not receive from some of his patients letters that touched his heart. In reading letters written to Berkeley by his patients it must not be thought that he was exceptional in receiving such tributes. But, because it is unlikely that any letters ever came to any surgeon expressing a deeper gratitude, the reader will surely know Berkeley better if he is allowed to see some of them. Berkeley gave the best of himself to every patient, and the letters came to him from persons of every sort — not alone from either public or private patients, but from every class and kind.

In the summer of 1921 Mr. Jack Hobbs — one of the greatest batsmen England has ever had, and one of the most beloved of the cricket crowds — was taken ill while playing in Leeds. He was operated upon by Berkeley, and the occasion made almost as great a stir in the press as would have done an illness of the most famous politician of the day. Berkeley was impressed by the modesty of the man who was the most outstanding figure in English

national sport ; he regarded his association with Hobbs
as one of the happiest events in his professional life. Pat,
then at school, basked in the reflected glory of a father
who had operated upon England's opening batsman.
Only those who know what England is like when in the
grip of Test Match fever can imagine the excitement there
must have been in the Moynihan family when this letter
was received :

" DEAR SIR BERKELEY,
    " I made a trip to the Oval on Saturday to see a
little of the Test Match and I brought the cricket ball I
promised you for your son away with me. At the same
time I got the autographs of both teams (England and
Australia) on a cricket bat for him. . . . I feel sure he
would like to keep it as a souvenir. . . . I'm sure you
will be glad to hear I am getting on splendidly. . . . I
should like to offer you, Sir Berkeley, my sincere thanks
and at the same time congratulate you on the successful
operation you performed upon me. I feel sure I can
never be grateful enough for your kindness to me and for
the kind consideration shewn to my wife. . . . I shall
never cease to wonder over the fact that I suffered so
little pain and inconvenience afterwards. . . .
                " Believe me, Sir Berkeley,
                        " Yours very truly,
                                " J. B. HOBBS "

Berkeley had operated upon so many wounded soldiers
that, in justice to them all, it would be a pity not to quote
a letter from one of them. This letter was written in
1920 :

" DEAR SIR,
    " It is just a year ago since you first operated and
removed the shrapnel from my lung, and is three months
since I was discharged from the General Infirmary at
Leeds. I have been away convalescent and have now

returned home greatly improved in health. Before having the shrapnel removed I was gradually getting worse, but I was told many times that it was in much too dangerous a position to be removed. I feel, therefore, that it is all due to your skill and the good nursing at the L.G.I. that to-day I am so much better. I can enjoy life now, and am steadily improving. I feel I cannot let the first anniversary of the operation pass without expressing my gratitude and sincere thanks to you, for all your skill and care, and your kindness to me during the last twelve months."

From a patient in the public wards of Leeds Infirmary came this letter to give reflection to Berkeley's treatment of the humble and obscure :

" SIR B. MOYNIHAN,
    " I take this my first opportunity since I left the Infirmary of writing you a few lines, hoping you will long remain a source of joy and comfort to the suffering humanity who is coming and will continue to come under your care, and that those who succeed you will be equally as gifted and successful as you are. I am delighted to inform you that I am out of all danger, and on the straight road to recovery, and that I can now enjoy a beef steak as well as I did at any time of my life. You are the only man who heartily recommended and then performed the operation on me on ——.
    " You are, therefore, the only man whom I can heartily thank for its successful end.
    " I have but very little more to say on this subject, except that words in my opinion would fail to sufficiently thank you. I should much prefer to make you a small present, only a token or keepsake on which you could look with pleasure in years to come and say, ' A man whose life I saved made me a present of this '.
    " If I had my choice the Keepsake would consist of a gold mounted ebony walking-stick. The inscription on the mount will faithfully represent, as far as the limited

space will permit, as much as possible of your acknowledged worth. If you think of anything more suitable,
you have only to say so, and you will be as welcome to
it as the flowers in May. Please appoint the time and
place, and I shall make it my business to go and present
you with either your choice or mine, I care not which."

How Berkeley must have loved that letter !

In the nursing home in Hyde Terrace, Berkeley would
spend hours — not working, but in talk beside his patient's
bed. He could never be persuaded to sit down : he
always stood — often for as much as an hour at a time.
There he would talk about everything under the sun
until, forgetting his or her own woes and troubles — the
inner secret of recovery —, the patient's mind would cease
to fret. Each of Berkeley's patients was to him a very
special human being, someone loving and loved, and not
just an exemplar of disease. Here is a story of healing
by mind as well as hand :

" Dear Sir Berkeley,

   " My heart is so full that it is difficult to express
adequately how truly thankful we are for all you have
done for my dear wife and also for your great personal
kindness to us in our anxiety.

   " You are so busy that it would not be kind to trouble
you with a long letter and indeed mere words cannot add
to the strength of our feelings of deep gratitude.

   " The extent to which your extraordinary experience
and skill enable you to be the means of relieving suffering
and changing trouble into happiness must be some com-
pensation for the enormous strain of your professional
life. . . ."

It is easy, and not entirely wrong, to say that the sentiments of those without medical knowledge are but a poor
guide to a surgeon's actual powers. The most crude,
clumsy, and ill-considered operation may bring from the

patient, in his pathetic ignorance, most heartfelt thanks. But in the opinion of his fellow doctors is true judgement ; if they approve, the surgeon, in honest endeavour, has touched the stars. Doctors admired Berkeley's skill, but those he operated upon even more admired the man. They then perceived better than ever Berkeley's essential attitude to surgery — the attitude that found expression in his remark to the surgeon who boasted that, in a series of operations, he had lost but one in every hundred cases, " You speak with pride of a mortality of one per cent. But suppose *you* were the *one* in someone else's hundred ! " The letter that follows was written to Berkeley by a titled physician — one of the most famous doctors in England. He had placed himself in Berkeley's hands. His words speak of the absolute authority of precise knowledge :

" DEAR SIR BERKELEY,
        " A line not only to let you know that I have duly arrived . . . but more especially to say how deeply grateful I am to you for your very great kindness to me.
        " I had quite made up my mind when the question of operation arose that there was no one in Europe (nor even in America for that matter, *pace* the Mayo brothers) into whose hands I could put myself with such complete confidence as in yours. You have not only spared me operation, but helped me in every way to recovery and made me feel that a great surgeon may be something more than a great operator. I wish that the rising generation of surgeons would realise this : I feel sure that those who are lucky enough to work with you must learn it from seeing it.
        " I shall not forget your goodness to me. . . ."

*   *   *   *   *

Without the confirmation of good nursing a surgeon's work cannot succeed. Upon the nurse's care depends the patient's strength to support the architecture of the surgeon's operation. It is the harmony of the surgeon and his nurses working in mutual regard that, in the patient's ears, sounds the music of health regained. Berkeley knew how much he depended for his good results upon his nurses' work ; and he paid to them the tribute of his appreciation. When a patient, upon leaving the nursing home, thanked him for his help, he would remind him that the debt was to the nurses as well as to himself. He always supported his nurses and would never let unjust criticism be directed at them. They held him in some awe, not because he was ever harsh, but because he was particular that every detail of his instructions should be exactly carried out. Although if things were wrongly done his reproof was given privately and not in unkind terms ; for the theatre sister in Hyde Terrace could say of him, " I never saw him cross, and he never found fault ". But he demanded of his nurses an application to duty no less strenuous than his own. He could not, at times, have realised the tax he placed upon their powers ; he, untired, would operate without interruption for many hours at a stretch, and during that time he would not submit to any relaxation in the efficiency of his nurses. He " worked them like galley-slaves ", but was always kind to them and grateful for their help.

He was careful to protect them from the burden of unreasonable responsibility. He never caused them to worry by leaving his sick patients for long unvisited. Most of the nurses who worked with him said that they never knew a surgeon who visited his patients so often. At night on his way home to Carr Manor, after having been to some theatre or dinner in Leeds, he would invariably call in at Hyde Terrace on the way. There, in the late night, he would prowl from room to room, seeing that all his cases were comfortable and that all was well. On one such night, when the nursing staff was short and there were many dressings to be done, he himself rolled up his sleeves and dressed the wounds of all his patients with his own hands ; when all was done he turned to the sister and said, " I haven't enjoyed myself so much for ages — not since I was a resident in the hospital ! " Hyde Terrace was his favourite place in which to operate. There he knew his nurses well, and they, by long usage, knew his every little habit — and by knowing it eased his way. But he still occasionally operated in a private house ; though he would only do so at the request of those faithful doctors who had sent him cases in his earliest days. When he did so go out he always took with him Miss Bertha Reid, his favourite nurse. He had perfect confidence in her and she helped him to perform operations even in remote farmhouses on the Yorkshire moors. Wherever they went his equanimity was never disturbed. He would operate by the light of an oil-lamp upon a patient laid on a kitchen table, with the same calm assurance that he displayed beneath the brilliant lights of the Infirmary theatre.

If one of his nurses should be taken ill and have to leave her work, Berkeley would show, by little acts of kind remembrance, that he hoped for her quick return to health and work. He would call in her sick-room with a bunch of flowers, a book, or just a cheerful word — leaving the patient with the happy feeling that she was needful to him in the best conduct of his tasks. Upon her he would, while in the room, focus his sincere attention, so that she felt his visit to be one of real affection and no mere casual courtesy.

Berkeley Moynihan

His thoughts about nurses he crystallised in a speech he made when presenting the prizes at the Annual Distribution to the Nursing Staff of the Leeds General Infirmary in 1921. He entitled his remarks " The Most Gentle Profession ", and this is what he said :

" The memory of unpleasing things is very tenacious. A century ago an operation was attended by a variety of circumstances calculated to arouse dismay and keen anxiety in every heart ; and to-day the very word ' operation ' sends a shudder through many of those who learn that it is to be their early destiny. And this dread continues, though you and I know that an operation is an act of gentlest mercy, guided and determined by the utmost skill, inspired and controlled at every stage by compassion for the sufferer. To the word ' nurse ' a similar obloquy attaches. Even now the word conjures up in some minds the picture of a bibulous and crapulous hag, unversed in the simplest rudiments of her art and indifferent and insensible to the needs of others. Her picture has been drawn by many hands ; it was coarsely exaggerated, no doubt, even in Dickens' day, but the recollection of it is still fresh in many minds, though you and I know that the nurse of to-day is one of the most gracious and most competent of women, and that the profession of nursing now attracts the best type of womanhood that this country can produce.

" But those of you who leave this hospital to go out into the world to nurse must not be surprised if you find that you are not welcomed with that open, eager enthusiasm to which your training and your experience will fully entitle you. In your hospital life you are the despots, most merciful despots it is true, of all your patients, who conform with no word of denial or contumacy to all that is demanded of them or imposed upon them. They accept without question the discipline of the hospital and the beneficent rule of its officers. Of your work in private much will have to be done in the

256

homes of your patients. Happily the day is almost past when an operation of any magnitude has to be performed in the unsuitable surroundings of a private house, with all the makeshifts and dangers inseparable from such work. But the convalescence of surgical cases and the whole course of a grave medical illness will be passed in a private house to whose rules and customs you will be expected to conform, in which, however great your competence and however congenial your society, you are an intruder. You will be compelled, looking only to your patient's welfare, to intervene between him and his friends, often running counter to their wishes and their normal practice as you shelter him from their well-meant but harmful attentions. It will be one of your many testing times, when you will require all the gifts, all the tact, and all the accomplishments that your natural aptitude, or your long training, have conferred upon you.

" How are you to fit yourself for such tasks, or to become competent to undertake with highest success all the manifold and arduous responsibilities that lie ahead of you ? First, you will need knowledge. To gain it in an adequate degree you will require intellectual powers of no mean order and industry above the average. There is much to be learnt of anatomy, of physiology, of medicine, and of surgery ; of the principles which underlie the technical work you will daily practise. You will have to avoid the little knowledge which is dangerous by delving as deeply as you can into those things which apply most nearly to your own tasks. It is better to learn intimately the relevant matters than to have a smattering of many things that it is not within your strict province to know. But knowledge which is within the reach of everyone who truly seeks it will avail you little unless it leads you along the way to wisdom. Wisdom implies the timely and rightful application of knowledge. Knowledge may even be a pitfall or an encumbrance unless you learn to use it justly. To gain wisdom is of all tasks in life the most difficult, and it is certainly no less arduous in nursing than in many of life's other activities. You will be foiled and rebuffed and disheartened, not once but many times, as you toil earnestly after it, for the application of the truths you have learnt may be so diverse, the reactions so unexpected and perplexing, and the personal aspects of them so capricious, that you may think of wisdom as Frascatorius did of the beating of the heart — that it ' is so difficult as to be only comprehended by God '.

" You will have duties, fewer than they formerly were, which may appear menial or degrading, and they will sometimes need to be carried out upon those who are the mere wreckage of humanity. But drudgery may be a blessed thing, and you may derive consolation from the remembrance of One who thought it no ill task to wash the feet of the humblest of people. And you will perhaps day after day, especially in your early years, be almost dead with fatigue, embittered by the disappointments of a case that has gone wrong, or wounded by a rebuke that has escaped from the lips of someone as weary and disheartened as yourself. Yet all the time you must show your best side, for you cannot give real help to others if you seem careworn or dejected. You must learn to bring an air of pleasure to the pursuit of duty. And so by degrees you will learn that it is not only knowledge, or even wisdom, but also, and chiefly, character that counts. You will learn to deal faithfully, stubbornly, and with untiring zeal with all your difficulties, and the word ' trouble ' will vanish from your vocabulary. No patient can ever cause you ' trouble ' if you remember that what is a daily and perhaps monotonous event to you is the great event and perhaps the sternest trial of a lifetime to him. Your patient's needs are your opportunity.

" You will soon divine the great secret that in many patients who are seriously ill the restraints which adult life impose upon us all, fall away. The qualities of child-hood again emerge ; there is a trustful dependence upon others ; there is great need of sympathy and understanding ; there may be a little petulance, a little fretfulness, a querulous demand for many things unsuitable. You may need great patience, infinite gentleness, unfailing forbearance, if you are to read your patient aright, and to serve him to the utmost of your capacity. Service is the noblest function of man. And to render the highest service you must attune yourself spiritually with your patients, so that you may read their hearts, discover their motives, divine their impulses, and lead them at last to realise that you stand loyally behind them, or beside them, to help them, not over against them to thwart them. And at all times you must keep reticence. Many secrets that have perhaps been most jealously guarded will be disclosed to you, and many of the most sacred mysteries will be revealed. You will preserve an inviolable silence. For taciturnity is an ornament, and in silence there is security ; if you repent once of your silence you will repent ten times of your speech. You will find help from the 39th Psalm, ' I will take heed to my ways that I offend not in my tongue. I will keep my mouth as it were with a bridle.' To chatter of those intimate things you learn under the seal of the confessional as you work is a degradation of your calling. Gossip tainted with slander is the last and meanest infirmity of empty minds.

" Such are some of the qualities required by a nurse, and this then is the nurse's office. To be ready in all emergency, quick and competent in action, courteous in speech, considerate in thought ; a comfort in hours of sorrow, an inspiration and encouragement in times of gloom ; to give ease to many a weary body and solace to many a troubled heart ; to lift with strong and gentle hands a heavy load of anguish from those who falter and stumble in despair. It is to be a beacon of hope, a rock of refuge and a tower of strength.

" If your attainments are these and your work of this high order, you are members of a profession than which none is gentler or nobler. Your watchwords become ' service and self-surrender '. You do not seek reward or selfish gain. Your work will be done in a professional spirit ; it will be done, not in the most meagre way for the utmost gain, but with all the energy and truth that you can put into it. The true rewards of honest work are neither to be seen nor handled, they are not measured by a gold standard nor by any material result. They are not acclaimed by the applause of the crowd. They lie within you ; in your own knowledge that you have done your best, that you have striven to reach your own standard of your highest powers. You will often, perhaps always, fail to reach your own ideal ; but be comforted. Ideals are not for attainment, but for pursuit.

" If you enter a profession and become adept and worthy members of it you should receive the proper recognition to which your work entitles you. The time is now ripe, in my opinion, for acceptance by some academic body which shall control the training and direct the teaching of the nursing profession, and in due time confer authority by licence, or diploma, or degree, upon those who have attained the standard of efficiency that is considered adequate. Your work, whether regarded as an intellectual task or a technical accomplishment demanding the exercise of fine craftsmanship, fully entitles the nursing profession to make such a demand as this. If such a recognition comes, then will follow a result I have long desired to see. There will be a grading of nurses by qualification as there is a grading of medical men. It is, I think, just as necessary that a sister in charge of a ward, a theatre sister, or a matron in a teaching hospital should bear evidence in her qualification of longer study and more careful training as it is in the case of the medical staff of a teaching hospital. Until some system of supervision of the training of all who may call themselves nurses and of the registration and qualification by diploma or degree is introduced, the nursing profession will not be cleansed from those impurities which still unhappily attach to it.

" In Leeds you are fortunate in your school. The training through which you pass here is as long, as arduous, as it is anywhere in the world. And the honour of your school is of the highest ; it has been created, maintained, and increased by the great multitude of your predecessors. Remember that you will carry with you, wherever you go, the honour and good repute of your school. Every one among you can add to that store of honour or detract from it. Leeds will be judged by your work and by your demeanour. And when the time comes for you to lay your work aside the highest praise that can be given to you will be that you have worthily upheld the high traditions of your own school and the dignity of the most gentle profession."

The State registration of nurses has since then come. The weaknesses to which Berkeley referred have been eradicated. And for the fact that these things have come to pass Berkeley deserves a share of the credit. He espoused this cause and brought to it all the persistent reformer's zeal that he brought to so many other medical causes. In this, as in many other things, by the stubbornness of his unwearied advocacy he helped to change the spirit and the rules that had dominated the world of medicine as he had found it when he first qualified.

*　　*　　*　　*　　*

In 1924 the University of Leeds came of age. One feature of the associated celebrations was a speech by Berkeley, which he entitled " The Contributions of Leeds to Surgery ". In it, after a brief survey of the history of surgery, Berkeley passed in review the surgeons who had been on the staff of the Leeds General Infirmary since its foundation. The lives of these men had for some time occupied Berkeley's interest, and two years earlier he had endowed a gold medal — to be given to the best Leeds student of the year in medicine and surgery — in memory

of William Hey, one of the surgical founders of the
hospital, a man whose son and grandson were also in
their turn upon the staff. The greatest charm of the
speech is in those passages in which Berkeley speaks of
the men who had been his own teachers, the men he
himself had known personally. These men came at the
time when Lister's principles of antisepsis were first
receiving general approbation : the greatest era in the
history of surgery. These were Berkeley's words :

". . . Surgery was now equipped for its great adventure. The science of pathological anatomy had established upon the only sure foundation, our knowledge
concerning the morbid processes responsible for the symptoms of which a patient made complaint and for the signs
which were disclosed when an examination was made.
Treatment could therefore deal with structural changes
which had been carefully studied. Operations were
rendered painless by anaesthesia, and safe by the
application of the antiseptic method. The advance that
surgery had made in its relief of human suffering, and
the prolongation of human life, is incomparable. Nothing
that has happened in the world since the birth of time
has meant so much in matters of human happiness and
welfare. What is the part that Leeds has played in all
this great revolution ? At the time when Lister was
introducing his methods Mr. Wheelhouse (1826–1908)
and Mr. Teale (1832–1923) were surgeons from 1864 to
1884. Both contributed new thoughts and new methods
to surgery. None of us who knew Mr. Wheelhouse are
ever likely to forget him. He was the most punctual man
alive. Arriving at the Infirmary less than one minute
before eight in the morning, he raised his hand to arrest
the porter hastening to sound his bell, and admonished
him to wait for the town-hall clock. His bell and the
hour struck together. His demeanour was of the most
solid gravity : his speech slow and of a solemnity that

made one listen with awe to the emphatic announcement of the time of day or the state of the weather. I heard him speak also at medical meetings. What he said seemed, as one afterwards recalled it, to contain no message of any value, but one almost held one's breath as one listened to its massive and deliberate utterance. I saw him operate on a few occasions only ; he moved, as he spoke, with the utmost deliberation and emphasis. On one occasion I helped him in a very minor biblical operation. I gave the baby chloroform and assisted at the same time. The operation was done in the ward, and as he walked away with the same brooding sense of the vast and profound significance of every act, I listened to the minutely detailed account of the difficulties that had been encountered in this very operation ; of cases in which the operation, full of hazards, had been abandoned by no less a man than Tom Nunneley ; and of the deaths that had followed upon delayed haemorrhage. By the time we stood upon the doorstep I was the victim of a profound nervous exhaustion, and I felt that the least I could do, in view of the threatening dangers ahead of me, was then and there most solemnly to vow that never would I suffer my own slender skill and my unripe experience to embark upon so menacing an operation as that which I had just witnessed.

" Once as I walked past the theatre door with him he asked who was operating. I said ' Mr. Teale ; and the operation is a lithotrity '. He stopped at once, and with a gentle push upon my arm he bade me enter the theatre and watch ' the most beautiful little hands in England ' at work. The description was not, I think, inaccurate. Wheelhouse's originality was shown in his suggestion of a new method for dealing with stricture of the urethra. ' Wheelhouse's operation ' is known to this day, and if not practised with such frequency as formerly it is because the conditions requiring it are prevented by more careful treatment of the disease in its earliest stages. Mr. Teale and Sir Clifford Allbutt formed the first alliance known

263

to me in this country. They were the pioneers of ' team work '. Sir Clifford, the most deeply learned physician of his day, master of a style of English which for sheer beauty and majesty is perhaps unmatched by that of any scientific author of our generation ; an orator whose speech makes Time seem hasty ; a cultured, upright, English gentleman, is the pride of the school he served so long and loves so well. Mr. Teale was the authentic product of Winchester and Oxford [to which Berkeley had sent his son], and I know nothing better than that. He was the flawless example of intellectual and moral integrity. He was modest, cautious, reserved ; free from any jealousies, ready with words of encouragement, and an occasional word of praise. . . . I learnt much from Mr. Teale, for whom I had a deep affection. He was a most courtly, truthful, upright gentleman — a man who honours his calling, and whose noble example is not soon forgotten.

" Mr. Jessop (1837–1903) was beyond question the most popular practitioner in Yorkshire for a quarter of a century. His experience was gigantic, in medicine no less than in surgery. He was in general practice during the whole of his period of office as surgeon to the Leeds General Infirmary (1870–90), and his consulting practice was almost as large on the medical as on the surgical side. He was the greatest man I have ever known in our profession, for to his massive qualities of intellect he added a grandeur of character unsurpassed. Though I knew him as well as any man, I never heard a heartless word or an ungenerous estimate pass his lips. But his silence could be full of awe ; and when need arose he could denounce with devastating emphasis the acts or the qualities he believed to be evil. In his examination of a case he left nothing undetermined ; he was methodical, comprehensive, deliberate. That completed, he would discuss the diagnosis, or the treatment, with the utmost circumspection ; nothing in the history or in the signs had escaped him ; there was never a need to look again or to feel again. Every detail was remembered and its value measured. All men considered his judgement as the final one, and popular sentiment was not alone in feeling that if Mr. Jessop had not seen a case there still remained something to be done and a gleam of hope was still to be found even in the gloomiest outlook. He was indisputably the best, and the safest, operator on the staff. He had developed a technique which for those days was good. His hands were strong, gentle, yet compelling. He was imperturbable. No crisis — and there were such events in his time — ever disturbed his perfect tranquillity of speech or action. He never knew the name of any assistant or house-surgeon, and addressed everyone as ' Mister '. This became in time his own title, and as ' Mister ' he was known to many generations of students and residents, who regarded him with the deepest admiration and respect, and with, perhaps, a shade of fear. He, too, was a pioneer. He recorded the first case of successful extirpation of a growth in the kidney in this country, and the first case in which an operation upon a patient with advanced extra-uterine gestation saved both mother and child. He was vice-president of the Royal College of Surgeons in 1901."

Then, after speaking of some other men, Berkeley came to his peroration — in which he summed up his fundamental views on surgery :

". . . Perilous as it may be to say so, I believe that the paths which we now follow have been explored nearly to the end. The methods of surgery can scarcely be made more safe than they are to-day. Operations of the utmost severity are performed by the great masters with an absence of risk that leaves little hope of betterment. The chief risk in surgery to-day comes from delay. But though as a measure of therapy the surgical art has now approached perfection, as the handmaid of medicine, as an instrument of scientific research, it has still very much to do. Immense though its achievements in this respect have been, we need in these days a broader method. Experimental research, in spite of its occasional fallacies, must march along with us, and the mass of evidence afforded by our surgical work must undergo a wider and closer scrutiny. Clinical and experimental research we needs must have, both extensive and intensive. These are functions of a university, and to our own university we have but now made our plea. When our centenary is celebrated I pray that the speaker who will then take this place of mine may be able truthfully to claim that, great as were the achievements in the early days of our School of Medicine, they have been far surpassed by the labours of our successors."

A few days after this speech Berkeley received a letter from Sir Clifford Allbutt — who had left Leeds to become Regius Professor of Medicine at Cambridge — in which the latter said :

". . . I must do more than thank you for your too kind words concerning myself. Such words from a friend, if too generous, are none the less very agreeable to read. And I was glad to see full justice at last done to my old friend Mr. Jessop. He was Resident Medical Officer at the Old Infirmary when I was elected on the Staff, and helped me in scores of ways, as I was a novice off whom he might have scored had he chosen to shew off ! He made so great a reputation there that on commencing practice he was almost mobbed ; and he and Wheelhouse both made the mistake of not cutting off the tail ends of their practices. Jessop nearly broke down in the first two or three years ; he came in to me late one night utterly exhausted — heart in extreme disorder. In later times I remember his coming into Meanwood near midnight, after a long country journey, to attend an ordinary case of childbirth ! Wheelhouse was as bad ; I remember seeing him going up the Chapeltown Road in his brougham, he asleep inside, the coachman asleep on the box, and the horses also asleep, all progressing by

' subconscious reflexes'. One night Wheelhouse was called to Wakefield [a neighbouring town] about nine o'clock ; hearing the shout ' Wakefield ! ' he got out to find it was 2.30 A.M. ! He had been taken to Wakefield, shunted, carried back to Leeds, shunted again, made up into a new train in a siding, and taken back to Wakefield. Luckily he heard the shout at last or would have gone on to London ! Just worn out ! . . . I saw William Hey's last few operations. . . . He was a marvellously accurate operator. In those days the Staff operated as a whole, all putting their dirty fingers into interesting wounds, and exhaling vapours from their unwashed woollen dressing-gowns ! They frankly criticised each other during operation. I remember Sam Smith say to Hey, ' Mind, mind, your saw is just through ! ' Mr. Hey turned the leg up and calmly said, ' Oh ! plenty of room yet ', and sawed on another quarter of an inch. . . . On one of my first consultations I was to meet Wheelhouse ; I arrived on the doorstep to see W., with his watch in his hand, saying ' Late, Sir, this will never do ! ' It was two minutes after the hour ; but it was a good lesson to me and I believe that I was never late again at a consultation by my own fault. If Wheelhouse had cut off his general practice he would have been a great man. . . . Again, did you know of his early — first ? — nerve repair ? The man who sat down three years before on a scythe ! and came with a solid puckered scar on the buttock and a useless leg. W. cut out the scar and drew the far apart nerve-ends together, with recovery of motion and sensation."

Once interest is aroused in earlier medical men and in the institutions that they built, it cannot help but increase in intensity, except in the most unimaginative minds, as the years go by. To the doctor's daily tasks it gives new colour ; as he employs each new discovery ghostly figures from the past share his excitement ; he works not alone but in a glorious company. This Berkeley felt ; this all those who love medicine also feel. In that fact is sufficient excuse — if such is at all required — for quoting another letter that Berkeley received in 1922. It tells of the early days of the Mayo clinic in America ; and because Berkeley loved the Mayos he treasured the letter, and would wish to see it here. The Mayo clinic is one of the greatest surgical institutes the world has ever seen ; its adventure was surgery's adventure — and so Berkeley's adventure too. Dr. R. C. Coffey of Portland, Oregon, — friend and admirer of Berkeley — wrote :

". . . I have just spent a few very delightful days in the home of W. J. Mayo at Rochester where I heard your name frequently and delightfully mentioned. He is the same charming great man we have known so many years and whose combined qualities of statesman, diplomat, captain of industry, financier and surgeon have been blended into one tremendous force, the like of which has never been known and probably never will be known again in connection with the science and art of healing.

". . . The hard times, particularly noticeable in the agricultural district of the middle west, has not failed to make its impression on this institution in some ways, but each time I go there I am amazed at the changes and improvements which have been made since my previous visit. Since I was there nearly two years ago, a most remarkable transformation has taken place. Buildings to the amount of millions of dollars have been constructed. Literally, hundreds of doctors and many hundreds of other employees are engaged in the various lines of research and clinical practice. Departments in all lines of medicine are being installed. Instead of being a purely surgical organization, scores and scores of people are employed in the department of internal medicine. The teaching and the scientific work is immeasurably better than I have ever seen there before. . . .

" While the Mayos themselves are just as skilful in

their work and just as fond of it, they have ceased to be the entire show. They still draw the largest audiences but the doctors and other guests now are scattered throughout nearly a dozen operating theatres which have just recently been completed.

". . . As I viewed this mammoth organization, I could not refrain from retrospection which led me back to the time when you and I first began to visit there nearly twenty years ago. The organization was small and consisted of two parts, Will and Charlie. The old doctor, who was then 90 years of age, sitting in the front office in his armchair, entertaining the visiting doctors with tales of early pioneer days which automatically led up to the present organization. Among these tales, I remember his story of the hanging of some forty or fifty Indians by the Vigilantes among which was a very large Indian, about six feet six. After the hanging the old gentleman procured the body of the big Indian and boiled the skeleton carefully and used it for teaching his boys anatomy. I remember that some doctor who was quizzing him suggested that he should feel very proud of his sons. ' Well ', he said, ' I don't know about that, I think they should feel very proud of me.'

" There was only one person in the Pathological Department, a woman doctor by the name of Dr. Herb, I believe. Miss Alice M'Gaw, Will's anaesthetizer, did the book-keeping and Old Jay, who helped to raise the boys, ran the offices with a rather high hand in the capacity of janitor.

" Very early in their development, they quit operating or attending patients on Sunday. A doctor from out in Dakota brought a patient and demanded to see one of the Mayos. Jay informed him that they were resting out in the country and could not be seen. The doctor became enraged and threatened to take his patient on to Chicago. Jay, not to be outdone, said, ' Take your patient and go to H——. We have all the patients we want anyway.' "

269

Berkeley's affection for the Mayos had grown steadily with the years ; they had now long been his friends. They had seen great days, and done tremendous things. Their work was in the grand style and manner Berkeley loved. He himself launched surgery on vast projects and laboured homerically. After Berkeley's death one of the most brilliant of his assistants wrote of him :

" There can be few men in the history of surgery who have influenced surgical procedure in Great Britain more profoundly than Moynihan. He arrived at the crest of the wave of surgical advance that has taken place during the last forty years, and he possessed qualities which enabled him to take supreme advantage of his opportunities. So far from suffering from ' provincialism ' in Leeds, conditions there enabled him to create surgical clinics, in hospital and private practice, such as he could hardly have achieved in London, where the one-man clinic is manifestly unsuitable. Moynihan's intellect and personality inevitably drove him to dominate his associates and surroundings, and he would not have fitted easily into the surgical community of a London teaching hospital."

*   *   *   *   *

During the years immediately following the war Berkeley's profession paid him many honourable tributes for the great services he had rendered to surgery and his country between 1914 and 1918. In the written word of one of his most famous colleagues was embodied the opinion of nearly all his fellow surgeons :

". . . for I took it you knew, and if not you *ought to know* that you are, in the opinion of those who are best able to judge, *facile princeps*, the member of the civil profession who has come out most brilliantly in connection with the War, and so far as I know, and I think I know pretty well, almost the only one who has not with his success collected a certain amount of jealousy and criticism — *and I always knew you would if your chance came !* "

Two honours that he dearly cherished came to him on the same day — October 11th, 1920. On that day, in the presence of the American College of Surgeons at its meeting in Montreal, he performed two great ceremonies : on behalf of the Consulting Surgeons of the British Armies he presented the American College of Surgeons with a Great Mace, and he delivered before the same body the first John B. Murphy Oration in Surgery.

The Mace had been carried to Canada by Berkeley and two other British surgeons — Sir William Taylor and Mr. Albert Carless. It was a remarkably beautiful piece of work. It was designed to tell in symbolic language of the close union between British and American surgery, and of the ties which unite Great Britain and Canada to the United States of America.

The speech with which Berkeley accompanied the presentation was one of the most felicitous of his life. It made a profound impression upon the company. These are the words he spoke :

" Three centuries ago, on this very day, a little sailing vessel, leaving England far behind her, was struggling against adverse winds and heavy seas towards America. On board were one hundred pilgrims fleeing from civil and religious tyranny to seek sanctuary and freedom in a new land. No voyage in history has been so fateful. Those who journeyed in that vessel, a chosen company on the horizon of your history, were the best of English stock. They helped to found here a small colony of people, grim and stoical in spirit, yet touched with idealism. Though all the great countries of the earth have since given of their best to build this nation, those few pilgrims have left their indelible stamp upon the culture, the institutions, and the laws of this land.

" Almost a century and a half ago that colony broke away from the Mother Country, with which it was long at war. But one hundred years of peace between the two nations had been celebrated when, in 1917, they stood together in arms. War is the Great Revealer. We learnt in that great testing-time of our race that ties of blood, when they mean kinship in spirit and an equal surrender to the noblest impulse, are never to be broken. In the Great War America and the Empire mingled their blood upon the same stricken field. The hope then grew strong in many hearts that a new understanding born of comradeship in battle, fiercely tested in the furnace of affliction, and sealed in death, would redeem the ancient blunders, blot out the bitter memories of wrong, and lead at last to a supreme and permanent reconciliation. For we seemed then to realise that deep down in the hearts, enthroned in the conscience of the two peoples, there was the same full eager devotion to eternal principle, love of justice, joy in liberty, hatred of oppression ; the same unselfish determination to strive for the redemption of mankind, and to establish anew the freedom of the world. On the fields of Flanders and of France, as in the cabin of the *Mayflower*, humanity recovered its rights.

" In the grave and anxious days of war, when we fought so long in fellowship, no associations were closer, no friendships more swift and intimate, no joint labours more fruitful than were those of the members of our profession coming from America and from every part of the British Empire. We then gained, each for the other, not respect and sympathy alone, but true affection also. Every lover of his country, every lover of humanity, must wish that the spiritual alliance then created shall endure to the end of time. In our desire to perpetuate the remembrance of those days of duty done together, we, the Consultant Surgeons of the Armies of Britain, ask the College of Surgeons of America, meeting in this great Dominion, to accept this Mace. We pray that you may regard it as a symbol of our union in the harsh days of trial ; as a pledge of our devotion to the same imperishable ideals ; as a witness to our unfaltering and unchanging hope that the members of our profession in the two lands shall be joined in brotherhood for ever in the service of mankind."

Colonel G. E. Armstrong, C.M.G., the President of the American College of Surgeons, replied :

" Sir Berkeley Moynihan : As President of the American College of Surgeons, I accept this beautiful Mace presented by you on behalf of the Consulting Surgeons of the British Armies, with thanks and a full appreciation of the care and thought bestowed upon its design and construction.

" We accept it as a token of the cordial relationship that obtains between the surgeons of the two great nations here represented. It is the symbol of the zeal and enthusiasm in our art that, originating in the Old World, has spread to the New.

" We shall endeavour in this western hemisphere to keep the ' Sacred Flame of Science ' burning not less brightly than have our forebears in Great Britain. It will remain with us as an emblem of unity, a work of art, a remembrance of the united effort of the two great English-speaking nations to give truth, liberty, and justice to all peoples and to all nations.

" The scientific fire represented in this gift welds another link in the chain that shall for ever bind us together in the great work of promoting the highest possible standard of surgery, as well as peace and good-will among men."

A few weeks later Dr. Crile wrote to Berkeley :

" My DEAR SIR BERKELEY,
" To-night I have read again your wonderful pre-sentation of the Great Mace. In that presentation you

presented a sentiment that embraces all that is worth while in our national life, in the aims of our College, and in the bonds of our cherished friendships — in that presentation you made us all feel nearer to you and all your colleagues and in the opinion of us over here you have turned a page in history.

" No splendid cause ever had a better ambassador or a more beloved. The occasion was too sacred for personal expression — and much too large in its meaning.

" Your various contributions made the Montreal meeting the greatest in the history of our College.

" Personally I was more proud of you than ever I have been and I, like all your friends — which includes everyone at the meeting — reciprocate every sentiment you expressed.

" With deepest appreciation,

" Always yours,

" G. W. CRILE "

Berkeley delivered the Murphy Memorial Oration immediately after his presentation of the Mace. In it he gave a brilliant account of Murphy the man, and told the story of surgery as it had unrolled itself until the day of Murphy's arrival. The address has been several times reprinted and will again be made available in Berkeley's collected speeches. How exactly Berkeley's estimate of Dr. Murphy's character tallied with reality has been frequently discussed by those who knew Murphy well ; but, to the occasion, Berkeley's words were beautifully appropriate. That Berkeley sincerely believed the words he spoke there can be no doubt. Berkeley desired intensely to see the best in every man. In Murphy he was satisfied that there did exist the finest attributes ; and he duly praised them. But, if he loved Murphy for the man he was, his admiration for him as a surgeon knew no bounds ; it was qualified by no considerations that admit of ques-

274

tioning. Berkeley, empowered by the authority of his own surgical supremacy, inclined to the view that Murphy was the greatest surgeon who had ever lived. Murphy, at work in his theatre, Berkeley described like this :

" And then Murphy would operate. Now, of operators there are many types, and, like every other work of art, an operation is the expression of a man's temperament and character. There are still among us ' brilliant ' operators, from whom I pray to be spared when my hour has come. For them it is the mere quality of effort that counts. Their ideal of operative surgery is something swift and infinitely dexterous, something to dazzle the beholder and excite his wonder that such things can so be done by human hands. The body of a man is the plastic material in which a surgeon works, and no art is worthy of such a medium unless it has in it something of a sacrament. Surgery of the ' brilliant ' kind is a desecration. Such art finds its proper scope in tricks with cards, in juggling with billiard-balls, and nimble encounters with bowls of vanishing gold-fish. But Murphy was of the true faith. He believed in safe and thorough work rather than in specious and hazardous brilliance. He was infinitely careful in preparation, and compared with many was inclined to be slow ; but every step in every operation which I ever saw him do was completed deliberately, accurately, once for all. It led inevitably to the next step, without pause, without haste ; that step completed another followed. ' In sequent toil all forward did contend.' And so when the end came a review of the operation showed no false move, no part left incomplete, no chance of disaster ; all was honest, safe, simple ; it was modest rather than brilliant. During the whole operation Murphy talked ; not wasting time, but expressing and explaining aloud the quiet, gentle, dexterous movements of his hands and the purposeful working of his mind. The operation over, he would draw his stool near to the front row of the benches, cross one

275

leg over another, rest his elbow on his knee, and talk, as only he in all the world could talk, of surgery in general, of this case in particular, of his faults, of any experiment made to clear a doubtful issue. In these quiet talks there was none of the earlier passion (as in his class) which had gleamed through him, and which, caught up by his audience, had made them throb or tremble with suspense or joy. In them all his former experience, all that he had learnt by contact with men and books, all his native ingenuity of mind, were now bountifully displayed ; the vast resources of the keenest surgical intellect of his day were now displayed, not with ostentation or with florid pride, but in such a quiet manner as to show that he rejoiced in the privilege of sharing with others so many fascinating and wonderful things. If, in answer to a request, a little intellectual gift were made to him, it was welcomed with frank, almost boyish enthusiasm, and with a delight and a humility obviously genuine."

That — as Berkeley's own pupils say — might be Berkeley himself at work. And his description of the appropriate usage for the " brilliant " operator's skill is a gem of polished definition : it is the perfect denunciation of dexterity divorced from conscience.

The next passage in the speech is given over to an account of Murphy's qualities as orator and teacher. Then comes a regret that Murphy did not succeed in training a younger man to take his place : that he did not evoke in another his own true evangelical fire. But even such modest criticism Berkeley tempered with kind explanation to justify the great surgeon's ways, and he was quick to follow it with other words of praise — words in which again we find reflection of himself :

" Year by year Murphy grew in intellectual power and in the dominion he exercised over the minds of men. A problem took on a different aspect if Murphy were engaged in it. He touched the common currency of surgical thought and changed it into gold. For no effort of his was meaningless or sterile, and all the powers of his mind and of his frail body were spent ungrudgingly in all his work. His well-stocked library and all new literature were searched for him, and dispatches made for his assimilation. He worked as all great men should work, with a clean desk. His great powers were used for worthy purposes and in due season, nothing was wasted in mere hack work, for all that could be equally well done by others was left for them to do. Yet all his life he overworked. He had an inner restless spirit, which drove him at full speed. He must work, and while at work there was only one speed, the highest he could command. ' I do not wish to linger after my work is done ', he said, and it was exactly what might have been expected of him.

" It is useless to wish that men possessed of his qualities and capacities should use them differently. A man must do as he must do. If we think that Murphy by spending himself with less lavish extravagance might have prolonged his life another ten years and so have achieved even greater results, to the benefit of all mankind, we are pondering over one who was not Murphy, and who could not in those early fruitful years have been so avaricious for work, or so generously have poured forth the new truths of which he was at once both parent and missionary. Our designs for another man's life are but futile exercises of an imagination lacking in full understanding.

" Such, then, was Murphy as I knew him. It is easy now to see how great a figure he was in the world of surgery of his day. When all his work is reviewed, when not only its range but the wonderful sincerity and the permanent and piercing accuracy of so large a part of it are considered ; when we remember his unequalled gifts as teacher, his power of lucid explanation and of persuasive or coercive argument, his devotion for many years at least to experimental research, it is no exaggeration, I think, to say of him that he was the greatest surgeon of his time. Great men are fitted to their times, and in many respects are a reflex of them. But as their times pass their work is seen in far perspective, and may appear to shrink in significance. It may then seem to have lost all its originality and boldness and force, and we who stand afar off, untouched by the magnetism of a great personality, marvel at its influence in its own day. For there are few indeed who enjoy both celebrity and fame, both glory and immortality. ' Mere talents are dry leaves tossed up and down by gusts of passion and scattered and swept away ; but genius lies on the bosom of memory.' How, then, will it be with Murphy ? Judged by the standard of his contemporaries he was an intellectual giant, but of what stature will he be when judged by the standard of history ? . . ."

Then comes Berkeley's survey of surgery down the ages ; each new discovery enlivened by his sense of the dramatic incident. At the last, bringing his story up to the present moment, Berkeley said those things he thought, had said before, and many times would say again :

" Our calling, by common consent the noblest of any, dignifies all who join its ranks. The honour of the profession is the cumulative honour of all who, both in days gone by and in our own time, have worthily and honestly laboured in it. In every generation there are a chosen happy few who shed a special lustre upon it by their character, their scientific attainments, or the great glory of their record of service to their fellow men, for it is, as Ambrose Paré said, ' beautiful and the best of all things to work for the relief and cure of suffering '. In our generation Murphy was one who by his full devotion, his complete surrender to its ideals, and by his loyal, earnest, and unceasing work added distinction to our profession, which in return showered upon him the rewards with which no others can compare — the approbation of his fellow workers, and the friendship and trust of the best among his contemporaries in every country.

> The mightier man the mightier is the thing
> That makes him honoured.

" As we look backward upon the long history of the science and the art of medicine we seem to see a great procession of famous and heroic figures, each one standing not only as a witness of his own authentic achievements, but also as a symbol of the traditions, ideals, and aims of the age which he adorns. The procession is sometimes thinly stretched out, or even rudely broken here and there, but in happier ages it is thronged by an eager and exultant crowd. In medicine the whole pageant is as noble and as splendid as in any of the sciences or arts, and it reveals the collective and continuous genius of a band of men inspired by the loftiest purposes and lavish in labour and sacrifice for the welfare of mankind. They have come throughout the ages from every land. They now belong not to one country but to every country, for they are the common possession and the pride of all the world. They have lost their nationality in death. They are men whose deeds will not be forgotten, and whose names will live to all generations. In that great order of men, small in number, supreme in achievement, the unerring justice of time will reserve an assured place for John Benjamin Murphy."

These are the high words Berkeley spoke in Montreal ; this is the laurel wreath he laid before the memory of J. B. Murphy and the surgeons of the past. Characteristically, too, before sailing back to England he paid one more tribute to the past — this time to a soldier : General Wolfe, who fell at Quebec in September 1759. In Berkeley's scrap-book is pasted a dried flower ; beneath it is written, in Berkeley's hand, " From Wolfe's tomb, Plains of Abraham, October 1920 ".

*   *   *   *   *

Berkeley Moynihan

In 1912 there was born the *British Journal of Surgery*.
It had been brought into being by Berkeley's conviction
that there was not in England a publication worthy of
the best work of British surgeons. It had been kept alive
during the difficult years of war largely through Berkeley's
own endeavours. When 1920 saw the formation of
Berkeley's long-desired Association of Surgeons of Great
Britain and Ireland the *Journal* came under the protective wing of this new Association. The *Journal* and
the Association — both in great measure Berkeley's
children — greatly occupied his energies throughout the
nineteen-twenties. Into them both he richly poured his
love of his profession and his fellow men. They remain
as twin monuments, raised by himself, and now standing
to his long remembrance.

Berkeley had made his first attempt to form the
Association in March of 1914 when he had written to the
then President of the Royal College of Surgeons :

" Dear Sir Rickman Godlee,
    " You may remember that I have once or twice
mentioned to you the need for a representative Surgical
Association in Great Britain and Ireland. Every country
that is counted among the ' first-class powers ' has such an
association with the exception of England. In spite of
the work done at the Royal Society of Medicine in the
Surgical Section, and at the meetings of the British
Medical Association, and elsewhere, it is I believe true to
say that no really adequate occasion is ever offered in
England for a fully representative and first-class debate
on surgical topics, nor is there any opportunity for the
general meeting of surgeons for the free intimate discussions, perhaps more valuable than public debate,
which result when a large body of men working in one
field meet together. I have gone quietly about during
the past year or two endeavouring to elicit opinions from

men who would certainly belong to such an association if it were formed. Almost everyone to whom I have spoken is in greater or less degree enthusiastic, but no one will come forward to give the requisite impulse and direction to the effort which must be made.

" So I appeal to you. Will you select the names of twelve men in London who would and could help to give the necessary authority and repute to such an undertaking ? Would you having made such a selection invite the twelve men and myself to your house for a general discussion of the proposal ? I have written and talked to Sir William Osler who helped to form the very flourishing Association of Physicians, and he has offered to come to the meeting, if you will summon it, and tell us of the experience he had in his early work in connection with that society.

" I know the mind of the best provincial men : there is no doubt at all that they would, without exception, give the warmest welcome to the suggestion that I have made to you.

" With kind regards,

" Yours sincerely,

" BERKELEY MOYNIHAN "

But, for the time being, nothing came of it. The proposition met with obstruction in some quarters, and then the war intervened to delay everything still more. Not until six years after Berkeley's letter did the Association come to life. This is Berkeley's own account of his idea and its realisation :

" In my early days I was struck by the lack of cohesion among members of my profession. Surgeons in one town knew little or nothing of surgeons elsewhere. A surgeon from Manchester had never, so far as I could hear, visited an operation theatre in Leeds, nor had one ever been asked in consultation. As a consequence it was not infrequent to have to listen to disparagement of one surgeon by another : and jealousies, openly expressed, were too often heard. I thought this was all wrong. If we were indeed members of a 'noble profession', as we most certainly were, then it was clearly an obligation upon us to speak well of one another. It seemed to me that, if by some means we could be brought together, it would be a great advantage to us all, and that we should then be made to realise that we were not competitors, one working against another, but comrades, each working with the other against a common enemy, disease. After much reflection I decided to see what could be done with provincial surgeons first of all. I thought they would be more likely to respond. London was not always friendly. My father-in-law, T. R. Jessop, when vice-president of the Royal College of Surgeons, had represented the College at the International Congress of Medicine in Moscow. On returning through London he visited St. Bartholomew's Hospital and asked permission to enter the operating theatre to see work there. Permission was refused, to his consternation. I knew a few of the provincial surgeons well, Rutherford Morrison had operated upon my aunt, Robert Jones of Liverpool was a friend of a few years' standing, and Harold Stiles of Edinburgh had stayed in my house. I therefore wrote to about twenty men asking them to come to spend a few days in Leeds. They came in July 1909 and stayed three days. I gave a dinner in the evening, and in speaking afterwards I expressed very strongly my views as to the necessity of friendship, good feeling, collaboration among surgeons, and I suggested (after a talk with Stiles) that we should have a meeting similar to this one in six months' time. Stiles asked us to Edinburgh and we decided to form the Chirurgical Club. [Since 1929 the ' Moynihan Chirurgical Club '.] We stayed in each other's houses on these visits, and Christian names soon became heard ; and visits were not uncommon when no arranged meetings were being held. Rutherford Morrison came to Leeds unexpectedly and brought young Grey Turner with him : I took my staff over to see Robert Jones, every few months, and so on. So far all was well. But I regarded all this as only a preliminary to the fulfilment of my cherished idea : that the surgeons of all England, Scotland, and Ireland should be fused into a brotherhood. After long consideration, and after many talks with Hey Groves of Bristol who was a constant inspiration and encouragement, I came to the conclusion that some bond must be made capable of holding us together before we were actually called to meet collectively. This bond was to be a journal. So Hey Groves and I decided upon a *British Journal of Surgery* and I began to talk to, and to write to, the leaders of our profession. I spoke to Godlee, Henry Morris, Makins, and others and wrote to MacEwen of Glasgow. Nowhere was there a sign of enthusiasm and I received the coldest reception. MacEwen wrote to say that there was little British surgery of any value, and few men capable of writing anything worth while. However, we pressed on, and the first number of our *Journal* appeared. I had desired to call attention to English surgeons and their work : at that time I thought MacEwen of Glasgow the greatest surgeon in Europe, and I arranged with Parry of Glasgow to write and illustrate an article on MacEwen. This appeared in the first number. A few days after its appearance I received a letter from MacEwen in which he said that ' If this is the kind of Journal you had in mind I feel sure it will succeed ', a delightful change of opinion. I had asked a surgeon in London, distinguished for his knowledge of surgical history, to write a note on Lister to inaugurate a series dealing with our famous men. The article was, of course, well written and accurate but it lacked a little enthusiasm. I exercised my right as Chairman and wrote an additional paragraph intending to add a little warmth to a cold summary. Watson Cheyne wrote an indignant letter saying that something better ought to have been written about his Master, and but for the final paragraph which contained a worthy tribute, he would never have consented to support the *Journal*. The *Journal* prospered and all credit is due to the little Committee who ran it, and above all to Hey Groves whose admirable skill and most earnest devotion have accounted for the fact that every number has been published at a profit and that we were able to carry on through the war. For one year Hey Groves was on active service abroad, and his place was taken by Sampson Handley whose ardent labour we all recognised.

" When the *Journal* had made a start and seemed assured of success I inaugurated my last desire, that of an Association of Surgeons which should carry out on a large scale what my little Chirurgical Club had done on a small scale. Sir Rickman Godlee was then President of the Royal College of Surgeons and I wrote him a letter making the suggestion that an Association should be formed. He was tepid in enthusiasm, cautious and sceptical. However, I urged him on, and asked him to give a Dinner where congenial souls might meet and a discussion be held, so that we might gauge the prospects of success. Godlee gave a Dinner to about twelve of us, himself, Watson Cheyne, Pearce Gould, Makins, Hey Groves, and others. We dined in Wimpole Street and after dinner I was asked to speak in the drawing-room upstairs. I tried to put some inspiration into my words and was quite content with the reception I was cordially given. We decided then and there to form an Association and I was asked to draft a constitution. This I did with the invaluable and devoted help of Hey Groves. Then the war came, and for about four years nothing could be done. Our interests had moved elsewhere. However, when the war was near its end I got to work again. Our draft constitution had meanwhile been completed, and was waiting a revival of interest when the war ceased. That draft constitution with hardly a word of change was accepted and the Association came into existence. Bland-Sutton was our first President and he gave a great Dinner for us at Claridge's and I think then that men began to

see that there was something in the idea which would be
of value to the men themselves and to the cause of surgery
we had at heart. I tried to expound my gospel that
surgery was a matter of ' team work ' (I believe that
before the war I had coined the phrase ' team work ' for
my own practice in Leeds, and I carried this into the
war, and was officially responsible for the team principle)
and that it was essential that we should come together
and keep together. The seed fell on fertile soil. The
later history of the Association is no doubt contained in
the Minutes. I will only recall one further incident.
When I was President and the meeting was held in Leeds
Sir George Makins proposed my health at the Dinner and
said that if three years before any man had told him that
the surgeons of the Country could be brought together
in amity in such fashion as he had seen at Leeds, he
would not have believed him. In three days in Leeds he
had seen the impossible performed under his own eyes,
and even while speaking he could hardly believe it was
happening, and he then paid a tribute to me that I
shall remember as long as I live."

* * * * *

In 1922 Berkeley, though determined not to leave
Leeds, found it essential that he should see some of his
patients in London. He was being frequently urged to
transfer his practice to London ; but he was restrained
from so doing by his loyalty to Leeds, his happiness at
Carr Manor, and by the recollection of the difficulties
that his old chief Mayo-Robson had encountered when
he himself made such a move. London medical circles
are not eager to welcome outsiders, and Berkeley knew
this.

So he made a compromise. He took a suite of rooms
at Jules Hotel and there, on certain days each week, saw
patients. The rest of the time he spent in Leeds. And still,

whenever possible, he tried to persuade his patients to come to Leeds for their operations — though he did operate in London. In a little while he moved to Portland Place, and there, while in London, both lived and practised. His consulting-rooms were in his flat and he operated in a nursing home near by. Almina, Lady Carnarvon, whose nursing home it was, became a close friend to him. He spent many hours in conversation with her and, when problems faced him, sought her advice and placed reliance in it. He enjoyed his days in London. In 1922 he wrote to General Goodwin :

" I'm deeper in work than ever — and loving it more than ever. I had a great time when the Association of Surgeons came to Leeds three weeks ago, doing all sorts of nice things for them."

He started to dine out a great deal and became fond of club life. He joined the Garrick Club and was seen there often ; for he liked actors and was always interested in stage affairs. Later, elected under a special rule that dealt with men distinguished in the arts and sciences, he became a member of the Athenaeum Club, and derived as much pleasure from it as he had done from the R.A.C. in earlier days. He delighted in the intellectual companionship of the men he met there — men distinguished in every walk of life.

Though attached to no political party he was usually ready, in his clubs, to join in political discussion. He was interested in electoral reform and wrote to the press in support of proportional representation. He was invited to stand for Parliament on several occasions ; he loved public speaking and only declined the invitations after some searchings of his heart. As late as 1926 he was still considering the matter, for at that time his friend

CARR MANOR

Lord Moynihan's home near Leeds from 1914 until the end of his life

Sir George Newman wrote to him :

" Take the advice of an old man and *don't go into the House of Commons*. The other House is another story. To do any good in the Commons needs a life of it, a life of that *sort* ; and there are the annoyances of election and partisanship — both provoking to a senior man who has won his laurels elsewhere, and has become sufficiently a philosopher to say ' a plague on both your parties '."

There was, too, talk of Berkeley becoming the Ambassador from Britain to America. He would have both adorned the post and gloried in it ; but, had such an invitation come his way, he would at the last most likely have asked to be excused, for he was convinced that surgery needed him. The possibility must have been mentioned in America, for it explains a later paragraph in this letter from Dr. Crile :

" MY DEAR MOYNIHAN,
        " May I tell you again how much I appreciated your putting on just what I wanted to see. Both operations were to me like a wonderful symphony — leaving absolutely nothing to be desired, and will be remembered by me as the most perfect thing in surgery I had ever witnessed. There is nothing more I wish to add than that I shall as far as ever I can adopt your technique. It would not occur to me to enquire about the patients — unless they have been struck by lightning I know how they are.
        " I was very glad to meet your colleagues at dinner and a fine evening it was. Your perfect house and gardens, and flowers, and the exquisite china and pictures and wonderful furniture, and the charming Moynihan family are equally in the symphony — the great symphony. The remainder of my trip will I fear be sort of a jazz.

" If your ears burned a bit to-day it was when Will spoke of a certain political possibility — that would be priceless — in such an event the post of interpreter is filled now. . . .

" Ever yours,
" G. W. CRILE "

All the American visitors, and there were many of them, who visited Carr Manor were charmed by the beauty of Berkeley's home and his possessions. Dr. Coley, of New York, wrote to Berkeley :

" MY DEAR MOYNIHAN,
" I cannot sail homeward without saying goodbye, and telling you again how very much we enjoyed our visit to Leeds. It was good to see you all in your beautiful old home which Osler so well described as ' Paradise '. I never dreamed of anything more perfect. How you must enjoy every hour spent in it and those wonderful gardens ! — I have written Helen all about them and about the house. How did you ever find so many rare and beautiful things ?
" Most of all I enjoyed seeing your work. I thought nothing in the way of operative technique and skill could surpass what I saw in Leeds twelve years ago, but you have been making progress all those years. I know of no one who has done so much for the advancement of surgery in this generation, and I rejoice that some measure of appreciation and reward has come to you. . . .
" Always faithfully yours,
" W. B. COLEY "

Berkeley's files are full of letters from his American friends. With these men he was much at ease and they were so with him. They did not often leave Leeds without writing to tell him of the pleasure they had felt while there. One of them writes :

" During my visit to your hospital I received so much

pleasure and inspiration that I would be very ungrateful if I did not express my appreciation to you. As I have gone about to various surgical centres trying in my small way to improve myself to carry on in my work nowhere has the 'patient' been so thoroughly emphasized. It has been statistics, tests of this kind and that, histories, and so on, the poor patient being an incident, seemingly. Perhaps this is not fair to other clinics. Perhaps I have not been given a proper view of them, but the fact remains that I have spent more time in some of them than I did in yours.

" I can only thank you and assure you that my patients are receiving the services of a better man through my contact with you."

Every letter that Berkeley received from his American friends, and from those others that wrote to him after visiting his clinic, he carefully stored away. The response of others to his enthusiasm was always a spur to him. He worked best before an audience. Many of his most fruitful ideas were the direct result of stimulating companionship. Silent contemplation in the study never appealed to him as much as did communion with his fellows. That is why, busy as he was, he managed to find time to attend the meetings of more than one society that had as its object intellectual exchange. In Leeds he was a member of the Conversation Club and the Leeds Luncheon Club ; the former met at regular intervals to fulfil the function of its title, and the latter listened to a brief address once each week during the University term. In London Berkeley was a member of Ye Sette of Odd Volumes ; which club satisfied his taste for the wittiest pyrotechnics he might desire.

Even so, with his mind so occupied in work and play, Berkeley's mental energy was not all consumed. He

U

still had to find something else to do. He let off a great deal of steam by writing to the press. His letters were full of ingenuity and of all his characteristic force. They covered a multitude of subjects of great variety. They were usually written to *The Times* and the *Yorkshire Post*. In these two papers, at one time and another, he pointed out such things as that Epstein's statue of Genesis was inappropriate to its title, that peas should be taken with sugar and as a separate course if their full flavour was to be enjoyed, that the Haig equestrian statue was unworthy of its subject, and that the streets of Leeds should be kept more clean. Berkeley had a ready pen and neat sentences flowed without hesitation from its point.

A beautiful example of his letter-writing is in this letter in which he airs his views on unorthodox medicine. For convenience I have partly abbreviated it :

" The lay mind seems to find it unaccountably difficult to understand the professional attitude toward the unorthodox practitioner. We accept the view of Bacon that ' The weakness and credulity of man is such as they will often prefer a mountebank or a witch to a physician '. We do not deny to such practitioner the possession of a degree of competence in manipulative methods : we do not doubt either his sincere devotion to his task or his personal integrity, nor do we disparage the irresponsible gay confidence he has in his own very limited powers. We do not grudge him success though we recognise its extreme infrequency, and are not unfamiliar with its perilous accompaniments, its fatal disasters. Our opposition rests upon something more fundamental than this ; upon his complete lack of training both in the most elementary principles which underlie all powers of diagnosis, and in the appropriate application of those principles to treatment. Such principles are not empirical, they are based upon a multitude of sciences, upon physiology, anatomy, pathology, radiology, and the like, and upon that trained clinical observation which seeks to determine not only the morbid local condition but also its correlation with the general state of the patient. It is only by such enquiry that an exact diagnosis can ever be made, and without accurate diagnosis, empirical treatment is mere guess-work, and attended by all the hazards and uncertainties of guess-work. The expert application of a method, good perhaps in itself but unsuited to the local or general condition, can bring no possible advantage and may be followed by irreparable harm. The fact that the untrained practitioner must necessarily be completely devoid of any knowledge of the nature of disease or of the methods by which it can be recognised and differentiated from those conditions whose signs and symptoms are mimicked by it, accounts for the multitude of grievous irremediable disasters that follow far too frequently upon his treatment. These are rarely told to the world, but doctors are very familiar with them : save for the anxiety and expense that would be entailed it would seem to be their clear duty to expose them.

" What should we think of an astronomer who knew no mathematics and had never seen a telescope : of a chemist who knew nothing of the nature of the elements, or of chemical reactions : of a physicist who spoke glibly of relativity and was ignorant of the constitution of the atom, the second law of thermo-dynamics or of the quantum theory ? Of the unorthodox practitioner of Medicine it is invariably true that his work and his writing betray a complete ignorance of those fundamental truths upon which alone a science or an art of healing can be based.

" There is surely no distinction between Medicine and those other fusions of Science and of Art which distinguish the theory and practice of Law, Divinity, Sculpture, or Painting. All sciences and all arts surely require for their profitable practice or perfect display, a stern preliminary discipline, an arduous training under masters of experience, with the gift of inspiring the mind or guiding the hands of the acolyte, who must ' act to-morrow what he learns to-day ' : and whose task is

> to watch
> The Master work, and catch
> Hints of the proper craft, tricks of the tool's true play.

" Is it only in medical mythology that the Scientific Minerva sallies forth fully equipped for her life's work ? Is the serious student of medicine merely wasting his time and emptying an almost jejune purse when he devotes years of his life to most exacting labour and to the painful acquisition of knowledge with which more fortunate rivals claim to be endowed by birthright ?

" The foundations of medicine in all its branches can be acquired in one way only. We must master little by little, step by step, with unflagging grim devotion, the preliminary sciences, we must acquire knowledge of structure and function in dissecting-rooms, wards, laboratories, and come at last to the great accomplishments of diagnosis, and safe and effective and rational treatment.

" Those who practise ' unorthodox Medicine ' are not practising ' Medicine ' at all. They are as competent to do so as a student would be who spoke in terms of higher mathematics without acquaintance with the elementary practice of arithmetic."

This letter proves that Berkeley did not write to the papers just for the pleasure of seeing his name in print. He was exuberant, but he was not silly. The press was often the best or the only medium through which he could achieve his end. It was the best place in which to expose unorthodox medicine certainly. When the flood of war novels was at its height, Berkeley again went to the press. He wrote a long letter in which he defended the private soldier against the calumnies that were being heaped upon him. Afterwards he wrote privately to a friend :

" It is just a week ago at this very hour since I ' boiled over ', on reading still another filthy war novel, and sat down (red-hot) to write to *The Times*. The Adjutant-General and a multitude of people, officers' widows, mothers, Tommies, have written to me."

Berkeley may have changed nothing, but many were grateful to him for his advocacy.

It sounds priggish to say that Berkeley was a fighter for the right. But that is what he was ; and he was not a prig. Something implicit in his nature always urged him on. This is how he described himself when in 1927 he was presented with his portrait :

" To me, on most sober reflection, it seems that throughout my life I have only attempted to do the day's work as well as my powers would permit. Fairies I am told preside at one's birth. They planted in me an almost uncontrollable desire for paths of dalliance. I was surely made for idleness, for the admiration and easy enjoyment of beautiful and gracious things in life. When I visualise my ideal of happiness I find myself lying on my back with my face to the sun, without a care, hearing the lap of water on the sea-shore, or on the side of a boat in which I am drifting lazily. But with the company of languorous desires bestowed by the fairies there intruded the most mischievous imp, who made it his task to see that I should have no spiritual peace except through toil. I have often hated the imp, and have been rebellious when I felt him growing active ; yet I hardly know what I should have done without him. I expect he is my best friend ; and for those who have eyes his portrait too is here. He has kept me, tyrant as he is, to a high standard of endeavour, and made me realise that I must cheerfully endure hardness. He would never let me compare my efforts with any other man's ; and so has kept me free from a single gust of jealousy ; he has made me compare my efforts with the best of which I knew myself to be capable. And he has rarely been pleased with me. But perhaps man's greatest intellectual happiness comes not from accomplishment but from effort."

*   *   *   *   *

From 1918 onwards public affairs of every sort commanded Berkeley's attention. It was always with him a regret that he had so little time to give to his home and to his friends. He delighted to be alone with his children ; particularly since, now grown up, they could give him full companionship. When his son went to Oxford, Berkeley visited him there as often as he could ; he vicariously lived the life that he himself would have so perfectly enjoyed if fate had given him the chance. His boy's successes meant the world to him ; the pages of his scrap-book tell of them every one.

He continued his intimate friendship with Sir Robert Jones, and when Lord Derby presided at a Dinner in Sir Robert's honour Berkeley was one of the principal speakers. On that occasion Berkeley said :

" What is it that makes a member of our profession regarded as among the great ones, not only of this generation, but of all times ? Least of the things that count is popularity, and the material prosperity that goes with such popularity ; it is not the spoken word that makes a man great, still less the written word. The thing that makes a physician great is not what he does by word of mouth or with his hands. It is the spirit which he puts into the pupils he trains to follow after. The war gave Sir Robert his chance ; it made every surgeon in the world his grateful pupil. A real monument to him was not one on canvas ; it could not be graven in stone or bronze or embodied in a tablet ; but it was to be found in the thousands of grateful hearts whose heavy load of sorrow and anguish his strong and gentle hands had lifted. In the name of all surgeons, both in this country and across the Atlantic, I honour him not only because of his superb and unsurpassed gifts of technique, and mastery of all surgical methods, not only because of his great intellectual attainments, and the superb dedication of the purest heart I know in the profession to-day to the welfare of that profession, but because of the magic and charm of his wonderful personality. We offer him from our grateful hearts the one supreme gift we can offer — we offer him our love."

And afterwards Sir Robert wrote to Berkeley :

" MY VERY DEAR FRIEND,
    " My heart is too full of gratitude to write you, for I feel very deeply your kindness. What your friendship has meant to me I cannot say in words. It has been a very close part of my life for years. Your speech which so thrilled everybody who listened to it has made a deep impress on my mind and heart. You are indeed an inspiration to everyone who knows you. But you are to me an ideal which no one approaches.
                " With deep affection,
                    " Your devoted friend,
                        " ROBERT JONES "

Berkeley, unlike so many of us, made his dearest friends only in his full maturity. As he grew older he shed his aloofness, and by so doing rendered himself approachable. Secure position, too, had changed his ways ; no longer did he fear rivalry or feel the necessity for exclusive, single-minded toil. To friendship he now opened inner doors.

Among the newer friends was Mr. Hey Groves, fondly regarded for his loyal partnership in the early, struggling days of the *British Journal of Surgery*. When the Bristol Medical School was reorganised in its association with the University of Bristol it was through Hey Groves that Berkeley was called in as adviser. Some of the opinions Berkeley then expressed were of the widest scope, and of interest not only to doctors. In his report he said :

" The view has, I know, been taken that hospitals are only concerned with the treatment of patients suffering from injuries and disease, that the presence of students is sometimes rather a hindrance than a help, and that it is not to the advantage of patients to submit to their enquiries and attentions. The truth is that the strongest safeguard of the patient is the presence of the student. A physician or surgeon who is engaged in the teaching of students cannot afford to do less than his best. He knows that his example will direct the tendencies and control the methods of all those who work for him. He will never consent to give his second best, for no one realises so fully as he how keenly critical a group of students can be. Of nothing in hospital work am I more convinced than this, that the student ensures that the best effort of all is given on behalf of the patient. A hospital that does nothing more than treat the immediate necessities of its patients will, however, remain of little or no account in the progress of Medicine. It is in the study of large groups of cases that many secrets as to the causation and the symptoms of disease may be disclosed, and lessons learnt as to the best methods of prevention, of cure, or of palliative treatment. A teaching hospital therefore is a research institution and the students as they learn to observe and record and collate the facts are a valuable part of the machinery by which progress is accomplished. The thesis that the teaching hospitals of the country have given greater service to humanity than any other research institutions in the last half-century would not be difficult to sustain."

Berkeley used his friendships to pursue his own ideals. When he launched the Yorkshire Campaign — an effort to investigate cancer in the light of modern knowledge and to bring it to early treatment — he invoked the aid of all his friends. To use friendship for high causes he regarded as a proper thing. There are many who now benefit through the friends that Berkeley made, and inspired to noble effort.

For his services to philanthropic ends, and for his achievements in the war, Berkeley was, in 1922, made a Baronet. From then onwards his descendants, by bearing for ever the title bestowed upon himself, would live in perpetual remembrance of his greatness and benevolence. None were more proud of his new dignity than the people of Yorkshire. In 1926 they paid him high honour — and the greatest his own city could offer — by making him a Freeman of the City of Leeds.

But of the honours that came to him in his middle years the one he prized the most, perhaps the one he most prized in all his life, was that it should fall to his lot to present Princess Mary to the University of Leeds when that University conferred upon her the honorary degree of Doctor of Laws. These are the words that Berkeley spoke in presentation :

" Mr. Vice-Chancellor, I bring to you the King's daughter, that we may render her great honour. Her Royal Highness Princess Mary Viscountess Lascelles, Imperial by descent, Yorkshire by adoption, has greatly endeared herself to all people by her loyal acceptance and faithful discharge of the manifold and heavy obligations which are her birthright. Tasks such as hers are never easy. They make exacting claims upon many qualities of mind and heart ; they are gazed upon with every eye. To succeed in them is but to confirm anticipation ; failure may bring injury to good causes. No family in this realm is so unwearied in the strict observance of high duty to the Commonwealth as that in which this heritage of the King has been so lavishly bestowed upon his children. Every member of our Royal House has made haste to seek an authentic mission, and in that has found life's discipline and fine adventure.

" The lot that has fallen to Her Royal Highness has deep significance. Her prerogative has been to awaken and sustain the interest of the younger generation of women in the ideals of public service. As Girl Guide, as nurse during the harsh days of war, as wife, as proud and happy mother, Her Royal Highness has acquitted herself with a demure and impressive dignity which leaves no hope or expectation unrewarded. Many daughters have done virtuously, but our Princess excels them all. Let her own work praise her in the gates. Inasmuch, then, as Her Royal Highness has been ardent in devotion to duty, compassionate with all who suffer, loyal to those who labour in good causes, and in all her virtues so womanly, I now present her to you, Mr. Vice-Chancellor, for that recognition which the degree of Doctor of Laws in our University will bestow."

PART VI

THE REWARDS BEFORE THE END

The Rewards before the End

THE Royal College of Surgeons of England is the parent body of British surgery. Its beautiful building stands behind Kingsway in the quiet of Lincoln's Inn Fields. From the heart of London it exercises dominion over English surgery and influences the surgery of the whole British Empire. It was founded in 1800 and it stands, above all things, as a memorial to the work of John Hunter in the eighteenth century. Of British surgery as we know it to-day John Hunter was the inspiration ; by placing surgery upon a sure scientific basis John Hunter elevated the surgeons of his day from their despised position as barbers' assistants to their new rank as gentlemen. He first revealed the extensive power for good the surgeon wields and turned the craft of surgery into a modern art. His spiritual memorial is a possession of every surgeon of to-day — the courage that is made confident by true knowledge of surgical first principles ; his physical memorial is the museum of the Royal College of Surgeons — the greatest collection of pathological specimens in the world.

In surgery Berkeley had two heroes : John Hunter and Lord Lister — the discoverer of antiseptic and aseptic surgery. For these two men he had a deep, devoted admiration. In him their spirit moved again ; in him was perfect sympathy with all their aims. When he was young, Berkeley, like many another junior surgeon, had regarded the College but as an examining body and of its ideals had been largely unaware. As he grew older, as Hunter and Lister caught his imagination, so did his affection for the College grow ; in his mind's eye he saw it once again, not reigning in dignified somnolence, but with vital energy directing the ways of surgery. That it should sink to the mere granting of diplomas was, to him, the abandonment of its birthright and the dereliction of its fullest duty : not for that had John Hunter laboured. It should indeed perform parochial tasks, but its highest calling lay in the promotion of surgical research, the wide training of young surgeons, and the maintenance of surgical ideals.

As a member of the Council of the College Berkeley had tried to implement these aspirations, but his authority was limited and such progress as he made was slow. After some years' service at the College he realised that only as President would he be able to exercise the power that could achieve considerable ends. That a man should be President of the Royal College of Surgeons may to the lay mind mean little, for that office is often filled by one who is neither the best nor the most successful surgeon of his day. But within the profession, it is regarded by all as the greatest honour that can befall a man. The President is a surgeon, chosen by his fellows — by those supreme in their knowledge of himself and his craft — to be the head of their calling and their symbol before the world. He must embody not one but many gifts — skill in his work, vision in his thoughts, and in his behaviour both diplomacy and honour. If at times there have been Presidents deficient in these attributes it is because, at those times, no better man has been available. In this at least the profession has been above reproach — they have always endeavoured to make their best man their President.

But endeavour can be, and usually is, beset by many difficulties. Of these not the least potent is tradition. At the College of Surgeons it had been an unwritten rule that the President should be a member of the staff of a London teaching hospital ; never had a surgeon from outside London been elected to the Presidency. This tradition was most tenacious ; before Berkeley's day it seemed beyond the bounds of reasonable probability that a provincial surgeon should ever be President. And yet against this background, and in spite of those jealousies that can misuse tradition for their private ends, Berkeley was in 1926 elected President. His elevation was almost universally approved : the good-will of the vast majority of the profession accompanied it. Had he been but narrowly successful his appointment would have been remarkable : but that he, the first provincial President, should have been so readily acclaimed was, in the history of the College, a tremendous happening. It was a tribute to the fundamental justice that rules the counsels of the College and it was the incontestable measure of Berkeley's magnitude.

To be President had been Berkeley's ambition for many years. Though he desired the office, and in his heart regarded himself as the proper person to occupy it, only to his most intimate friends had he spoken openly to that effect. Not only wisdom but true modesty as well had placed restraints upon that vanity that he, as well as others, knew to be a weakness of his flesh. His delight in his election was so great, the response of his emotions so strong, that at this, the highest triumph of his life, he behaved most decorously. At this moment when he might indulge his boastfulness he stayed his tongue. Surgery was his life ; he had raised it to the level of a faith, and had served that faith with the utter selflessness of a true disciple ; and now his reward was this ; by his peers he was confirmed in his faith ; in their eyes were his services approved. Here was something that a man could not — must not — speak about.

Even in the company of his much-loved Robert Jones, Berkeley's delight was silent ; even there he must not let pride despoil his joy. A few days after the election he was talking to Sir Robert and the latter, within a few hours of that conversation taken ill, later wrote to Berkeley from his bed :

" MY DEAR OLD FRIEND,

" When I parted from you at Lime Street on that day a short while back — a day for me divided by an abyss from this (I know the date of neither) — I felt I had left something unsaid : that you were expecting me to say something more, and you spoke of friendships.

" You told me of the elections to the R.C.S. ; but in my ignorance I had not known that the election of President had also fallen due, and that you had reached the Throne of British Surgery and had become King of our Faith and our Craft.

" You must have indeed wondered why I never mentioned the subject !

" Since yesterday when I learnt the great news on coming back to this interesting world after a fight beset with rigors and rocketing temperatures, I have been overjoyed, and this condition has stimulated me to disobey orders — Sister is using terrible threats — and write myself to you. Damn the consequences !

" I have much in my mind to say of the wonderful things you will do, and the wonderful way in which you will do them ; but, for the present, my hand is stayed. . . . Good luck ; and may the sun always smile upon you.

"Your affectionate,

"R. J."

That was a cherished letter. And there were many others which, if not as intimate, had each of them a special interest that made them highly prized. Sir Humphrey Rolleston, the Regius Professor of Medicine at Cambridge, sent a card that contained the graceful phrase " Only to-day have I heard that you have become the nominal in addition to the actual head of the Surgical Profession ". One of his old assistants wrote :

" Nineteen years ago when I had the honour to be your House-Surgeon you told me that your greatest ambition was to be President of the Royal College of Surgeons. And that that has been realised may I offer you my very heartiest congratulations."

Another old student followed his congratulations with the sentence :

" May I remind you that about 24 years ago we wore caps for the first time as Surgeon and H-S together in the Theatre ? I look back on this with some satisfaction."

The Secretary of the Chirurgical Club wrote words that in different forms appeared in many letters :

" The soul of every provincial surgeon will rejoice that at last the College have seen fit to appoint a provincial surgeon to its highest honour. I suppose one might put it that there is a chain of office in every pair of rubber gloves."

A student, then working in Leeds, followed his congratulations with these sentences :

" I am conveying the glad news to my father, who will be extremely delighted to hear it, as his chief desire was

305   X

that I should be the student of the celebrated Sir Berkeley, who has a great name in Hyderabad. I am sure thousands of your admirers in the East will hear the news with great joy. . . . Yours obediently, M. A. RASHID (of India)."

But most touching of all was the letter from his sister Ada. Here was a reminder of those enshadowed student days when she alone in all the world believed in him, and had for him ambitions that to others must have appeared fantastic in their rash presumption. But she — remarkable woman — was right, and the others wrong. What a moment this must have been for her !

" MY OWN DARLING,
    " A thousand loving congratulations on this last and greatest of all your many honours. I say greatest — for there is only one President of the Royal College of Surgeons at any one time — you stand alone at the very apex of your great profession. And again greatest — because you've been elected by your ' Peers ' — those who know best the value of your powers. That you will excel as President we with them expect of you. . . . I am prouder and happier about you than ever.
                    " Your loving sister,
                                " ADA "

Yes, she was delighted. But, sister-like, she was not overawed by her distinguished brother's fame. When she next met Berkeley, as had always been her habit, it was with corrections and admonishments that she pursued him ; he must not think that he could now sit back, he should find still greater heights to climb. And then the fur would fly ! Really, was not even this enough ? — did she still ask for something more ? These two loved each other, but they could never meet without reviving the old argumentations, without resuming the endless friendly

bickerings that had first started around the table over
which their mother had presided so many years ago.
Eva was gone, their mother was gone, but these two —
both now over sixty — still fought the heated battles of
their childhood. They were battles of spirits ardent and
untouched by age ; the bodies that encased those spirits
might now show the batterings of time, but, in their
deeper selves, Berkeley and Ada were unchanged : they
were still Moynihans — loving, quarrelsome, fighting the
world, proud of their Moynihan heritage. And now — as
ever — though behind the family ramparts they engaged
in internecine war, but let an outsider attack or criticise
their name or ways then in an instant he would find them
united, tremendous in defence. In Ada's eyes nothing
was too good for Berkeley, but — likewise in her eyes —
nothing he did was quite so good as to justify his indulgence, in her presence, in self-satisfaction.

Another memory, this time of long-gone student days,
was awoken by the congratulations of Berkeley's first
great friend, by the words of one who in affectionate and
faithful admiration had stood by Berkeley all the years.
Here was no sleek flattery, but something spontaneous,
flowered from the heart of a friend :

" All hail ! Imperator Chirurgiae. My very dear old
Moyne ! *Magnificent.* I have lived to see your glorifica-
tion, and old friend, the best pal ever man had. Always
yours, Tommy."

There are, after all, compensations in being a provincial surgeon. No doubt London surgeons enjoy the
love of friends, but London is big and those same friendships can never so partake in local loyalties and in the
delight in laurels carried home. In addition to his personal pleasure Berkeley had the happiness of bringing an

honour to Leeds. And Leeds responded nobly. It wrote
him robust, Yorkshire letters, instinct with native good-
will ; it gave him dinners in his honour ; and it welcomed
him like a king. As no London surgeon ever could,
Berkeley came home in triumph. The news of his
election to the Presidency had not long been out before
Berkeley received this wire, " Please let me know time of
your arrival as students etc. meeting you at station and
taking you to Carr Manor. Mackill."

A few minutes before Berkeley's train was due there
drove up to the station at Leeds twenty motor-cars filled
with white-coated students. Up and down the platform
these young men stormed until Berkeley himself arrived.
No sooner did he step down from the train than they
seized him and carried him shoulder-high past the barriers
into the station hall. There to Lady Moynihan — who
in laughter demurred — and so instead to Sir Berkeley,
they presented a bouquet : it was composed of flowers
of inflated rubber gloves, leaves of cotton-wool, and a
stem of Berkeley's own designed, special abdominal
clamp. Berkeley and Isabel were then escorted to their
car and the whole procession drove to Carr Manor ;
there, upon the lawns, the students paraded in Berkeley's
honour, so on this day giving immortality to old Carr
Manor. Not till late in the evening were Berkeley and
Isabel, tired and happy, left in the quiet of their home.

* * * * *

The Hunterian Oration is one of the great occasions
on the calendar of the Royal College of Surgeons. Yearly,
from the Fellows of the College, one is chosen to speak
in honour of the great John Hunter. It fell to Berkeley's
lot to deliver the Oration in the first year of his Presidency.

The Rewards before the End

Upon the same day Berkeley, as President, admitted Princess Mary to the honorary Fellowship of the College, and before Her Royal Highness he delivered the Oration. The year was the centenary of the birth of Lister, and Berkeley gave to his lecture the title " Hunter's Ideals and Lister's Practice ". In language free from obscure technicalities he told the story of Hunter's and Lister's work ; he described the revolutionary effects of their labours upon mankind's well-being ; and he concluded by planning the future course that should be taken by the surgeons of the day. His opening words were :

" Man's life is warfare. The individual, the whole race, is beset by foes, unresting, relentless. Against them our defence, if we are ever to subdue them, must be carefully planned and diligently strengthened. But defence, however stubborn, is not enough. Attacks designed after scientific study of the enemies' strongholds and methods, and launched with impassioned zeal, must never for one instant falter. Not all our attacks meet with success. We are cheered when we gain some notable victory ; yet when we suffer defeat, as wave after wave of our advance is checked and repulsed, we do not lose heart. Failure inspires us to fresh and still more eager endeavour.

" In this year, the centenary of Lister, we rejoice to acclaim the greatest victory ever won by man against his enemies. We, who are in active work to-day, are perhaps unable to measure the full extent of that victory ; for during the long fight, lasting almost exactly sixty years, our standards have been so changed that we cannot truthfully compare our work with that of our intellectual ancestors. Operations from time immemorial so mortal as to be prohibitive are now freely performed without anxiety. Operations formerly unimaginable are now matters of everyday occurrence. The mere tale of such work done does not adequately illustrate the change. On my last day as surgeon on the full staff of my hospital, I performed six abdominal operations. Not one of these was practised by any member of our staff during the year in which I became house surgeon, nor had such a diagnosis as was made in three of these cases, and verified at the time of operation, ever then been attempted in the history of medicine. Above all, a statement of facts and a comparison of methods does not in adequate degree convey to our minds the difference of outlook of the intellectual and spiritual approach of a man to his daily task, as between the surgeon in the days before Lister and since. It is barely possible for us to imagine how men felt about their daily work when an eminent surgeon could speak of his hospital as a ' house of death ' ; when hospitals ' were little short of pest-houses ', as Lister said ; and when the oppressive mortality compelled the closure of wards or of a whole hospital for months, until the curse was lifted from them. The change, of incalculable benefit to humanity, is due to one man, Lister."

Berkeley's veneration for Lister was the factor which most controlled him in the conduct of his professional life. He regarded Lister as the greatest benefactor the world has ever known. It was his desire to impress his own acute consciousness of this upon every surgeon that he met. In the little span of his own life Berkeley had seen the marvel of antiseptic surgery revealed ; alone, to his generation of surgeons, belonged this glorious sight. When Berkeley, the student, entered his hospital surgery was rude and menacing ; when Berkeley, President of the Royal College of Surgeons, walked for the last time down the steps of the Leeds Infirmary, safe and perfect surgery was at the command of any surgeon that to sufficient training would submit himself. Berkeley had seen this wonder ; before it, in humility, he stood perpetually amazed. That anyone should take all this for granted he could not bear ; here should the puniest imaginations find astonishment.

Vanity and hero-worship are, in the constitution of a single character, inimical. He who sees the greatness that rests in others does not too much esteem himself. Berkeley, in the fullness of his years, talked much about himself. At his dinner-table, surrounded by his guests, he loved to recount with egotistic anecdote the tale of his rise to fame ; much would he dwell upon his own opinions and his works ; the guests, as they departed, might at times complain amongst themselves of Berkeley's habit of self-praise. And yet it was a habit only ; there was no corrosion of Berkeley's mind. The adventure of the doctor's life enthralled him, he was fascinated by medicine's heroes of the past, and of them would talk for hours. His own life too had been adventurous, he was the hero of a saga of his own. If he was an egotist, his was but the egotism of a child — a child that is more concerned with the circumstance and trappings of adventure than with the valuation of its individual role in the romance. Berkeley was a hero-worshipper, and of his heroes he was one. His vanity was in the things he had done — and these were many — and not in the rewards he won ; the adventure was the thing that mattered, not the prize at the end of the road. Berkeley was proud of being President, but when he came home he said, " I am glad to have brought this back to Leeds ". When he was later made a peer he naturally was pleased, but from his heart he said, " I am happy that this honour has come to the profession ". In each remark he was essentially sincere. The vanity that is false pride of place and title, that saps and disorientates the mind, he did not have. What he did have were the foibles of a mind that refused to grow old ; an Irish mind, infinitely susceptible to romance, whether in his own life or another's.

Isabel had a Yorkshire practicality that Berkeley never had ; not by romance was she inflamed as Berkeley was. Her values, though not as colourful or visionary as his, were often much more real. Of Hunter and Lister she knew nothing, about them Berkeley might be right ; but about the affairs of every day she had a stable wisdom that transcended his. The glitter of success never appealed to her ; in it she could see no enduring happiness. Not for his delight in the emoluments of fame had she loved Berkeley ; she had loved him, and still did, for the qualities that had made him strive towards that fame. Berkeley — titled, brilliant orator, successful surgeon, President of the College — was everywhere in demand ; public ceremonies and public dinners stole nearly all his leisure hours. To many of these duties Isabel, though now delicate in health, accompanied him ; but whereas he, susceptible to flattery, enjoyed them, she for her part often found them irksome and meaningless. She did not resent Berkeley's pleasure in them, but she feared lest he should be injured by his too ready accept-ance of smooth words, and she tried to protect in him the boy that had never grown up. He was so easily captured by success ; and she was not. To be seen in the company of a famous actor, athlete, or any celebrated star shooting to oblivion through the heavens of the press — such things delighted him ; but to her they gave little pleasure. For her, infinite worlds of quality separated one who, a great doctor, had varied and cultivated gifts of heart and hand and mind, from those people who through some single talent enjoyed a moment's notoriety. So, with good sense, she steadied Berkeley on his way. And Berkeley knew that her wisdom in these things outdistanced his (though not in accordance with it did he always conduct himself), and he recognised it to the full ; for this — and many other things — he loved and needed her, and at her going was desolate.

Not in the rattle of public places but in the Royal College of Surgeons walked again the young doctor Isabel had loved. There, in the service of surgery, Berkeley was at his best. There, too, he loved to be. To his friends he said that within the walls of the College he discovered a happiness he had never known outside his home. The year of his election as President coincided with his retirement from the Leeds General Infirmary. He had hoped, when 1926 came, that the Infirmary would have found some occasion to prolong his term of office ; when it did not, as indeed it hardly could, he was sadly disappointed. On his last afternoon there, before an audience of distinguished surgeons from all over the country, he performed six of his famous operations, but as afterwards he left the hospital he did so not only with affectionate regrets ; the Infirmary had held so large a part of him that without its ties he felt a new loneliness. So to the College he gave all the devotion that until now he had given to the Infirmary. With plans for its advancement he occupied his mind.

Under his direction new research laboratories were built at the College ; there, in accordance with his cherished and long-envisaged plans, anatomical, physiological, and surgical researches were to be conducted. Later on — finding his enthusiasms shared by the Conservator, and great anatomist, Sir Arthur Keith — he worked with this eager colleague towards a still greater end. He and Sir Arthur Keith, with whom his friendship

soon went deep, together sought the means and opportunity to establish outside London an institute, under the
direction of the College, where vital surgical research
could be conducted. Berkeley was convinced that in
free association with research work lay the proper training of the surgeons of the future. In an address inaugurat-
ing the student year at King's College Hospital in the
autumn of 1927, he had said that—

" Were my days to come again I should, after leaving
examinations behind, spend the time necessary to make
an adequate knowledge of human anatomy my permanent
possession, and I should then escape to experimental
research, and in a community of like-minded people
endeavour to train myself for the high destiny of a
surgeon, the one man who may engage in direct research.
My time would be spent in the laboratory, where a youth
of plastic mind may learn the methods of approach to
new problems, or to new extensions of old problems ;
where old knowledge is merely an impulse to the search
for new ; where intellectual dissatisfaction is victor over
narrow complacencies ; where the religion of research
inspires him and equips him for his work in days to come.
If surgery is to be something more than a wonderful
craft, if it is to be the instrument of research which I
believe it to have been, and to be destined to be in the
future, those who practise it must have their minds shaped
and strengthened by contact with unsettled problems,
not cramped and sterilised by monotonous exercise within
a narrow province of static knowledge."

Now that he was too old to have this experience he wished
to make its realisation possible for the generation of
surgeons on its way. Berkeley at sixty-two had not been
made cynical by the world ; he still regarded the surgeon's
mission as a high vocation, one only to be followed by
those who, as to priesthood, had dedicated their lives to

surgery. This, his faith, Berkeley never did more beautifully confess than in the words with which he closed that same address :

" No training of the surgeon can be too arduous, no discipline too stern, and none of us may measure our devotion to our cause. For us an operation is an incident in the day's work, but for our patients it may be, and no doubt it often is, the sternest and most dreaded of all trials, for the mysteries of life and death surround it, and it must be faced alone. Those who submit to operation are confronted, perhaps after long and weary days or months of suffering, with the gravest issues, and far more often than many of us suppose they pass into the valley of the shadow of death, and, in stark dismay, wonder with Beatrice in her aching solitude and panic, what will come to pass

<blockquote>
If there should be
No God, no Heaven, no Earth in the void world,
The wide, grey, lampless, deep, unpeopled world.
</blockquote>

To give courage to those who need it, to restore desire for life to those who have abandoned it, with our skill to heal disease or check its course, this is our great privilege. Ours are not the mild concerns of ordinary life. We who, like the Happy Warrior, are ' doomed to go in company with pain and fear and bloodshed ', have a higher mission than other men, and it is for us to see that we are not unworthy."

So, giving practical application to his words, he worked for the promotion of surgical research. He found in Sir Buckston Browne, himself a surgeon, a generous benefactor ; one who was willing to provide the institute that Berkeley and Arthur Keith desired. At Downe in Kent, where the great Charles Darwin had lived, the Buckston Browne Research Farm was built, and there research in the very manner Berkeley planned is now being carried on.

Surgical research required vital experiment ; discoveries are made by discerning the effects of operations upon the living organism. And, because it is not right to operate on man himself while the operation's efficacy is yet unproved, experiment must confine itself to lower animals until its issue is out of doubt. At the Buckston Browne Farm such work as this is done, and it is done with the same humane and technical care as in the operating theatre of a great hospital.

In his Romanes Lecture *The Advance of Medicine*, given at Oxford in 1932, Berkeley discussed the experimental method of research. In an appendix to that lecture in its published form he expounded his views on vivisection. He revealed himself sensitive to the feelings of those who were opposed to that method of research, but demonstrated that the method was essential if surgery was to advance. These are his own words :

" Here let me frankly face criticism that has been directed against the methods of our laboratories, and has resulted in a most lamentable impediment to the advance of medicine. Without experiment on living animals, that advance, already greatly hampered, cannot continue. I recognise and endeavour to understand the motives which animate powerful bodies of noble and highly gifted men and women who are opposed to experimental methods. No right-minded man ever wishes to inflict suffering upon man or animal. That is abhorrent to us all. Opposition to animal research, I firmly believe, is based upon lack of appreciation and understanding ; as it is certainly supported by grievous and, I think, unpardonable mis-statement. Day by day for many a year it has been my happy duty to operate upon men, women, and children who now number a goodly company, in order to save life or bring relief. My heart is full of compassion. I cannot bear to cause or even to hear of suffering. Everyone who has experience of laboratory work knows how little pain is inflicted, and what steps are always taken to minimise or abolish it. Yet the slight distress we must occasionally impose in our work upon man is greater in intensity, and far more protracted, than any suffering in our laboratories. It is simply not the truth to say that pain is wantonly, or avoidably, inflicted there. The experimenter who excites suffering defeats his own aims : for pain changes the issues he seeks to discover. Physiologists and surgeons are the most humane of men. The necessities of their work would impose this quality if it were not already possessed. The whole anti-vivisection campaign, though a great testimony to the tenderness of heart of its supporters, has no slightest foundation in truth, and is a witness to their shut-mindedness and credulity."

To be invited to give the Romanes Lecture is to be the recipient of one of the greatest honours that Oxford can bestow. The Lecture has, in the past, been delivered by Gladstone, Asquith, Balfour, the first President Roosevelt, Winston Churchill, and famous men from every intellectual calling. Berkeley was the first surgeon to receive the invitation. When he was invited he was most doubtful as to whether he had at his command such erudition as would permit him to acquit himself in a manner fitting to the Lecture's great tradition ; it was only after much consultation with his friends that he finally accepted. Even after several months of careful preparation he remained, for him, unusually nervous. But, as those who knew him well only expected, when the day came he spoke with power and assurance. Before a gathering mainly comprised of the laity, he told the story of medicine from its infancy. Throughout a long speech he fully sustained the interest of his audience. Than this oration he gave none more famous, yet never

Berkeley Moynihan

did he give a better one. Before the Lecture the University had bestowed upon him the honorary degree of D.C.L. The day was in every way a happy one for him. Berkeley had been accompanied to Oxford by his friend Sir George Newman, Chief Medical Officer to the Ministry of Health. Two days afterwards Sir George wrote to Berkeley :

" DEAR BERKELEY,
" The more I reflect on our pleasant visit to Oxford the more I recall with great satisfaction the benign and dignified bearing of the great man whom Oxford desired to honour. Standing in the middle of the Sheldonian Theatre it was a gracious, decorous and pre-eminent figure, looking as he would have wished to look, and of which his family and friends were justly proud. . . .
" Ever yours,
" G. N. "

*   *   *   *   *

As the nineteen-twenties went by so did Berkeley's friendship with Sir George Newman grow. At each state of his life Berkeley had looked up to someone — had found in some particular person his inspiration and ideal. When he first qualified, Jessop had moved his thoughts, then from Murphy and the Mayos he had drawn his strength ; during the war his two chiefs, Keogh and Goodwin, had been his model — loved and faithfully served ; now, as he day by day more deeply entered the world of affairs, with affection and admiration he turned to Sir George. In him he found a friend most perfectly atuned : one loyal but candid, one who could love without forgoing his power. Sir George, unlike so many of Berkeley's friends, did not, in returning Berkeley's love, renounce his right to criticise. When Berkeley did well, Sir George was first with praise, but when he was wrong Sir George gave him a greater gift — the honest warnings

318

of a true friend. And for this, even more than for the easier things, did Berkeley love his friend ; and in so doing he showed the bigness of his mind. For Berkeley this new companionship was a source of comfort and delight ; in it he found a mind stimulating, eager as his own ; from it, when the shadows crowded round, he drew solace for his heart. Sir George, like Berkeley, enjoyed an intellectual fight, but, like Berkeley too, had a nature basically sincere. In the study he was an opponent, keen in controversy — but before the world he was an ally, faithful in encouragement.

Berkeley's doings in these later years are all punctuated by his letters to Sir George. At many and different times he writes to his friend : in the gaiety of holidays, in his doubts seeking advice, in his troubles easing his burden, in kindness offering sympathy — and in every letter he reveals himself. Before Sir George he delineates a picture of a many-sided man ; one human, understandable, and ready to be loved. Here are no stodgy letters full of unleavened news, but brief, sparkling, loving, spontaneous notes — links forging a chain of friendship stretching across the years.

Anniversaries and days of celebration always invoked in Berkeley feelings of strong sentiment, so it is not surprising to find him sitting down to write to his friend on Christmas Day in 1929 :

" GEORGE DEAR,

" Here we are on Christmas Day — a few fugitive moments of sunshine, and then tempest. So I am driven indoors and what better thing can I find to do than to write to HIMSELF.

" I did once intend a postcard telling you you were a great man ! but instead I'll send this letter to tell you

you're a beast. Listen ! ! ! Here am I in the north, happily housed, overfed, and longing for a scrap with you : and there are you far far away in the south lusting for a chance to riddle me from stem to starn with your argumentative fire ; and proposing to yourself a problem — 'how can I make his red cells stretch from here to Centauri ? ' George dear — how can you so desert me ! And then insult me!! You tell me X has spent 3 HOURS with you. Well ! Perhaps his soul's welfare does require it. . . .

"George dear I'm very fond of you — and SHE loves you — so there.

"Ever and ever,

"B."

One February Berkeley writes from the South of France :

"MY DEAR GEORGE,

"I hesitated — and hesitated — whether to write to you about *your* speech at the dinner — and now as Artemus Ward says 'You've got your blow in fust' it is really odd how a few days shews up the difference between froth and substance. B's speech has gone for ever ! Yours moves me still, because it reached my soul. The real immortality is of the spirit. . . . You know my dear friend how I value your opinion — its sagacity is I think above that of any man in our profession : and I am cheered by your kind words. Bless you.

"The weather here is quite perfect and I bask in the sun about three hours daily. I wish you were here to talk Keats !

"Ever affectionately,

"BERKELEY"

And here is Berkeley as he so often was, full of affectionate fun :

Friday after you left
In the train

"GEORGE DARLING,

"Boo hoo ! What am I to do without you ? I

320

never guessed your heart was so cruel that you would leave me forlorn and lonesome on the very edge of the desert ! But

> Love is not love
> Which alters when it alteration finds
> Or bends with the remover to remove.

So I must go on loving you. To think of Whitehall and official frigidity. Ugh.

" Your own,

" B."

" She says ' Give him my love, it's sure to be George you are writing to '."

In 1928 Berkeley wrote a letter to his friend that, read in these after years, does much to exonerate him from an accusation that was levelled at him in the last years of his life. The trouble had arisen through an illness of Berkeley's. The story of the ailment is told in a truly remarkable document written in Berkeley's own hand. He was taken ill — seriously ill — in December 1927. He told no one about it, but day by day, until he was compelled to place himself in his doctor's hands, he wrote down the history of his disease. The document is long, it contains much precise medical observation, but here is the essence of it :

" On Thursday evening December 1st dinner with the Skinners' Company. I had had no lunch, was hungry, and thoroughly enjoyed an excellent meal [which he describes] . . . and then a pear, with less than a glass of champagne, a tumbler and a half of iced water, nearly all the jug provided, and one glass of port. I left the Skinners' Hall at 9.30, called at Portland Place, picked up my wife and D. and went to May Fair Hotel. Danced and enjoyed it all. At or about midnight the party went to supper. I had [again a description] no wine, orangeade

only. Danced and talked till about 2 A.M. Went back
to the flat feeling fit. Woke as clock was striking eight.
Breakfast [description]. Went to nursing home and had
to climb to top as lift not working : felt a little breathless
at the top ! otherwise perfectly fit. Worked and idled
at the flat afterwards till 1.30 when I went to Christie's.
Stayed there till nearly 3 P.M. and then walked to near
Charing Cross Hospital and took a taxi to R.C.S. . . . In
committee till 5.15. Walked to Underground, then by
it to King's Cross. Had first dinner in the car [descrip-
tion], ½ bottle Graves. Enjoyed it, but was not very
hungry ! After dinner went back to another car, seats
like dining-car, not to my carriage, read *Four Just Men* —
fell asleep. Woke feeling a little faint, and found food
regurgitating into my mouth and quickly escaping on to
my shirt and clothes. Went to lavatory. Very sick —
four times — and thought vomit very dark — was certain
at this end that there was both fresh blood and old blood.
Noticed that I looked very pale and was sweating
about the forehead. [Then follow similar details for that
evening and the following morning.] During all this —
not the slightest pain. The psychology is interesting.
The diagnosis of carc. vent. [cancer of the stomach] seems
probable. Yet I am undisturbed. Wondering how the
diagnosis can be true, for up to the dining-car incident
I was very fit, and thoroughly enjoyed every meal : and
had kept my weight. My thought was of T. and the
children, and I was thankful that they were likely to be
fairly comfortable financially."

But Berkeley had not got cancer. Two things, both
not uncommon occurrences in the lives of doctors, had
happened to him : he had misdiagnosed his own complaint, and he was, in fact, suffering from the very disease
upon which he himself was the great authority. He had
a duodenal ulcer. When the diagnosis had been correctly
established Berkeley, as doctors often are, was most secretive
about his illness ; he did not like others to speak of it,

nor would he speak of it himself. It was not long, however, before medical circles were saying that he was silent because he would not submit himself to the operation of which he had been so great an advocate. But the accusation was unjustified. Here, in this letter written to Sir George from the nursing home where Berkeley was, is the refutation of an unfair attack :

" MY DEAR GEORGE,

"Thank you so much for a charming little note. The trouble is over ! Shortly after I wrote you last, at the end of a year of really hard unbroken work, an acute duodenal ulcer began to bleed. I disregarded its activities for a week or more : but in the end had to give in. My surgical experts refused to deal with me : so I came here for a rest and treatment. . . . I shall be good and go slow for another 4-6 weeks and then, judging by my experience of others, I should be like a young lion again. I'm not going to work so hard at so many jobs in future. You see I've been doing the R.C.S. work (as Keith will tell you) ardently and unceasingly. I've been operating in London, running a large 'home' in Leeds, building up the Yorkshire Cancer Campaign (we have now over £150,000, a research institute and a research farm), looking in at the War Office (I'm still Chairman of the Army Medical Advisory Board) and so on and on. . . .

" Ever affectionately,

" BERKELEY "

Berkeley's recovery was very good. But from that time onwards he made some efforts to conserve his strength. Since that eighteenth birthday on which he had become a medical student, he had worked with unrelenting and prodigious zeal ; a few hours for golf on Sundays and some irregular holidays had been his only rest. Now, at sixty-two, he modified his ways ; he started to take vacations, regular and prolonged.

*   *   *   *   *

It is difficult for a famous surgeon to escape his trade. Wherever he goes he cannot elude, nor easily resist, the call of patients who need his aid. Berkeley found that only upon the sea was he fully emancipated from his work. And the more he voyaged the more he liked it ; cruising became his great delight. It gave him both his needs and his desires : rest for his body, and for his mind the joys of travel in a friendly company. From 1927 onwards he used his holidays to travel by ship all over the world. He visited South America, India, Jamaica, Canada, and all the Mediterranean ports. He loved the gaiety of life aboard ship and into all its activities entered with boyish glee. The rest that is languid he never knew, even at sea he could not idle like other men ; in constant reading, writing, talking, and playing games he passed his time ; it was upon the change that his body throve.

He liked to travel with a party of his friends, and then with them to spend the hours in the jokes and chatter of his youth. From him bubbled a ceaseless stream of fun. All that his companions need provide was a mood congenial to his own — he would invent the games.

Even when travelling Berkeley's pen was never stilled. In letters sent to friends at home he did not bother with the detailed movements of his journeys, he tried rather to communicate to them his own experience. To Sir George he would write like this :

" Ah ! How we missed you in Egypt. The trip to the second cataract was simply perfect, in weather, company aboard, things seen, thoughts aroused, emotions stirred. Abu Simbel with the full moon and before and during the dawn ! Oh my dear, it was quite the most wonderful experience of its kind : and my little wife (who loves you and says so !) was stirred to her depths. We had a day in the laboratory and in the tomb with Howard Carter : and a day with Winlock, who is digging for the Metropolitan at New York. I was called in professionally and reduced the subcoracoid dislocation of the shoulder of a sphinx. The accident occurred 1450 B.C. and there was a compound fracture to complicate matters ; but with pullings, power, and persuasion we got the head of the granite humerus into its socket. The last news is that all is healed. So we had a day with each of the 4 men doing excavations, with the result that I'm tempted to abandon medicine and go in for the resuscitation rather than the creation of corpses. . . . Isn't the country a fascination: and the lore of it ! ! I can't rest till I go deeper."

Visits to Egypt became a favourite jaunt, and the reading of Egyptology became Berkeley's hobby. He looked forward to the day when he would be able to give to its study the greater part of his time ; but that day never came. For each time Berkeley returned to England from abroad he found new duties, and new demands upon his time, awaiting him. From the very trip about which this last letter was written Berkeley returned home to be laden with a duty that would be with him to the end of his days. It was certainly a duty that he loved and one that he had longed for, but it was one that he took seriously and to which he gave his leisure time. At the beginning of 1929 he was elevated to the Peerage ; the second surgeon in English history so to be honoured. His distinction was well deserved, for he was in English surgery already almost a legendary figure. Every aspect of surgery had been touched by his endeavours. By his researches, teachings, organisation, and surgical mastery he had suffused the whole of surgery with the colour of his personality. Not for a single activity was he honoured, but for the multiplicity of his outstanding contributions. It was his tremendous versatility that had brought this prize to him, that same " massive " quality that he himself in Mr. Jessop had admired. As it had been with the Presidency so it was with this, he was moved more to awe than pride. He wrote :

" But George dear, I feel so humble ! To follow Lister ; and in this to be alone. You know what I feel, and have so often yet so imperfectly tried to say, about him. To be put, not alongside, that would be sacrilege, but near him — it simply brings a lump to my throat, and drowns an eye unused to flow. I can only say to myself ' this is to be used for the best ends — to help the Profession ' if I am ever able to help."

But his first thought was of his son. Through all his life he had enjoyed his work to the very full, but, true Moynihan that he was, it was his family and his family name that mattered most to him. Even in his greatest success he did not think that to his own efforts alone it was attributable. He never forgot that his days had been easier than those of his parents and that for him Andrew and Ellen had made great sacrifice. His father he had never known, but of Andrew's struggles and hard times his mother had often told him ; and what his mother had done for him he never could forget. With one little ceremony each year he paid tribute to their memory. Each year, on the day on which Andrew won the Victoria Cross, he dined at home alone with his family. His daughter Dorothy prepared the decoration that adorned his table — red roses arranged in the form of the Victoria

Cross. When dinner was over, Berkeley would get out his father's sword and V.C. and, talking the while of his parents' lives, would show them to his children. Then, more than at any other time, would he reveal what the name of Moynihan meant to him. So it was that on the day he became a peer the first thing he did was to sit down and write to his son. His heart filled with emotion, he wrote this — perhaps the most beautiful letter of his life :

MY DEAR OLD SON,

" You will see by the address on this envelope what has happened ! I have been given a peerage, which some day will be handed on to you. I want you to know that it is this which gives me the greatest happiness of all.

" Before you came to us I prayed to have a son, so that my father and mother, and Mother's father and mother, could have a boy to carry on their name and tradition. And when you came I wanted to work harder than ever so that I might leave you something to shew you our love and our hopes for you. When I got the knighthood I wrote to Aunty Eva, with whom you were in Norway, to say ' Now I must make it a baronetcy for the sake of my boy '. The baronetcy came, and now the peerage. I am happy to have them both to hand to you, for I know that you will be worthy of them, and that you will bring your own son up in such a way as to make him a worthy follower of yourself.

" The greatest regret I have is that you could not know my mother, the most beautiful, kindest, most lovable mother in the world. You would have loved each other, and you would have learnt much from her. She was the gentlest, sweetest, most considerate of people. I never heard her say an uncharitable thing of anyone ; she never did an unkind act : and at immense sacrifice to herself she gave me my chance. She was terribly poor, and my education was more than she could afford : but she denied herself everything for me. And she showered love on me, and helped me so gently and tenderly in every possible way. It was her influence that made me want to work, and to succeed, for my son, as she had laboured and sacrificed for me. So you see, old son, it is to her that I owe everything ; and you must always remember that : and ask Aunty Ada to tell you about her. For though it is forty years since she died I could not talk about her, even to Aunty Ada, without breaking down. If only my son, and your son, and his son can have something of her character we shall help the world to be a better place for others.

" Mother and I have watched you so jealously for years, and have tried to help you to be the son we so much desired to see you. I must tell you to-day, my dear boy, how glad we are to have you just as you are. You are the heir we want, and the peerage is safe with you. It is a great trust, as well as a great honour, and you will always so regard it. You will hold it for longer than I shall, and you will tell your son in turn, to use its power for others, as well as for himself.

" Your mother and I love you very dearly and trust you ; and it is our great happiness to have a son who so fulfils our hearts' desire.

" Bless you, my dear old son,
" Your own most loving,
" DADDY "

Since the day of his son's birth Berkeley's devotion to the boy had been passionate. He strove to give Pat's youth all the opportunities that his own had been denied. He wished, too, to give his child security ; the hardships with which his mother's home had been surrounded had painfully taught him the value of that prize. A father cannot satisfy all of his son's desires, but it was Berkeley's ambition to give to Pat at least that happiness that comes from a good education and a freedom from the restrictions of poverty.

The Rewards before the End

Berkeley had always set great store by excellence ; perhaps more so than thoughtful wisdom should dictate. Lack of money and an inborn love of precedence had been the two influences that had driven him forward in his own career. He sometimes forgot this. He forgot also that neither of these influences bore upon his son. He was too ready to think that by the mere taking of sufficient pains his son could emulate his own performance. That is why, when Pat approached manhood, he did not urge the boy to follow medicine ; for he knew that, in that field, he himself could not be surpassed. He wished rather to see his son imitate his own achievements in some other walk of life. When Pat, with an aptitude for figures, elected to follow the study of finance, his father immediately visualised him as destined to be in but a little while the master of the Stock Exchange. Berkeley never did understand where the rewards of effort ended and those of natural powers began.

But he was a devoted father, dearly loving his children. In spite of his over-anxiety to see them shine, he worked for nothing harder than he did for their happiness. When Pat married Miss Candy in 1931 Berkeley knew profound joy in the thought that his son was to have the quiet delights that the years had brought to him and Isabel. His love of children had never waned. As time went by he became again in the company of his grandchildren that Berkeley who, as R.S.O., had romped in the children's ward. No one could rightly claim to know the best in Berkeley who had not seen him at play with Pat's children and with Shelagh's son. He understood children. Their affection for him was always spontaneous.

*　　*　　*　　*　　*

Men have called Berkeley vain, self-centred, eager for recognition — and, truly, in appearance he could be all those things. He spoke so easily, in bearing was so confident, that the world was disposed to think that he, hampered by no shyness, displayed before it his fullest self. Surely one so effervescent, so full of ardour, could hide nothing of himself. But the boy in Berkeley that never grew up here sometimes betrayed the greater man. Before an audience Berkeley, boy-like, could not resist the temptation to cut a dash. He saw himself the famous surgeon, great orator, and handsome man, and with romantic Irish enthusiasm heartily played those parts. Of the effect his behaviour caused he was not always a discerning judge ; he was too impetuous to think that the tones might sometimes ring false. One day, carried away by a recent achievement of his own, before Sir George he entered on one of his parts. " Have you ever, Berkeley," Sir George interpolated, " heard of the Remembrancer?" Why, yes, he had ; wasn't he something to do with some ceremony ? " Yes, Berkeley, he was. But it was an old ceremony, and its story goes a long way back. When Caesar, returning from victory, drove through the cheering streets of Rome, he rode not alone in his chariot, for another, by the multitude unrecognised, sat on his right-hand side. And, Berkeley, do you know who this was ? It was the Remembrancer. His duty it was, as the roars of praise rose up, to whisper in Caesar's ear a single phrase, ' Remember, Caesar, thou too art human — remember, Caesar, thou too art human — remember, Berkeley, thou too art human '." Sir George — good friend — could say these things. He, wiser than the world, knew the real, the lovable Berkeley, and would not let the boy despoil the man.

The Rewards before the End

It was when Berkeley wrote to his son, or when in intimacy he talked to his friends, family, or patients, that he showed the inner beauty of his nature that had been the power behind his throne. There were many things, deep hidden in his heart, about which he was closely reticent, and about them he could only with difficulty bring himself to speak ; but they were the best of him, the things that made him so loved by those who knew him well. If indeed he was an actor he was no mere thespian husk. When he left the stage of his activities it was to enter his home a man of generous passions, and of a character rich, thoughtful, and devoted.

About nothing was Berkeley more reserved than his religion. There were few who heard him speak about his faith. And yet, though he was but seldom seen at church, his life was ruled by true piety. But of his beliefs he would never talk ; asked about them he would reply that a wise man would not, nor could he, openly discuss such things. His mother and his sisters had been persons of devout mind, faithful in religious practice. There can be no doubt that in his early life at home with them he absorbed and shared their main beliefs. But in his grown-up years, unlike his sisters, he performed no public religious exercise. This greatly troubled Ada and Eva, for they saw in it evidence of endangered faith. Even when Berkeley was seventy Ada was adjuring him to mend his ways. Perhaps she need not have disturbed her mind so much, for Berkeley's thoughts were pillared in humbleness. Though his voice was silent his behaviour proved his thoughts.

He read regularly in the Bible ; and this not only for the loveliness of its words. With quotations from the Scriptures he would often illustrate his opinions and advice. His favourite passage — one that he many times used — accorded well with a surgeon's life: "What doth the Lord require of thee, but to do justly and to love mercy, and to walk humbly with thy God?" So did Berkeley strive to conduct himself.

He had a profound belief in man's innate essential goodness. He was impatient with those who doubted man's inborn power to follow the paths of virtue. When a Prime Minister publicly spoke of the "tiger instinct" as being part of man's nature, Berkeley seized the first opportunity that came his way to say, also in public:

"I don't believe that vice is in the smallest degree an inherited quality. I believe that children are born the purest thing the world knows, and that whatever vice creeps into the life of a child is something that creeps in from outside. I believe there is far more of the saint than of the tiger in mankind at large. Perhaps, as a surgeon, I have greater opportunities than come even to a parson for judging the qualities of men and women. I meet people, as every surgeon does, in the great crises of their lives, in the great testing-time of their characters, and I am quite sure than when people, under my own eyes, are put in the crucible of affliction it is solid gold that most often comes out. That is my consistent experience of mankind. . . . The man of science has a God far bigger than the God that can be contained within the four walls of any creed. I would ask you never to measure your God with a foot-rule. The cross Christ is bearing to-day is made by ignorance, the stupidity, the apathy, and the superstitions of mankind; and I am not quite sure that the fetters that bind Christ are not the fetters of the doctrines of many of the Churches. I think that where science in the end will come in will be to set Christ free from that cross and to undo those chains that tether him."

The Rewards before the End

Berkeley's surgical work was closely related with his faith. He felt himself to be the servant of a high calling, and an operation was to him a sacrament. No wonder then that he could not bear, nor would he tolerate, criticism of his science by the Church. To a bishop, who from the pulpit had made adverse comment on the ways of science, he wrote :

" The reign of spiritual authority was so long, its tyranny so complete, that for centuries its question or denial was impossible. Any enquiry into the problems of natural science was heretical and was punished by torture and death. For more than a millennium the spiritual masters had matters all their own way. Then the mind of man slowly and dangerously found freedom and in the last 50 years has gained incalculable intellectual victories, though it is still in the infancy of its power. Because, under such discipline, spiritual and moral development was so deadly slow, is the progress of science to be slowed down also to keep languid pace ? ' Man's power over nature far outstripped his moral and mental development ' (up to the twentieth century) you quote from Trevelyan. Well, those responsible for our moral and mental training, having had their chance for a millennium and having so greatly failed, must not now even in fun call a halt in our increasing efforts to gain still further ' power over nature '. . . . There is no fear that Science will bring ruin. It may lead to momentary disasters, but it embodies perhaps the only universal truth. The greatest of truth seekers and of truth tellers are the men of Science, for without flawless intellectual integrity no progress can be made. . . . But if the Church wants to ' increase the sum of human happiness ' I claim that the greatest happiness is to be found in intellectual unrest, leading to the pursuit and on the triumphant days to capture of the tiniest fragment of ' truth '. Before you feel a dread of Science or any apprehension as to where it will lead, or even allow the thought of its delay to enter your witty

333

mind, will you not concede that it is not the advance of
Science which leads to peril, but the impotence of moral
teaching over 2000 years that has left man weak and
vulnerable? Our spiritual pastors have had their long
time, free to themselves for the ' remaking of man '.
How little they have done! It is time that Science had
its chance. I have no doubt as to the result."

*   *   *   *   *

Berkeley had another brush with the Church towards
the end of his life. It was the result of his advocacy of
euthanasia. For many years he had inclined to the view
that the employment of the so-called " mercy death "
was, in certain painful and incurable diseases, justifiable.
But it was not until his period of office as President of the
College of Surgeons was concluded that he was able to
give much of his time to the furtherance of this interest.
He remained President for six years, having had the
honour of holding the position for longer than any other
man had ever done, and, unfortunately, the years that
were left after his retirement were not long enough to
allow him to do full justice to this new cause. They were,
in fact, just long enough to allow him to excite criticism
without giving him time enough to make the public
adequately understand his case. The ignorant and ill-
informed did not appreciate that he desired the practice
of euthanasia to be most carefully hedged about with
protective legislation ; they thought that, without due
consideration, he was seeking to place a dangerous tool in
the hands of every doctor.

Berkeley was right when he said that no doctor had
seen more than he himself of the suffering caused by
incurable disease. In the matter of surgical ailments he

had been for so long the final court of appeal that thousands of such cases had passed before his eyes. Not until they had seen Moynihan were many patients upon whom sentence of death had been pronounced satisfied that everything possible had been done. So to his rooms there came a constant stream of men and women in the grip of fatal disease. It was only after years of thought that Berkeley put forward his case for euthanasia ; it was not, as his detractors said, a sudden enthusiasm of a mind grown old, the child of his desire to keep in the public eye. Berkeley's mind did never degenerate ; apart from an accretion of vanity he was, right to the very end, as clear-sighted and quick of thought as ever he had been. His support of euthanasia came only after careful examination of all the issues and an enquiry, keen and clear-sighted, into its every implication.

That, however, is not to say that he was entirely right. Amongst the great doctors of the day — amongst learned men that understood him generously — there were few that came over to his side. Of the majority it was their view that the wise doctor did even now give to the death of his suffering patients merciful expedition ; they held that the legalisation of euthanasia, though voluntary in principle, was unnecessary and must lead to dangerous abuse. But, whether right or wrong, Berkeley's case was at least formulated with wise solicitude.

Nevertheless, when he put forward his plan many of his friends took him to task ; not only because they thought he was wrong, but even more because they feared for his reputation. They were afraid that, like many another famous man before him, he might in the last few years of a great life do irreparable damage to a name that a lifetime's work had built. As soon as the news of

Berkeley's intention reached America, his old friend Dr. Lobingier wrote from Los Angeles :

" I have been deeply interested in the movement you are leading in England for legalizing Euthanasia for the hopelessly ill. This is in such contravention of the canons of medical and surgical practice into which we have been born and bred, that one who has known you as long and favourably as I, is startled at this direction your thought and interest has taken.

" I have always believed this issue could best be met by discovering the cause of disease ; and by the orderly processes of research prevent its occurrence. . . . I am persuaded that the medical world has achieved sufficiently outstanding results of its labours to be content to rest its case in the scientific processes now under way to prevent and cure almost all forms of disease which afflict mankind.

" May I not, as your lifelong and devoted friend and admirer, beg you to go slowly in this movement? Your illustrious name makes the entrance into this hitherto forbidden domain more dangerously impressive. One can only venture to suggest the vast medico-legal complications which may easily arise amongst those emotional peoples such as the American, French, Italian, and Spanish. In judicial, sedate, well-ordered England these incidents would be greatly minimized. An Euthanasia Act will probably not meet with serious opposition from the liberal branch of the Anglican Communion. But Rome of course will oppose it with all its implacable power.

" You are embarked on a noble venture, inspired I know by the sincerest idealism and humanitarian purpose. But I am baffled as to how such a Bill may be drawn so that it will not violate every motive and principle of life-saving effort to which, for more than a generation, you have dedicated the cleverest energies of your illustrious mind. I beg that you will forgive me, but I cannot visualize your brilliant mentality lending itself to this dangerous measure."

The Rewards before the End

To this letter, from one who had long held his affection, Berkeley replied :

" It is just over thirty years since first we had the pleasure of meeting. Since then you and I have had occasional correspondence and I have read the many Reprints which you have been kind enough to send me. I think, however, I never had a letter which I so greatly enjoyed as that which has just come. You give me in the most tender and gracious manner a scolding for my Voluntary Euthanasia campaign.

" I quite understand that there are people who take a strong objection to the lines we are advocating, but there is, in my judgement, no doubt whatever that the day is not far distant when opportunity will be given to those suffering from irremediable and excessively painful diseases of seeking relief from their agonies. The position will have to be very strongly safe-guarded, of course, and we are quite willing that anything in that direction should be most strongly established. We accept the opposition from the Roman Catholic Church and we shall have to say that if this Voluntary Euthanasia is permitted the Roman Catholics are under no compulsion to apply it themselves or to any of their people.

" With what you say in regard to a multitude of other diseases I most cordially agree. Step by step, or rather stride by stride we are advancing, and I have no doubt whatever that we shall, within the next decade or so, have other conquests to record, but meantime people go on suffering to an almost illimitable extent and I really think that we cannot wait for the advance which you foresee (and I agree) will come before very long.

" These, however, are only comments upon one of the kindest, most generous, and most sympathetic letters I have received. I see that you do not agree with me but I hope at any rate that I have not wounded your feelings with my advocacy of what I believe to be right."

Before Sir George — to whom he took so many of his

337   z

problems — he tried, too, to justify his case. What most
people thought he did not care, but his ardent nature was
always grieved if he was not in perfect accord with his
friends. So he wrote :

" It was a thrill to see your beautiful script again ! It
would be still more delightful to see you. . . . I'm dis-
tressed to hear of your being tired. Take a long holiday and
go on strike. Your only defect is that you haven't a few
trifoliate hibernian red cells which incite you to rebel
now and again. I can spare you a few. That's the cause
of my taking up Euthanasia. It's righteous and necessary
and will come in a generation or two if *we* start the
racket. It will rarely be necessary, but *sometimes* desper-
ately necessary. I know all about St. Paul and all that
he did and said before his head bounced three times and
my chief respect is that he did know how to write the
English language !! I never set great store by some of
his teachings and I am sure I know far better than he
did what a suffering tortured creature needs. In some
respect he was ignorant and in this (and other) respects
just stupid. It will be adherence to the ' doctrines ' of
such as he that will stay Christianity if the Church
doesn't take care (or rather Churches don't). Then we
shall be left mainly with our old friend Socrates : no
bad companion. . . . The divinity of Hippocrates (and
Galen) held intellectual advance back for a thousand
years. We must be careful that other divinities don't do
the same. Now get up and hit me !! Have I roused
your tranquil Quaker soul ? "

Berkeley would pursue his friends to the last ditch with
good-natured argument, but as soon as they were in
trouble the dispute would be swamped and washed into
forgetfulness by the waves of his abundant sympathy.
All suffering saddened him : but the sufferings of his
friends moved the depths of his heart. There can have
been few doctors whose charity was more profound —

and practical — than Berkeley's. If his friends needed him he awaited no last cry before coming to their rescue; eager to help, the first intimation of trouble brought him to their side. A few days after writing to win Sir George to euthanasia his letters took a very different tone. One near to Sir George was taken ill and Berkeley, on hearing of this, wrote at once to his friend. He continued to plead his cause, but he wrote like the Berkeley that his friends — for all his failings — the more loved as they knew him more :

" George Dearest,

" I can rag you to my heart's delight about your old friend St. Paul (or anything else) but I am moved to tears when I hear of your trouble. I do hope there is nothing wrong, really wrong . . . but if there is the remotest chance for God's sake see somebody who *knows*, before you go abroad. One cry stirs me to my depths, ' Too late '. There may be nothing wrong, or there may be just some little thing — but find out. Guess-work, and hopes, are no good. Get to know. . . . You with your compassionate heart would suffer miseries if you saw what I have seen, and see still : and you would lead the ' Euthanasia ' stunt. We shan't get our way for a genera-tion at least : but after all even the Greatest one needed an Evangelist. And other leaders in our profession are timorous folk, whereas I care ' nothing for nobody ' if the cause is right, or I, however misguided, think it is. I've always thought of myself that I should have made a reasonably good mediaeval martyr. I think I could die cheerfully for faith.

" George dearest, I do miss you. Other men seem so little and so . . . ignoble by comparison with you. There was something about you very saintly and wonder-fully attractive to me. That's why I used to pick little quarrels with you — to get you to spread yourself. And, you know, you write our language better than any doctor alive ; so don't delude yourself into the idea (how stupid ! !) that you've written enough. I've been reading you lately, once again, and I marvel at your erudition (far more than knowledge, you know) and the grace and flow of your majestic pen.

" Bless you, dear George. . . ."

And yet again, how different Berkeley's letters were when the skies were clear, and work and the world went well. Then he is writing to his friend from the Savile Club :

" Matters are coming to a crisis. I simply cannot, and will not stand this studied and incoercible neglect. The remedy is not apparent, but the punishment is maturing. In my loneliness, I come here to lunch — better food than the Athenaeum — so, when your long period of neglect is over, if it ever is, I must bring you to have a little fried sole and Vichy."

The old teasing Berkeley was always bubbling up ; if there was no friend immediately at hand upon whom Berkeley might exercise his lively spirits, then he must seize the moment to sit down and write one of those little notes that so revealed the lightness of his heart. A little message, a few words — that was enough — something off on an errand of fellowship.

Many who knew Berkeley only from afar marvelled at the spell he cast over those in his immediate circle ; to those distant ones he seemed too powerful, almost too over-powering, to be comfortable as a friend. But in intimacy he was very different from the man who strode to success through the streets of men. Sitting before the fire, when the curtains were drawn and the warm logs glowed, his nature — sweet as had been his father's — reached out to his gathered friends. His bantering humour — for so in self-defence he needs must use it — hid a very passionate heart. The core of him was never hard ; he had an abundant love of friends. He knew, too, how easily, by his own and others' troubles, his eyes were filled with tears, and these no tears of metaphor, but the physical emblems of a strongly emotional mind. The little joke, not always gay, was sometimes armour against too great display.

In friendship, as in all things he undertook, Berkeley matured to the end of his days. As an ageing man he made a better friend than as a youth. Kind he had always been, but in the thrust of young endeavour for long he masked himself. As he grew older so did he reach more easeful concord with his fellow men. That something aloof, superior, segregate, in his later years he lost. He became a friend — if not perfect, then by so much the more loved for the imperfections he now ceased to hide.

* * * * *

No man can escape disappointment ; and, when it comes, it is often most keenly felt by those who have commanded great success. There were, of course, many things about Berkeley's life that he would have liked to change, but major frustrations were few. After his youth it was not until his last few years that he suffered such disappointments as would really cause him bitterness. He could never easily tolerate a thwarting of his desires, and when he was in danger of such obstruction he would fight the opposition to the last. In his middle years by the vigorous weight of his personality he had in nearly all ways moulded circumstance to suit his wish ; so much so that with the passage of time he became apt to think that his wish alone was law. From the day of his first struggles he had taken life by the scruff of the neck and had forced it to bend to his will. When the hour came, as sooner or later it inevitably must, in which he was driven to contend with intractable things he found bitterness in his defeat. He never won to a philosophy so serene that he could accept, without in some degree reviling, a fate that went against his wish.

By the end there had fallen into his hands nearly all the honours upon which he had set his heart. One by one, in regular succession, they had come within his grasp. But not all ; one in particular never came his way. And when, after struggling, he was compelled to the realisation that it never would, he could not in calm reason console himself. His provocation came not from unsatisfied greed but from the pain of the admission that he could not in all ways form his world.

Over all branches of scientific activity in England the Royal Society remotely presides. The bestowal of its rewards is as much as may be uninfluenced by those imperfections that contaminate all high reward. Without appropriate merit, outstanding and unquestioned, a man has little hope, by the mere pressure of friends at the court of that body, of receiving its dignities. Those only gain its recognised approval who have done great scientific work. No true labourer in the scientific field finds any reward more estimable than that he should be made a Fellow of the Royal Society. If honours mean anything at all, then it is certain that the man who can write the letters F.R.S. after his name is a scientist, original and of the first class.

Berkeley coveted this honour. He thought that his investigation of the nature and symptoms of duodenal ulcer and his work on the " pathology of the living " rendered him eligible for election as a Fellow of the

Society. In this, if not right, he was at least almost so. His might be called a borderline case ; it was one that merited, and probably received, careful considera-tion. But it was Berkeley's hastiness that prejudiced the issue ; he did not rest in quietness and let his claim fructify. Instead, both in conversation and in letters to the press, he pleaded for greater recognition by the Society of those doctors who elucidated scientific prob-lems in the wards. He announced that too much atten-tion was paid by the Society to the laboratory and too little to the operating theatre and bedside.

Now it may not be fair to say that, even though some of his letters were anonymous, he was seeking his own advancement ; the interests of the profession as a whole were always forward in his thoughts. But, since his case was foremost amongst those of the doctors that the Society would review, to behave as he did was manifestly dangerous ; it was inescapable that the world should suspect his motives. When finally, in a letter to *The Times*, he criticised the President of the Society, his friends foresaw that he had for ever blocked his path. They knew then that the Society could not — nor did they ask that it should — forgive. When Berkeley saw what he had done he told his intimate friends that he would not, even if offered it, accept the F.R.S., and that he would have abided by this there is little doubt. But to the event he never reconciled himself ; to the last it was a bitterness. And the pity of it is that all this might not have been ; had his eagerness been less, he might have reached the goal he sought.

Another disappointment was one over which he him-self could exercise no control. He had for long been an admirer of the Royal Family and his personal contacts with them had confirmed him in all his thoughts. In his professional capacity, to have an official association with the Household was a happiness he most desired. But as a provincial surgeon this satisfaction was not for him, and it irked him that this should be his lot. There were mountains that even he could not move ; but he did not like it when he encountered them.

Sometimes he would almost wilfully disregard them, as if determined to persuade himself that they did not exist at all. For many years his blood-pressure had been high ; towards the end it left the average far behind. That it should be so was no reproach — these things are not of man's choosing — and indeed to his high blood-pressure he owed in part his enormous energy. But it was a fact that with an almost obtuse resistance he would not acknowledge. That he, Berkeley, should be so afflicted savoured of an affront deliberately put upon him by malignant Nature. It raised the old fighting spirit that had carried him to the top. This too must submit to his will. And so, by every sort and kind of apparatus, he had his blood-pressure measured, hoping always to discover one that would find him normal. But none ever did. His state even he must admit.

But no — there was yet another loophole. Suppose that there was no reliable apparatus, suppose that none of them spoke the truth ? Into the medical press he plunged, hoping against hope for the answer for which he craved. In a letter cloaked with anonymity he said, and characteristically began,

" I am a surgeon. I am tempted to say with Lord Moynihan that I am a physician doomed to the practice of surgery. Recently being concerned with the maladies of a patient a little over sixty years of age, I thought it right before operating to take the opinion of a physician upon the question of blood-pressure. . . . Can anyone tell me if blood-pressure readings are of any real value, and if so, of what value ? . . . Is there any English evidence available to show whether a high blood-pressure involves an added risk to life or health, or are we once again the victims of tradition, hearsay, or prejudice ? . . . Every week as I incompetently play my round of golf I watch the highly accomplished performance of two rounds by a friend whose blood-pressure has not been known to fall below 285–170 in the last ten years ; and one of the most eminent of my professional colleagues frequently repeats to me a statement I first heard him use during the war : ' I feel a worm if my systolic pressure falls below 200 '. . . ."

A rare fighter, Berkeley !

Towards the end of life troubles, when they do come, cruelly crowd in. It seems as if fate, waiting until the mind and body are too tired to stem the tide, chooses her hour with grimmest skill. In September of 1931 a disastrous fire consumed Berkeley's consulting-rooms in Leeds. Almost all his possessions there were destroyed. But he bore the blow with fortitude. To a friend who had sent sympathy he wrote :

" I am glad to say that, almost alone, the notes of my operation cases, with drawings, are intact. But the lares and penates have perished, and a good library that on January 1st next was to become the property of the Medical School, engravings and photographs, too, are destroyed. In a very selfish sense I am glad that after 38 years of happiness, my rooms perish ! "

And then but a few years later he was writing to General Goodwin :

" I've just started the U.S.A. Memorial to Robert

Jones, with the help of Osgood. Poor old G'andpa was
ill for months before he died . . . but his courage, charm,
and high spirits never faltered or flagged. The Memorial
did not go well in England. People are soon forgotten,
and indeed few people seem to have heard of Robert
Jones. I was shocked and grieved."

Sad days — the shadows growing very long as they reach
across the grass. Gone the stored treasures of a doctor's
life, gone friends, tarnished the glowing energy of earlier
days — and at the end, what ? By the world so much
endeavour, the striven-for benefactions of a whole life's
span, forgotten before the leaves turn brown.

There is no doubt that, as the sands ran low, even
Berkeley could not continue in the homeric labours that
had been his way. Sheer force of mind may urge the body
on but the steps are hesitant and lack the sufficient energy
to make them sure. All his life Berkeley had said that he
never felt tired, and had said it truthfully ; but in his
last years, because courage and vanity would not let
him change his words, he made the statement with
bravado instead of calm assurance. To the last he went
battling on. When he was sixty-nine, he was vigorously
resisting in the House of Lords a Bill that had as its
purpose the registration of osteopaths, which, if passed,
would have given them a status akin to that of doctors.
He was strongly opposed to this measure ; in it he saw
the denial of the validity of the whole of the doctor's
training. His old enjoyment of conflict welled up again,
and when the Bill was sent to Committee, he was writing
from Leeds to Sir George :

" You will help me to draft amendments ; and we
will set to work to make trouble ! ! What a spell the
osteopath casts upon men. I've just had a letter from an

old patient (abdominal) in Ireland who, for over twenty years, was under Robert Jones. She says she was ' cured ' in 10 minutes !! by finger treatment. We're at fault somewhere. Give my love to the Sun, and say I'll see him soon. He doesn't live in these parts now.''

But in the Lords his oratory never captured the glory of his speeches in the world at large. It lacked the incisiveness that is effective in debate ; it was almost too carefully prepared. Though in the House he only spoke on matters concerning which his feelings were intense and genuine, he did in his heart hope to take it by storm. But he never did. Perhaps he came to the task when he was too old, perhaps his gifts were never of the kind to appear to advantage in Parliament. Though really not a failure there, it was a secret disappointment to him that he did not enjoy in the House such triumphs as he had won in surgery.

And yet, even if the night does draw near, the evening brings with it peculiar pleasures of its own. When Berkeley reached man's term of years the manifestations of love that were showered on him by his friends astonished him and caused his heart to swell with happiness. If this was what they felt, then, after all, everything had been worth while. He had made mistakes — most not viciously, but from the extravagance of his enthusiasms — and now they were forgiven. Others then did know him as he knew himself — and were compassionate. For a little while he had, by an over-zealous pursuit of a single purpose of his own, been separated in spirit from his old assistant Braithwaite. Now came an affectionate letter from his pupil to show that in the hearts of those who knew him well his greatness was not obscured by his fallibilities. He was deeply touched by the words of the

347

one who, in his succession, was now representing Leeds on the Council of the Royal College of Surgeons, in the buildings of which Berkeley's portrait hung in these latter days. So, still — and as always — exhorting his disciple to carry the banner high, with sentiments reminiscent and restored to happier days, and with moving thoughts, he wrote :

" Many letters, and as many telegrams, have brought me messages of congratulation and good wishes from all sides. But, of the personal greetings, none could give me deeper joy than the affectionate greeting of the very best assistant I ever had. I am still conceited enough to think that of all operations I ever watched none ever went so smoothly, or with such technical accuracy, or with so little vocal disturbance, as those we did together. Our spirits no less than our hands seemed in perfect harmony, each adjusted to the other ; and both of advantage to the patient. They were great days ! I have never ceased to miss them and to lament their end, however inevitable.

" You still have heights to climb. In your journeys upward no man has been so proud as I. If you have energy, devotion, and desire, the highest place in our profession awaits you. If I am not here to see your exaltation I will descend from my frame, in my robes, and grasp your hand.

" Ever yours affectionately,

" MOYNIHAN "

It was to Leeds that in these days of his seventieth year his thoughts all went. He hoped that, even though forgetfulness should at the last come, for a little while after his going the old spell would linger over Leeds. He cherished the desire that as long as there was life in the mouths and hands of those who had stood beside him in the theatre, the Infirmary should know his memory. He supposed, too, that others about their own lives probably

348

felt the same, for to Miss Innes — who had been Matron of the Infirmary in his day — he was writing :

" We have had great times together in what seems to have been a very short period, but is counted in three decades ! Nobody would believe us after looking at us !! They were happy days, full of activities of all kinds, and I think we both left our mark on the L.G.I."

At this time, Ada and Berkeley were very close ; Moynihans together. For both of them the long road was winding to its end. The boy Berkeley had become the man of Ada's dreams, and she tried to tell him so :

" No words can express my love for you — but I *do* try ! What you have been to me always is the very best of brothers — the very kindest of helpers — and the very truest of friends. I think how our precious mother must rejoice over you — and love you more and more — when she knows (as I believe she does) all you have been to me and to our dear children. . . . 70 years ! I remember *that* day so well ! and Eva's and my excitement, and our own darling mother's happiness. I love you . . . ever more and more, and I wish for you — a grandson ! the only thing that now waits to come."

In the spring of 1936, while at sea, Berkeley heard that a son had been born to his son. The Moynihans, that had so tenuously held their line, were again secured. He never knew in his life a greater felicity than this. In the succeeding days he seemed to be restored to the Berkeley of many years gone back. And a new restfulness possessed him ; ambition and fear were stilled. Upon thoughts of the many Moynihans of the past and those now coming, he reposed his soul in peace.

* * * * *

The summer of 1936 found Berkeley almost as busy as

ever in his round of public activities. At dinners, theatres, and social gatherings of every sort he was frequently seen. He would still leave Leeds for London by the ten minutes to eight train in the morning and travel back again in the evening in time for dinner at Carr Manor. As in every other year he went to Wimbledon to see the tennis that he so delighted in. He continued to operate and sometimes, alas, regretted the encroachments that younger men made upon his practice ; it is not easy to let go a grip that has been most hardly won. He continued to bathe in the pool in his garden, and each Saturday and Sunday, unless restrained alone by great compulsion of events, had his regular game of golf. In his later sixties he became much interested in bridge, a game he had never played before. Now, after the round of golf, he liked to play cards with his friends in the club-house. He took to bridge with the same ardour that he had brought to all the other undertakings of his life. Gradually his book-shelves filled with row upon row of text-books upon the game. He wrote analytical notes about bridge and plied the Portland Club with questions concerning the nice points that arose in the course of his play. Altogether he appeared to the world so strong and lively that it seemed as though he had many good years ahead. Only those doctors who knew him intimately feared for his lasting health.

By happy inspiration both those two children of his trade — the Association of Surgeons and the *British Journal of Surgery* — chose this year of 1936 in which to honour him. In May, the Association informed Berkeley that thenceforward its grant to young surgeons was to go by the name of the Moynihan Scholarship. In July, at a reception held in his honour at the Royal College of

Surgeons, he was presented by the *British Journal of Surgery* with a cheque and silver statuette. The cheque he himself presented to the College. The statuette, most beautifully designed by Omar Ramsden, was entitled Vigorous Youth. No gift he ever had he more closely treasured than this. At the presentation, emotion overwhelmed him ; he was so disturbed that he could not speak with his old-time ease. At his request by his side sat Braithwaite, and more by the pressure of his hand upon the knee of the younger man — so long his associate — than by his speech did he reveal how overcome he was by memories of the rich, gone years. He was a great man, greatly honoured in his time, and nothing he could say could empty the flood of gratitude that rose up in his full, tired heart.

The month of August was spent at Carr Manor. Towards the end of it Isabel, whose frail body was now drawing on its last reserves, was overtaken by sudden collapse. She was ill for but a few brief hours, and died on August 31st. Berkeley was stricken. His fire barely flickered before its embers started to cool. Lonely and desperate he strode through the rooms of his house. Grief tormented him and an anguish of sobs he could not stay destroyed the foundations of his wonderful frame. He would not be comforted. The day after Isabel died he withdrew to his room and in that lovely, precise, and flowing hand — now for the very first time irregular — he wrote what follows :

" I daresay some of our successors in the titles may care to hear a little about the first holder of the female title. Here it is. She was the daughter (2nd) of Thomas Richard Jessop, D.L., F.R.C.S., of 32 Park Square, Leeds. He was appointed Surgeon to the L.G.I. on a day in 1870, and became consulting surgeon in 1890. He had the busiest and best surgical practice in Leeds. When I left the Infirmary as resident surgical officer in 1893 I was already engaged to his daughter Isabella Wellesley. She was then 20 years of age on June 15, 1873, was short and very slim. After her marriage and before we sailed from Liverpool on our honeymoon, she weighed with all her clothes on 6 st. 3 lb. She was extremely beautiful with a lovely profile and exquisite complexion, for which she very rarely used any cosmetic, and never till over 30 years after her marriage. She was lively and accomplished. She played tennis well — her sister was Yorkshire champion for years and she could occasionally beat her. She skated well and was lithe, supple and active. She had had trouble with her ears owing to scarlet fever when young, and was always a little deaf. She danced divinely, indeed everyone agreed that she was easily the most accomplished dancer in Leeds, and in those days one could judge, for it was considered almost improper to dance more than once with any girl ! She settled down to married life at once. I was very poor to begin with, and her housekeeping allowance was 2 sovereigns in gold. She kept house splendidly on this meagre amount. Indeed all her life she was distinguished by her skill in housekeeping and she was unequalled in the management of servants. Though so small and slight she had a most remarkable personal authority and was obviously 'someone', a very great lady, who expected her word and instruction to be faithfully observed. We kept servants for years, Emily for nearly 36. A chauffeur who has now been with us 28½, Dowding ; another, Stringer, for 15. Housekeepers — cooks have been with us for 10 and 15 years and been reluctant to leave because of age, or desire to go abroad.

" Until she became deaf in recent years, my little wife was generally beloved. She could ' keep people together ' in social intercourse, and override frictions and discordances by a charm and quiet authority that were as remarkable as they were acceptable, always with an air of personal distinction. She might have been the descendant of a hundred kings. Yet she always held a shade aloof and was invariably the pursued rather than the pursuer. As a companion to me she was adorable. There was always something in reserve that I was constrained to strive to capture, yet rarely ever attained. Of sagacity, wise judgement and foresight, she was past-mistress. Her judgement of people was almost infallible. I always found her wiser in 2 minutes than I might be in 2 years. Her accuracy was literally unfailing. Her help to me in these matters has been of immeasurable value.

" I am sure she was proud of my career to which she contributed so much. But I think if the choice had been left to her it is possible that she might have chosen a more obscure life in which we two would have been even more together than was possible with my so many engagements.

" She was a small yet great and lovely lady worthy of all honour and remembrance."

Not till the last sentence was written would Berkeley admit to himself that Isabel was gone. Then, as he laid down his pen, he knew he must continue in the world alone. The knowledge overbore him. The memory of all the hours that Isabel had spent alone while he was at his work was in this hour a bitter agony to him. It was a mortal one. The terrible desolation of his mind quickly called upon, and fast destroyed, the last of his physical reserve. Before the eyes of his saddened children he dwindled hour by hour, shrank, and finally collapsed. An attack of unconsciousness overtook him ; he was discovered lying helpless upon the floor of his little study. It was impossible to move him from this room. Here — surrounded by his books, pens, pencils, and the spirit of all his written words — he was made comfortable. Unable now to move about, he lay on his couch with the dreadful dignity of a great and fallen oak. He would permit no voice to bring him consolation. He travelled into a solitude beyond the reach of help. Six days after the death of his wife he himself also died.

His son was asked to allow that Berkeley be buried in Westminster Abbey — the supreme and final honour that the British people bestows upon the tiny group of its most illustrious sons. But the family found themselves unable to accept this high distinction. It would not have been Berkeley's wish. Leeds had been his home, his love, the scene of the long march of his endeavour from obscurity to fame ; here, resting beside his wife, it had been his desire to remain. His funeral was in Leeds. He went to his grave through streets silently massed with those upon whose selves and families his gentle hands had bestowed the gifts of health and continued life.

Six weeks before his death he had been writing to one of his oldest friends. His letter had been full of recollections of his past. He had looked back upon his life. These were his words : " It has all been great fun, and I would willingly have it over again ".

THE END

There are men and classes of men that stand above the common herd ; the soldier, the sailor, and the shepherd not infrequently ; the artist rarely ; rarelier still, the clergyman ; the physician almost as a rule. He is the flower (such as it is) of our civilisation ; and when the stage of man is done with, and only to be marvelled at in history, he will be thought to have shared as little as any in the defects of the period, and most notably exhibited the virtues of the race. Generosity he has, such as is possible to those who practise an art, never to those who drive a trade ; discretion, tested by a hundred secrets ; tact, tried in a thousand embarrassments ; and what is more important, Heraclean cheerfulness and courage. So that he brings air and cheer into the sick-room, and often enough, though not so often as he wishes, brings healing.

—ROBERT LOUIS STEVENSON

Printed in Great Britain by R. & R. CLARK, LIMITED, *Edinburgh*